THE

Russian-American

Company

S. B. OKUN

Edited, with introduction, by B. D. Grekov
Member, USSR Academy of Sciences

Translated from the Russian by Carl Ginsburg
Department of State

Preface by Robert J. Kerner
Director, Institute of Slavic Studies
University of California, Berkeley

Harvard University Press
Cambridge, Massachusetts
1951

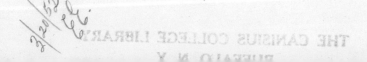

JV
3029
.N62R7

DISTRIBUTED IN GREAT BRITAIN BY
GEOFFREY CUMBERLEGE
OXFORD UNIVERSITY PRESS
LONDON

A Volume of the Russian Translation Project
Series of the American Council of Learned Societies

Russian Translation Project Series
of the American Council of Learned Societies

1. *Tolstoy as I Knew Him*, by Tatyana A. Kuzminskaya. Macmillan. 440 pages. $5.00.
2. *The Law of the Soviet State*, by Andrei Y. Vyshinsky. Macmillan. 749 pages. $15.00.
3. *Economic Geography of the USSR*, edited by S. S. Balzak, V. F. Vasyutin, and Ya. G. Feigin. Macmillan. 620 pages. $10.00.
4. *History of the National Economy of Russia to the 1917 Revolution*, by P. I. Lyashchenko. Macmillan. 880 pages. $13.00.
5. *History of Early Russian Literature*, by Nikolai K. Gudzy. Macmillan. 546 pages. $10.00.
6. *Natural Regions of the USSR*, by L. S. Berg. Macmillan. 436 pages. $10.00.
7. *Russian Folklore*, by Y. M. Sokolov. Macmillan. 760 pages. $10.00.
8. *History of the Russian Theatre*, by B. V. Varneke. Macmillan. 459 pages. $6.50.
9. *The Russian American Company*, by S. Okun. Harvard University Press. 296 pages. $4.50.
10. *Soviet Legal Philosophy* with an introduction by John N. Hazard (a volume in the 20th Century Legal Philosophy Series of the Association of American Law Schools). Harvard University Press. *In press.*
11. *Lomonosov: Russia's Universal Genius*, by Boris Menshutkin. Princeton University Press. *In press.*

PREFACE

THERE ARE FEW regions in the world whose past history
and whose future role are as important as those of Alaska
and eastern Siberia. Thousands of years ago it served as a
bridge from Asia to the Americas when the ancestors of the
American Indians migrated to this continent. In the eighteenth century it became a part of the story of the rise and
expansion of Moscow, which began as an insignificant block-
house on an insignificant river ruled by an insignificant
princeling and which emerged in the course of time as the
pivot of an empire extending into three continents. Eighty
years ago a queer twist of world politics made Alaska a part
of the United States. Today--in the age of air power--this
area is one of the strategic crossroads of the world.

It is in this perspective that we may best observe the discoveries of the Russians on the shores of the North Pacific,
the organization and activities of the Russian-American Company, and the significance in Russian-American relations of
the possession of Alaska by the United States. Important as
Alaska and eastern Siberia were in the past relations of Russia and the United States, a guess may be hazarded that they
will be more important in the future. Will they serve as a
bridge of friendship between the United States and the Soviet
Union in the future, as they served in the past--to mention
only two instances--in the decade when Russia sold Alaska,
and again, in the Second World War, when the United States
sent airplanes and other urgently needed military supplies
by way of Alaska and eastern Siberia to Russia proper?

To understand the establishment, development and activities of the Russian-American Company--in other words to
know one-half of the history of Alaska--one must go back to
the rise of Moscow, to the origin and development of serfdom
and the feudal regime, and to the remarkable eastward advance of hardy hunters and trappers, of bureaucrats and
priests, to the shores of the North Pacific. All these left
their impress on eastern Siberia and the northwestern shores
of America.

S.B. Okun's "Russian-American Company" is the most re-

cent of the solid research contributions on the subject. The
greatest value of his work lies in the use for the first time
of many scattered documents in the archives of various departments of the Russian government, which by accident found
their way into them and which, because of the loss of the same
materials by the departments where they were originally deposited, have heretofore remained undiscovered. As a result
the author is able to reconstruct certain phases of the Company's history.

Okun very properly stresses on a broad scale Russia's use
of the Russian-American Company as a screen for ambitions
in world politics to establish a vast Russian empire in the
whole of the Pacific north of the Hawaiian Islands. With
Marxist zeal he criticizes also the Company's financial poli-
cies, its exploitation of the natives, and its failures in the
social and cultural domain. Okun has rendered a significant
and outstanding service to scholars from these points of view.

One very valuable and extensive source, the Sitka Archives
which were transferred to the United States at the time of the
purchase of Alaska and are now to be found in the National
Archives, Washington, D.C., and in photographic copy in the
University of California at Berkeley, were not available to
Okun. To a very limited extent these significant materials
were used in the two other outstanding and more extensive
works of research on the history of the Russian-American
Company. The one by the Russian, P. Tikhmenev, "Historical Survey of the Formation of the Russian-American Company and its History to the Present Time," published in two
volumes in 1861 and 1863, indicates a slight use of them from
the Russian side. The other by the noted American historian
Hubert Howe Bancroft, "History of Alaska" (San Francisco, 18
has at least a dozen references to the Sitka Archives, which
he states his agents consulted. Evidently here is the great
opportunity of the future for significant contributions in the
field.

Whether because of the inaccessibility of the numerous
and fundamental works of non-Russian scholars (chiefly
American, British, Canadian and Spanish) beginning with
Bancroft, or whether for some other reason, Okun's work
shows little or no acquaintance with them. They were for
the most part surveyed by the present writer down to 1930.[1]
It is because of this that Academician A.I. Andreyev, in his
introduction to the valuable set of documents edited by him

under the title of "Russian Discoveries in the Pacific Ocean and in North America in the Eighteenth and Nineteenth Centuries,"[2] indicates that "the decisive problem of historical science in this field appears to be in the discovery and survey of all existing materials relating to the history of Alaska, California, and the northwestern shores of America. This work may be carried out best by the joint efforts, primarily, of American and Soviet historians having access to the largest collection of materials for the eighteenth and nineteenth centuries." As one, who has for some time in various periods examined the extensive Sitka Archives in our possession, I fully agree that only extensive labor, as well as much collaboration and joint effort, will result in the fullest development of research in this field.

American scholarship is much interested in the significant volume by Okun. It is for this reason that an excellent translation has been prepared by Dr. Carl Ginsburg of the Department of State under the auspices of the American Council of Learned Societies through its Russian Translation Project of which Dr. W. Chapin Huntington is editor.

> Robert J. Kerner,
> Director,
> Institute of Slavic Studies,
> University of California, Berkeley.

CONTENTS

INTRODUCTION

THE STORY of the Russian-American Company constitutes
one of the most remarkable episodes in the process of
Russia's penetration to the shores of the Pacific. Yet, this
interesting and significant chapter in the history of our
country has remained virtually unexplored. While the complex of contradictions in the Pacific during the era of imperialism has repeatedly been a subject of study on the
part of our historians, the political aspect of the Pacific
situation during the preceding period has remained well
outside their range of vision.

The only monumental work dealing with the activities of
the Russian-American Company, namely, that of P.
Tikhmenev,[1] throws light only upon the commerical aspect
of the history of that company; it overlooks the whole complex of political problems relating to the Tsarist expansion
along the shores of the Pacific.

Without, however, taking into account the policy of the
Tsarist régime, there is much that cannot be resolved in
the general field of Tsarist foreign policy. Just as Great
Britain waged war for two hundred years for the possession
of India, hiding behind the name of the East India Company,
so did Tsarist Russia fight intensively for nearly a hundred
years for the acquisition of the shores of the Pacific, behind
the name of the Russian-American Company.

The policy of Tsarist Russia was not, however, one of
direct imitation of British policy; a similar pattern of expansion was widely in use in the period when the struggle
for the partition of the world had not yet entered the climatic stage. In an era of imperialism, though, when the
battle for the division of the world has been joined openly,
there is no longer any need for such a subterfuge. And it
is no mere accident that the three similar monopolistic
combinations--the English East India and Hudson Bay Companies and the Russian-American Company--were liquidated
at about the same time, in the 1860's, at a time when they
had lost their usefulness.

The story of the Russian-American Company is, at the

same time, an epic of the great geographical discoveries made by Bering, Chirikov, Shelikhov, Krusenstern, and by many other Russian navigators who opened up new ways, discovered and studied new lands and waters which no one had seen heretofore.

The history of the Company is furthermore important as a page in the life of the peoples that were an object of colonial exploitation by Tsarist Russia and which, through the activities of the Russian-American Company, came to be included among the peoples depending upon Russian capital, --with all the consequences resulting therefrom.

Thus the study of the history of the Russian-American Company is an undertaking of considerable scope and importance. The author has utilized for his purpose much new archival material that is not yet known to scholars, and has thereby lent to his book the quality of novelty and persuasiveness.

B. Grekov

AUTHOR'S PREFACE

THIS STUDY is based upon archival material preserved in the Moscow and Leningrad State Archives. Our work on the history of the Russian-American Company was rendered difficult, however, by the circumstance that the greater part of the archives of the Main Office of the Company is to be regarded as lost.

After the Company had been liquidated, the archives were, under the law, to have been transferred to the Minis-try of Finance. But for some reason this transfer was never effectuated. [1]

An inconsiderable part of the documents from the ar-chives of the Main Office, in the form of single papers, detached from the cases in question, came into the hands of the naval historian F. F. Veselago. Later on, these documents, together with Veselago's own archives passed into the archives of the State Geographical Society, where they are preserved at the present time.

The so-called Archives of the Central Administrative Board of the Russian-American Company in Russia, pre-served in the archives of the Council of People's Economy in Leningrad, contains only ten items which came into the archives after the revolution.

As for the other part of the collection of the Russian-American Company, the sources to be found in Novoarkh-angelsk "concerning the colonial administration," the terms of the 1867 Convention on the sale of the Russian settlements, provided that it should be surrendered to the United States of America.

Unhappy, too, is the situation with regard to the personal archives of the individual promoters of the Company. Such sources might have compensated, if only in part, for the absence of the archives of the Russian-American Company itself. These archives, it has been proved, are widely scattered and, to a considerable extent, irretrievably lost. Part of the records, the least valuable in our opinion, those belonging to Shelikhov, the founder of the Company, and to Buldakov, its first director, were transferred from Vologda (where they had been discovered) to the State Archives

of Feudalism and Serfdom in Moscow. Another small part
of the same collection--and the most valuable--was accidentally obtained by the Academy of Sciences of the U.S.S.R.
and deposited in the Archives of the Historical Institute.

It was, therefore, found necessary in assembling the
source material for this work to focus our attention on the
collections belonging to those government departments--
such as the Department of Manufacture and Domestic Com-
merce--or belonging to those with which the Company
maintained a correspondence, such as the Senate, the State
Council, the Ministry of Foreign Affairs, the Navy Department, and the like. Now and then we succeeded in uncover-
ing some valuable source material among the collections of
certain government departments with which the Company,
by the nature of its functions, had no connection whatsoever.
Thus among the collections of the Ministry of Public
Instruction we came across material illustrative of the
economic situation of the Company in the '40's. The papers
had apparently found their way to that Ministry by accident;
the problem of the Company had been on the agenda of the
Ministerial Committee, and copies of the records were then
distributed among all the ministries.

Of great help to the investigator in his search for original
source material on the history of America is the "Guide to
Materials for American History in Russian Archives," com-
piled by the outstanding historian F. Golder.[2] While the
Guide is not exhaustive, it facilitates in many ways the
study of the history of Russian-American relations and of
the settlements on the American continent.

The literary sources utilized in this work fall into two
groups. The first more comprehensive group, includes
the memoirs dealing with the numerous round-the-world
expeditions of the Russian navigators. The notes on the
voyages of I. Krusenstern, O. Kotzebue, V. Golovnin, and
others, contain much valuable material also on the history
of the Russian settlements in America, although they are primarily concerned with the organizational aspect of the
activities of the Company and with the condition of the
Russian and native population in the colonies.

The second group of sources, investigatory in character
and devoted to the activities of the Russian-American
Company, is extremely limited. Apart from a number of
brief notes scattered through periodical literature, we have

only one real work of research, that of P. Tikhmenev.[3]

Even though that work was a purely "departmental" history and was intended to glorify without reservation the activities of the Company, it has considerable interest for us, since Tikhmenev was able to utilize the records of the Archives of the Main Office of the Company, records that are now lost. To be sure, he drew only on the material relating to the economic aspect of the Company's activity, and did not examine the collections belonging to government departments.

The work of K. Khlebnikov, Director of the Company, partakes of the nature of a work of research and of personal memoirs. To a certain degree it approaches Tikhmenev's study in importance. A part of the book was published, under the title "Zapiski o Amerike" (Notes on America), in "Materialy dlia istorii russkikh zaselenii po beregam Vostochnovo okeana" (Materials for the History of the Russian Settlements along the Shores of the Eastern Sea), as a supplement to "Morskoi sbornik" (Navy Journal), St. Petersburg, 1861, vol. III. The greater part, however, is preserved in manuscript copy in the Archives of the State Geographical Society and of the Historical Institute of the Academy of Sciences of the U.S.S.R.

One of the most valuable contributions on the subject of the Russian-American Company is the article by S.S. Shashkov.[4] While he does not introduce anything new in the sense of utilizing the sources, and while he limits himself primarily to the notes left by travelers who, at various times, had visited the Russian settlements in America, Shashkov was the first to bring up again a whole series of questions pertaining to the activities of the Company, including the question of the methods it employed in administering the colonies. In describing the commercial activity of the Company, Shashkov notes that the very monopoly which brought prosperity to the Company reduced it, in the long run, to a state of depression and finally to complete economic collapse.

Valuable source material mainly on the history of the Company's final period may be found in the departmental publications of the Russian-American Company itself and in those of the Ministry of Finance.

The printed accounts of the Russian-American Company contain information not only about its financial condition, but

also about the size of the Russian and the native population,
the state of agriculture and trade in the colonies, and so
forth.

Of the publications of the Ministry of Finance the one
worthy of especial mention is "Otchet po obozreniiu russkikh
amerikanskikh kolonii v 1860 i 1861gg. deistvitelnovo
statskovo sovetnika Kostlivtsova" (Report of a Survey of the
Russian-American Colonies in the years 1860 and 1861 by
Actual State Councillor Kostlivtsov), in "Prilozheniia k
dokladu komiteta ob ustroistve russkikh amerikanskikh
kolonii" (Supplements to the Report of the Committee on the
Establishment of the Russian-American Colonies), St.
Petersburg, 1863; also in a separate edition.

Kostlivtsov, who had been sent in 1860 on an inspection of
the colonial administration, describes not only all the
branches of the Company's activity, but also the condition of
the dependent native population. The material communicated
by Kostlivtsov is supplemented by Captain Golovin's report
and by miscellaneous correspondence relating to the final
period in the activity of the Company, both published in the
same "Supplements to the Report of the Committee."

It is not the main purpose of this book to examine the
economic side of the Company's activity; that was investi-
gated, fully though somewhat tendentiously by P. Tikhmenev.
We shall devote most of our attention to the expansion of
Tsarist Russia in the Northern basin of the Pacific in the
first half of the nineteenth century, a process carried on
behind the screen of the Company.

The second purpose of this book is to study the specific
form of economic dependency created by the Russian-
American Company in the territory it occupied, and endured
by the Russian fur-hunters and by the indigenous population.

The history of the brilliant geographic discoveries
associated with the round-the-world expeditions that were
organized by the Russian-American Company and the
ethnographic problems of the tribes native to the region
colonized by the Company, inasmuch as they are a subject
of study in the special literature of their field, have not
been treated in this work.

Chapter I

THE FIRST RUSSIAN "PROMYSHLENNIKY" ON THE NORTH AMERICAN CONTINENT

"RUSSIA just like Western Europe, had her period of great discoveries. Her sphere of action," notes correctly the outstanding Russian ethnographer L. Ya. Shternberg, "was the whole of Northern Asia from the Urals to the Pacific. Like America before Columbus, that whole vast region on the continent of Asia had been absolutely terra incognita to the European world prior to the advent of the Russians in the sixteenth century."[1]

The knowledge of this almost unknown region has its origin in the sixteenth century, at the very time that Russian Cossacks, in quest of gain, made their first appearance on the northern shores of the Pacific Ocean. The active advance of the Russians in the northerly direction, around the Pacific basin, began in the first decades of the eighteenth century.

As far back as 1716 Colonel Yelchin was commissioned to explore the islands that are strung out opposite Chukchi Point and Bolshaya Zemlya. His expedition, however, was not accomplished.

In 1719 the geodesists Yevreinov and Luzhin, on a mission to explore and describe the Kurile Islands, proposed to determine whether "America and Asia join."

The same problem was also put before the first Bering expedition, the dispatching order for which dates back to 1725. In 1728 during the course of his first voyage, however, Bering was unsuccessful in solving the problem. By the order of 1732 concerning the equipping of a second expedition under Bering's command, he was charged to proceed "to find out about" the land which, it was surmised, was the American continent; to learn "what kind of people live there, and what they call the place, and whether those are really the shores of America."

Yet even before the second Bering expedition had started, the geodesist Mikhail Gvozdev, who had set out from the mouth of the Kamchatka River towards the mouth of the

Anadyr in June, 1732, drew near to Bolshaya Zemlya (close
to the Cape of the Prince of Wales) in August and rode at
anchor there. That was the first visit by Russian navigators to the American coast.

Finally, though, the way from Kamchatka to America
along the Aleutian chain was prepared by the two distinguished
Russian travelers Bering and Chirikov.

Bering's expedition, consisting of two vessels, set out in
June, 1741. But, approximately at latitude $49^o50'$ it ran into
thick fog and savage winds. The "St. Peter" with Bering in
command and the "St. Paul" with Chirikov in command lost
one another.

Bering came up close to the American continent and could
see, not far off in the distance, the snow-capped mountains
which were subsequently to be called the "St. Elias Mountains." He also saw Kodiak Island, discovered some groups
of hitherto unknown islands, was the first Russian to observe
the Aleuts at Nagai Island, reached the vicinity of a number
of islands in the Aleutian chain, and died on one of the
Komandorsky Islands, named in his honor.

Chirikov also saw the St. Elias mountain range; he, apparently, came near Umnak Island or Unalaska. The following
year, 1742, on his second voyage, he came up to the island
of Attu.

And following in the footseps of Bering and Chirikov, there
went, attracted by the reports of a rich fur-"trade," scores
of bold, fearless fellows who were to convert the passage
from Kamchatka to America into one of the most bustling
sea-lanes of the time. At first they confined themselves to
the Komandorsky Islands and the Aleutians. The first one
to make up his mind to set forth in search of sea-otters was
Yemelyan Basov, a sergeant in the Lower Kamchatka Command. He formed a partnership with A. Serebrennikov, a
merchant from Moscow, built a small, decked boat, and in
the summer of 1743 set sail for Bering's Island. Basov
spent the winter there and returned to Kamchatka in 1744.

The following year, Basov, subsidized by the merchant
N. Trapeznikov, again set off for Bering's Island. The
merchants supported these expeditions quite readily, hoping
for large profits.

That same year 1745, Mikhail Nevodchikov, a peasant
from Tobolsk, who had participated in the second Bering expedition, started out for the Aleutian Islands in a boat built

by a group of merchants. Luck turned against him, his boat
was wrecked on the return trip and, in July, 1746, he came
back to Kamchatka, having lost thirty-two members of his
crew.

In 1746 a group of merchants again built a ship which they
dispatched in search of new sources of furs, under the command of Adrian of the Tolstoy family, a seafaring merchant
of Selenginsk.

So from year to year numerous seekers for gain made
trips to the Aleutians, boldly surmounting all the obstacles
on that difficult crossing.

The fur-hunters* would generally stay in the Aleutians for
several years at a time. They obtained the greater part of
the pelts through barter with the native population, or by rob-
bery. A small quantity of the pelts was secured through their
own efforts, by hunting. Government agents would also come
along on the merchant ships to collect furs.

By the end of the '50's, when the Aleutians had been thoroughly stripped, they began to search for new places where
no one had been before.

In 1759 the fur-hunter S. Glotov was the first after Chirikov to visit Umnak Island and Unalaska. In 1761 the boat
belonging to the merchant Bechevin of Irkutsk penetrated as
far as the Alaska peninsula, discovering in the Issinakhsk
Strait the so-called Protasov Bay which is very suitable for
anchoring.

When the reports of the successes attained by the Russian
fur-hunters and of their moving forward into "new lands"
reached St. Petersburg, Catherine II issued a secret order
in 1764 to the Board of the Admiralty, which called for the
immediate equipment of a secret expedition, without informing even the Senate, for the purpose of obtaining a description
of "some hitherto unknown islands, in order that it may be
possible to derive the greatest benefit from them."

The secret expedition under the command of Lt.-Capt.
P.K. Krenitsyn was named, with a view to concealing its
true nature, "Commission for the Description of the Forests
along the Kama and Belaya Rivers and Their Tributaries."
The members of the expedition were to proceed to the

*"Promyshlenniky," fur-hunters, trappers.--Tr.

Aleutians on a hunting ship or an a merchant vessel, and only in the capacity of passengers. Only as a last resort, in the absence of ships of the type designated, were they permitted to build new ships. According to the instructions of the Board of the Admiralty, Krenitsyn was to sail to Umnak Island, gather information about the Aleutians, particularly about Kodiak, and determine its distance "from the American mainland."

Krenitsyn's expedition consisting of four ships visited the Aleutians in 1768. One vessel, with Levashev in command, spent the winter in Unalaska; the other, under Krenitsyn, stayed on Unimak. These were the farthest two points reached by Krenitsyn's expedition.

Even before this, in 1764, Lieutenant Sind set out for Okhotsk by order of the Board of the Admiralty to obtain a description of the American coast. Sind sailed off far to the North, to latitude $64°50'$, but did not see the shores of America.

In the meantime, the merchants, obsessed by the lust for profit, familiarized themselves with the difficult crossing to the American continent. The government, furthermore, encouraged their spirit of enterprise in every way; they were rewarded with medals and their debts to the government were remitted.

This special attention that the Tsarist government paid to the progress made in the northeasterly direction was anything but accidental. The tribute in furs, in its natural form, had lost its former importance by the second half of the eighteenth century, that is in the period of greatest activity in the forward movement of Russian merchants toward the North American continent. Furthermore, the expenses connected with organizing the collection of the fur tribute almost equaled the receipts.

Still, the abundance of furs and the sparseness of the population in that region opened up wide possibilities for Russia to secure a strong foothold in the Asiatic market--provided the hunting were properly organized. This had a bearing, first of all, upon the Chinese market. where sea-otter skins--the principal type of fur procurable on the North American coast--very soon met a ready sale. At the same time, Chinese foods, such as tea, silks, and so forth, played a tremendously important part in the Russian market, and the Chinese evinced a lively interest in trading with Russia.

In the eighteenth century people were already fully cognizant of this. "The discovery of new and unknown lands has at all times had an effect on general commerce and has produced in all those states that were bound by mutual advantages great changes in their relations with each other and in their trade, handicraft, wealth and abundance," wrote the Secretary of State P.A. Soymonov to Catherine II in a report "O torge i zverinykh promyslakh v Vostochnom more" (Trade and Hunting in the Eastern Sea).[2]

But, in its aspiration to consolidate its position in Alaska and on the adjacent islands, the Tsarist régime did not intend to confine itself to this alone; Alaska was to be only a base for further expansion.

This expansionist aspiration of Tsarist Russia was also clearly reflected in the literature that made its appearance in the book-stalls of the day.

"The discovery of America" by Tsarist Russia in the second half of the eighteenth century coincided with the propagation in that country of the ideas of the mercantilists who regarded foreign trade as the most important source for the enrichment of the state.

The writings of the mercantilists, and especially those of the popularizers of the ideas of mercantilism, were being translated into Russian and published in Russia.

One of the most characteristic works dealing with what was then a real problem is the treatise, published in 1776, by the French Mercantilist J. Justi, entitled: "Torguyushcheye dvoryanstvo, protivu polozhonnoe dvoryanstvu voyennomu, ili dva rassuzhdeniya o tom, sluzhit li to k blagopoluchiyu gosudarstva, chtoby dvoryanstvo vstupalo v kupechestvo" (Trading Nobility, Contrasted with Fighting Nobility, or, Two Discourses on whether it Serves the Welfare of the State for the Nobility to Enter the Merchant Class). The translation of the work was made by Denis Fonvizin, the future author of "The Minor."

Justi's treatise represents a very vivid paraphrase of the ideas of the most prominent representatives of the economic thought of the eighteenth century, particularly those of its classical representative William Petty. One hundred years before the appearance of Justi's "Discourses," Petty notes, in describing the merchants who are engaged in domestic commerce, that "properly speaking, they do not give the state anything.... They represent nothing but the

veins and the arteries that distribute the blood and the nutri-
tive juices of the state organism."[3]

To the Russian nobleman, however, the compilations of
the French Mercantilist were, for a number of reasons, more
acceptable than the works of his English predecessors. What
appealed especially to the Russian nobleman--and to the
French aristocrat--was the fact that Justi regarded foreign
trade as one of the forms of State activity. While trading in
the very same furs and the very same tars as the low-born
trades, the Russian nobleman still did not wish to be regarded as comparable to him. Domestic commerce, he thought,
was the affair of petty shop-keepers, while foreign trade was
the prerogative of statesmen; for, as Justi notes, "the full
weight of commerce and of the power of the government are
one."

Justi has recourse to a picturesque parable to illustrate
his thought: "'What shall we do with the sword,' the children
reply to their father who has handed them a sword of the
nobility, 'when, with the exception of hunger, we have no
enemies?'" Having put this question in the name of the
children of the impoverished nobility, the author concludes:
"Their father would, perhaps, have acted more wisely if, in
expounding his genealogy to them, he had said: 'My dear
children, many roads to happiness are open to you, the army,
the courts, the Church; if we should consider only happiness,
then we also have merchantry in which through little things
great things are attained. Merchantry procures for us great
wealth, for which no one can reproach us."[4] "Merchantry,"
in this connection, signifies foreign trade.

In that period, when Tsarist Russia was entering upon the
road of broad colonial expansion, some phrases in the treatise
sounded like a battle-cry: "Europe is opening her harbors to
us, Asia is calling us, Africa is awaiting us, and America
is counting on us."[5]

The mention of America along with other parts of the
world, as early as the 1760's-1780's, was not without particular significance to the Russian nobleman. The economy of
the landed class came to be more and more deeply affected
by the condition of the market, and was thus caught in a net,
of insoluble conflict with the natural basis of its very being.
This longing to engage in business on the part of the nobility
in the last decades of the eighteenth century was particularly
manifest under the favorable economic conditions then pre-

vailing both in the domestic and foreign markets, and because of the depression which was already perceptible in the serf economy.

Thanks to the privileges it enjoyed, the nobility had a number of advantages over the merchant class in the second half of the eighteenth century, both in the domestic and in the foreign fields. A series of reports prepared by some of Empress Catherine's commissions speak unequivocally of this situation. They note that "instead of the expected improvement, greater burdens are being prepared for the Russian merchant class," to the extent that the nobility will be given the opportunity "to enjoy the right to engage in commerce wherefor the merchant class will inevitably come to ruin."

The merchants were unsuccessful, of course, in their attempts to have limitations put on the trading privileges of the nobility.

There were, however, certain branches of commerce in which at first the competition of the nobility was not felt. Of such nature was also the highly developed trade in furs imported from the northwestern coast of America and the adjacent islands. The tremendous wealth, however, flowing into the country in the form of a countless quantity of little skins from the American settlements, could not but attract the attention of the enterprising spokesmen of the nobility. The Tsarist government and the "trading nobility," on the alert for the possibility of further conquests both in Europe and in Asia, contemplated with profound interest this new market, where Russian merchants were already pursuing a definite course of action. The Vice-President of the Board of the Admiralty, Count I.G. Chernyshev, had even built a boat in a government shipyard, and was preparing to dispatch it to America in 1781, all loaded with his own merchandise.[6]

The statesmen of the time of Catherine II understood full well, however, that the American settlements, which were actually the first Russian overseas possessions, might involve Russia in an open struggle over the colonies with other great powers, particularly England.

"Since Russia is situated on the edge of Europe," wrote P.A. Soymonov to the Empress, "she could retain her trade with the peoples of Asia without harmful competition on the part of other nations. And, to judge by present circumstances, she may even entertain the hope of being free from danger in that quarter for a long time to come. But her hunting-posts on the Eastern Sea, which until now have been in her hands alone should be excepted from the above condition. The most recent discoveries by Cook lend ground to such a conclusion."[7]

Tsarist Russia which, in her immutable desire to gain possession of the Straits and of Constantinople, had constantly run up against opposition on the part of England--powerful on the seas--, attempted more than once to utilize England's difficult position in the Pacific to weaken her rival. Hence, too, Russia's armed neutrality in 1780, during America's War of Independence with England,--a neutrality that was directed toward undermining England's sea power. As a result of the loss by England of a considerable part of her colonies on the North American continent and her concurrently intensified expansion in a northwesterly direction, the Pacific area, together with the Near East and the Asiatic markets, became a new source of Anglo-Russian conflict.

The Russian government was seriously disturbed by Cook's voyage to the coast of America, and it was not out of mere curiosity that Catherine immediately ordered L.I. Golenishchev-Kutuzov to translate into Russian the great navigator's journal which had just come off the press. James Cook, who in 1776 sailed to the shores of America on the initiative of the East India Company, recorded on the map under new English names all the places he visited. By that very act he staked England's claim to "primogeniture" in the matter of the discovery of those places, although, as he himself notes in the description of his travels, he found Russian hunters in a number of places. Thus he renamed "Nutka" Cape King George, Cape Chutkotsk--Cookshaven, and so on.

The Russians for their part also tried to prove their priority in the conquest of Alaska and the islands. In a secret order to the clerks of the merchant Shelikhov, who were to set out for Alaska in 1787, Governor I. Yakoby of Irkutsk enjoined them to raise the emblems of the Russian Empire in those localities "where in 1784 an English boat had stopped and the crew had made a rich haul." He ordered them at the same time to bury in the ground a number of iron tablets "with the image of a copper cross superimposed and the following words in copper letters: 'Land under Russian Domain.'" These tablets were supposed to be buried so "that not only were the native inhabitants not to see them, but they were also to be hidden from every one of our Russian workers, so that, by keeping this secret, the inhabitants might be prevented from guessing that the tablets were placed there in the present time."[8]

A little later, in 1800, under Tsar Paul, a royal rescript was sent to Count S.R. Vorontsov, Russian ambassador in London, together with a note "Concerning the doings of the English traders on the shores of North America, who are doing harm to establishments of Russian subjects in places originally occupied by them." The explanation that S.R. Vorontsov had on this question from Lord Grenville who headed the Foreign Office leads to nothing. Grenville denied categorically that English ships were proceeding, with the knowledge of the government, to places occupied by the Russians. Grenville's denials, however, were only a diplomatic dodge. It is known that, apart from Cook, the following navigators reached the North American shores between 1787 and 1789: Captain Meares on the "Notka," Dixon on the "Charlotte," Portlock on the "King George," and between 1791 and 1794 Captain Vancouver on the "Discovery" and Lieutenant Puget on the "Chatham."

The accounts of these expeditions, written by the navigators themselves, speak eloquently of their purpose. Dixon, in his account of his own expedition, published in Paris in 1789, wrote as follows, in telling of the insufficient exploitation of the wealth of the region on the part of the Russians:

"After the accounts I have already given of this kind of business, you can imagine how considerable the profits could be if the business were established on a firm footing. The means to attain this end is, in my opinion, the setting up of trading-posts along the coast, and the northern extremity of the Charlotte Islands seems to me to be the most suitable place for them."[9]

Captain Meares considered it advantageous to England to gain a firm foothold on one of the Kurile Islands (erroneously, it is clear, Meares says "Korean Islands"):

"Setting this plan into motion will not present any great difficulty and will not require any strenuous efforts....

Besides exporting English goods--an advantage we always
enjoy--we could utilize the same facilities to give greater
stability to the trade in better quality hard lumber. We
should then be powerful enough considerably to reduce the
profits that the Russians derive from that branch of
trade."[10]

The rivalry between England and Russia was also manifested in clashes between them in the Chinese market which
was one of the chief markets for American furs. And, while
on the American continent there was a struggle between
those two powers for the possession of the sources of the
furs and for their exclusive purchase from the native population, in China the contest was on for the sale of the furs.
The closing down, in the second half of the eighteenth century, of the trade with Kiakhta rendered very difficult the
entry of Russian furs into China. Competition with the
English merchants did not slacken, however, since Russian
furs, which penetrated into the holds of ships "under any
kind of suitable flag," still sold considerably cheaper than
the English.

The mission of Lord Macartney to Peking in 1792 for the
purpose of concluding a commercial agreement and obtaining
a monopoly on trading in furs ended in a failure. The English
did not obtain exclusive rights, and in 1794 Russian trade
with China was officially reestablished, which aggravated
still further the relations between England and Russia in
that area.

"The successes of the Russians with their discoveries in
the Northeastern Sea," N.P. Rezanov, a correspondent of
the Russian-American Company, wrote a little later, (in
1800), "have always roused the envy of all the European
powers doing business in America. So much the more did
it rouse the envy of the British Court, which now possesses
the establishments closest to the Russian acquisitions, both
because of the similarity of their trade with the Chinese and
the nature of the rivalry between them."[11]

In the second half of the eighteenth century Catherine made
an attempt to resolve the rivalry between Russia and England
on the American continent by a little saber rattling. On
December 22, 1786, Catherine, "on account of the encroachment on the part of English traders on trade and hunting in

the Eastern Sea," ordered the execution of the measures proposed in the memorandum of A.P. Vorontsov, President of
the Board of the Trade, and A.A. Bezborodko, Steward of
the Household. In their representation Vorontsov and
Bezborodko took as their point of departure the consideration
that "to Russia must indisputably belong the following: 1) the
American coast from 55°21′ latitude extending northward,
skirted by Captain Bering, Chirikov, and other Russian
navigators; 2) all the islands situated near the mainland and
near the Alaska Peninsula that were discovered by Bering
and Cook, called Montague, St. Stephen, St. Dalmatius, the
Shumagin Islands, and others located between the course of
those navigators and the mainland; 3) all the islands extending thence westward in a chain, called the Fox Islands and
the Aleutians, and others stretching northward, that are visited annually by Russian fur-hunters; 4) the Kurile chain of
Japan, discovered by Captain Spanberg and Walton."[12]

Vorontsov and Bezborodko, considering, therefore, that
the discoveries made by Cook had no "validity," insisted on
the necessity of informing all the maritime powers that the
territories above delineated belonged to Russia. At the
same time they considered it necessary to inform the same
powers that Russia could not allow foreign vessels to touch
at any of the enumerated harbors. Since, however, a declaration of this kind would, without being sustained by main
force, "be hardly sufficient, and might even jeopardize in
some way the dignity of the Court," the authors of the memorandum affirmed that it was indispensable to maintain a
Russian naval squadron in the Pacific waters.

According to this plan Captain Mulovsky's squadron, consisting of four naval vessels, was designated to be dispatched
from the Baltic. Upon arriving in the Eastern Sea it was to
be divided into two forces, with two of the vessels proceeding to the American coast and the other two to the Kuriles.
But the war which had broken out with Turkey, and later
also with Sweden, compelled Catherine to renounce the
sending of a military expedition. As to the construction of
men-of-war in the area of the conflict, that was hampered by
purely financial considerations; for, as was pointed out
correctly by Soymonov, "the equipment of three or four
frigates in these waters is just as costly as that of a whole
fleet in European waters, and furthermore no little time will
be needed for such an undertaking."[13]

It became necessary, then, to abandon this method of combatting Great Britain, a method fraught with a multiplicity of diplomatic complications, and one that was wholly dependent upon the political situation in Europe, and which, in addition, entailed the diversion of armed forces from the Baltic area. Furthermore, it became apparent that it was impossible to limit oneself to sheer force; for the contest would, in the first place, have to be joined with the enterprising foreign merchants and with a mighty monopolistic organization like the East India Company in particular. The situation called for the utilization of a different method, one consisting, in the words of Soymonov whom we have frequently quoted and again, "in securing for ourselves such a position that would render us forever immune to any danger from the competition of other nations." The method he had in mind was that of creating monopolistic associations, similar to the East India Company, which would be able to resist both the business competition of foreign merchants and the attempts of the foreign governments to employ armed force.

The East India companies, both the Dutch and the English, had long been known in Russia. Even in the days of Peter the Great attempts were made to start some monopolistic companies in Russia, patterned after the East India companies. The Archangel Whaling Company was intended to be such a company. Article 4 of the decree of November 8, 1723, reads as follows:

"So it is necessary for the whaling trade to establish companies out of the City of Archangel for the aforementioned, and the most powerful company in Hispania, in which a few officials with ranks above that of hunter should be given positions, as is done in Holland, in the East India Company."[14]

In 1739 the Swedish engineer Lorenz Lang, who had gone over into the Russian service, had carried out a series of diplomatic missions in China, and was then appointed Governor-General of Irkutsk, presented a plan for the formation of a monopolistic stock company for trade with China.

In the 1750's a number of trade associations were already actively engaged in trading with the Orient. Such were the

Russian Trading Company in Constantinople, founded in 1757, the Company for Trade with Persia, founded in 1758, the Trading Company of Bokhara and Khiva, established in 1760.

The desire of the government to create in Russia some organizations which would not only have a monopoly in trade but would, at the same time, after the manner of the East India companies, perform the functions of administering and defending the colonies put at their disposal for exclusive exploitation, was expressed with particular clarity in the decree of Peter III of March 28, 1762:

> "Trade or commercial companies are of the greatest benefit both to commerce itself and those states where they are established on a firm foundation and set up after careful consideration, as, for example, in England the companies for trading with India. These companies are of such great importance that the nation comes to their aid every year with a considerable sum of money in addition to the fact that these companies maintain fortresses there and armies, and wage war against the nation's enemies; and in that way they enhance the power, fame, and eminence of their fatherland. Consequently, since they render such great service to their country, it is absolutely necessary that the increased subsidies they receive should spread over the whole nation, since it comes to their aid with considerable sums of money. Finally, the great distance involved in the voyage, the tremendous difficulties and perils, and the considerable expenses entailed which no individual could shoulder by himself, all this has rendered the companies indispensable in that country."

At the end of his decree Peter wrote: "We do not deny that here, too, the necessity may arise to follow the very same examples."[15]

The history of the Dutch, French, and English companies of the colonial type and their advantages were widely known in Russia at that time. A special chapter, entitled "Sur les compagnies exclusives," in "Essai politique sur le Commerce" by the French mercantilist Melon, published in Russia in 1768, demonstrated the necessity of organizing similar associations under two sets of circumstances; first, "in the case of all new establishments, both as a reward to those who originated them and as encouragement to those who decide to engage in such undertakings," and secondly, "when private individuals, united under a superior authority, do not find sufficient strength within themselves to carry out some important enterprise, and when the co-partnership of others may do them injury or give rise to trading that would be detrimental to the people."[16]

In the latter case monopoly was justified by its indispensability to the needs of the state as a whole. "Exclusive rights," wrote Melon, "seem to the merchant as something odious, something that threatens to deprive him of his freedom, but when, after due consideration and experience, freedom proves to be injurious to the people, then that exclusiveness becomes quite necessary."[17]

The creation of such associations was justified, as it were, by considerations about the subordination of private commercial interests to the general interests of the state, and by the necessity, in extraordinary cases, of having recourse to monopolies, --at the very time that Catherine was proclaiming the eradication of privileges of any kind. Finally, no less convincing was the argument that the Dutch and the English had followed the same course, and they "are so zealous about every sort of liberty, especially commercial."

There was one other circumstance which favored the creation of monopolistic associations for the exploitation of the Russian colonies in America. Direct knowledge of the situation of the fur-hunting posts on the islands and on the American continent brought to the fore most forcibly the problem of the defense and acquisition of that vast territory, as well as of the exploitation of its resources. It was evident that the exhaustion of these, what seemed at first, incalculable sources of profit was a matter of the near future. Those places that were easily accessible had already been stripped bare. Under date of 1785 V. Berkh records the following data in the "Chronological History of the Discovery of the Aleutian Islands":

"It is now possible to observe how the enterprising spirit of the merchants from Siberia has gradually grown weaker. In 1784 not one ship was put to sea." True, Berkh attributes it partly to the fact that "the sizable profits made by many of those engaged in that pursuit induced them to leave it and to

enjoy in peace the fortune they had acquired." Yet he notes
at the same time that a part of the fortune-hunters "having
suffered several setbacks, were compelled to give up the
occupation in which fortune no longer smiled upon them."[18]

In 1785 only one ship, belonging to the merchant Panov of
Totemsk, set out for the islands. Two years later that ship
brought back 1388 sea-otters and 183 blue foxes,--figures
which, according to Berkh's testimony, "will astound the
reader," since in past years some vessels would bring back
more than forty thousand sea-otter skins.

The same ship set out for the islands again in 1787. It
stayed there until 1793 and again returned with an insignificant cargo. "Hardly," testifies the same Berkh, "did the
skins brought on that boat cover the cost of the round trip
and of maintaining the ship for eight years."[19]

The reduction in the quantity of furs available in accessible places brought ruin upon the small companies and the
individual merchants. It was now beyond the reach of small
groups of fur-hunters to take possession of new areas. When
in 1783 a group of hunters with the navigator Zaikov at their
head attempted to effect a landing in Chugatsk Bay, they met
with resistance on the part of the natives. "The fearless
natives of Chugatsk," writes V. Berkh, "who had, by their
raids, spread terror among all the surrounding tribes, and
especially among the inhabitants of Kodiak, were not to be
frightened by Russian guns. They performed so successfully
and so bravely with their arrows that in many skirmishes
they got the upperhand over their enemies, and, to make
matters worse, they blocked their way to the trading-posts
and to subsistence.... In order to defend themselves against
the enemy, one third of the entire ship's company remained
the whole night under arms, fearing a sudden attack."[20]

The seizure of new places on the continent required not
only immense expeditions but also the establishment of
strong settlements. It was impossible to plunge deeper into
the interior of the country without setting up fortified bases,
without the systematic dispatch of expeditions to supply those
bases, and without planned action.

Chapter II

THE ORGANIZATION OF THE RUSSIAN-
AMERICAN COMPANY

IN THE LATER 1770's there appears a new name among the
names of the Russian traders operating in the Pacific Sea,
that of Grigory Ivanovich Shelikhov, Honorary Citizen of the
town of Rylsk. Shelikhov, who, in the course of two decades
became one of the wealthiest merchants of Siberia, had
started his business career with almost no means at his disposal. F.F. Veselago makes the conjecture that it was the
capital which Natalya Shelikhov brought her husband that enabled him to open up his operations in America.[1] Shelikhov's
commercial successes belong primarily to the end of the
1780's and the first part of the 1790's. It is known, at any
rate, that even in 1783, when Shelikhov set out to survey
the condition of the trading-posts on the islands, he was
compelled to resort to a loan. He obtained fifty thousand
rubles from N.N. Demidov, who owned some smelting works
in the Urals.

Shelikhov returned from his "American voyage" in 1787.[2]
This "Russian Columbus," who announced "the discovery of
the islands of Kyktak and Afognak, newly acquired by him and
which had not been reached even by the renowned English
navigator Cook," returned from America firmly resolved to
obtain from the government the pre-emptive right to exploit
the fur-resources of the region.

In view of the exacerbated competition that had developed
in the colonies, the sending of an expedition on the same
basis as before might have led to the complete destruction of
the trading companies. By the end of the 1780's the small
trade associations hardly ventured to send their boats to the
islands and to the American continent. Even for the large
trade associations, which were engaged in fierce competition
among themselves, business conditions were becoming more
and more difficult from year to year.

At that time, Shelikhov already occupied one of the most
important places among the large associations that were

active on the islands and on the American continent. Beginning with the year 1777, upon the return of the "Nicholas" which was partially equipped at Shelikhov's expense, a considerable part of the peltry brought from the colonies belonged to him. He was a stockholder in most of the expeditions that made their way to America. He participated with his capital in the equipping of fourteen out of the thirty-six ships returning from the hunting-posts in the twenty-one year period from 1777 to 1797; one ship ("John of Rylsk") belonged to him completely. Each of the vessels that belonged jointly to Shelikhov and Golikov, a Kursk merchant, brought back more than 300,000 rubles worth of peltry. The considerable quantity of game bagged was due to the fact that the company in question possessed a number of solid settlements on Afognak Island and in other places.

However, some serious rivals to Shelikhov did appear at that time. Nine of the thirty-six ships we have mentioned were equipped by the merchants Panov. In contrast to Shelikhov's practice only two of their ships were sent out in company with the other merchants, while the remaining ones set out for the hunting-posts independently. The value of the furs brought back on the Panov vessels also reached considerable dimensions,--the value of the peltry brought back in the course of a single year not infrequently came to 200,000 rubles.[3]

There also grew up a number of other large companies with considerable assets. One of the well known companies was that of Lebedev-Lastochkin, which was distinguished by a spirit of enterprise and which also went in for establishing a network of permanent settlements. The competition between this company and Shelikhov's was subsequently to lead to armed clashes between the two.

There ensued a period of fierce struggle between the large associations, which, in view of the vast funds at their disposal, were in a position to enter upon new forms of exploitation of the region. This competitive battle, complicated as it had become by the increasing penetration of foreign fur-hunters into the Russian sphere of operations, was to set before the rival associations a whole series of pressing problems, lacking a solution to which their further activity would become unprofitable. It was necessary to assure the consolidation of definite areas for hunting purposes. Otherwise there was no justification for the exploration and seizure of new regions--

both carried out at a tremendous cost--for, on the heels of
the large companies came the petty traders who, at no expense to themselves utilized to the full the results of the
various expeditions. Directly bound up with the question of
consolidating the new regions was that of establishing permanent settlements on the islands and on the continent itself.
This required considerable investments, which only an
economically powerful association was capable of making.

It was also necessary to obtain a maximum reduction in
expenses, first of all in the remuneration of the Russian
fur-traders, which absorbed one half of the cost of the furs.
The situation with respect to the natives was quite different;
the trading companies were not in the habit of treating them
with excessive solicitude. The systematic exploitation of the
labor of the natives, on the other hand, required government
sanction; for acts of violence against the natives, which
formerly went unpunished under the conditions of competition
then existing among the several companies that accused each
other of cruelty toward the indigenous population, could now
lead to most unpleasant results. The fear of such consequences tended to restrain, to a certain degree, the extent
of the exploitation of the native population and of the violence
against them on the part of the companies. Finally, it was
indispensable for the definitive consolidation on the islands
and on the continent to maintain an armed force which would
be capable, when necessary, of offering resistance not only
to the natives but to foreign hunters as well.

The realization of these conditions, which were closely
related to government measures, was naturally contingent
upon the granting of definite advantages to some one company
over others. An economic monopoly was, from the merchants' point of view, an indispensable prerequisite to a new
stage in the exploitation of the islands and of a portion of the
American continent. As an example of the benefits derived
from such a monopoly they would cite the operations of the
East India Company, whose ships more than once visited
the Russian settlements in America, and even Kamchatka.

In the given case, the interests of a group of merchants,
particularly those of Shelikhov, who were endeavoring to
obtain exclusive advantages for themselves, coincided with
the interests of the government as a whole. The latter, not
wishing to take the risk of international complications which
might result from the official annexation of the American

colonies to the Russian Empire, saw in the creation of a mighty monopolistic company a way to mask its own expansion along the shores of the Pacific.

If a crown administration were to be established in the colonies, the most trifling conflict might easily be transformed into an armed clash with foreign powers; the situation would be different, if a commercial company were to attempt to realize the very same purposes. In the latter case the possibility of diplomatic complications would be considerably smaller--the government could always keep in the background and attribute the sporadic clashes to the activity of the merchants acting at their own peril and on their own responsibility.

Shelikhov took account of the favorable circumstances as they had developed and, fearing lest he be outmaneuvered by the representatives of the competing associations, immediately upon his arrival in Irkutsk in 1787 presented to the Governor a detailed plan for the formation of a strong company.

Shelikhov's plan consisted of nine points. The first and the fifth points were devoted to the question of the subordination of the company to some government department. It was Shelikhov's thought that the company in order "to prevent confusion," should not be dependent upon the administration of Kamchatka or Okhotsk, but, being regarded as under "the highest patronage," should be wholly subject to the Governor-General of Irkutsk. At the same time, the company should be granted the right, in special cases, to communicate directly with Empress Catherine, by sending reports to her via its own couriers. The last provision was apparently intended to protect the company from any arbitrary measures on the part of the governor-general of Irkutsk.

Points 2, 3, and 4 dealt with questions that were of the utmost importance to the future company, the recruiting of an armed guard and of the necessary labor force. Shelikhov wrote as follows:

"For the further assistance of the company's enterprises in the future it is of the utmost necessity that the company be provided with means of maintaining the existing fortresses, and furnished with up to a hundred military men, adept in discipline, for the purpose of protecting and defending the peoples brought by me, in

the name of the Company, under the rule of her Imperial
Highness."[4]

These men were to include five cannoneers, several can-
non-smelters and armorers from Tula, a few anchorers,
three officers, one of whom with a knowledge of "mountain
science" (i.e., mining), a number of sailors with a knowledge of rigging, a few master workmenffamiliar with shipbuilding, and others. In other words, these one hundred
men would constitute that indispensable nucleus of technical
and military specialists that would guarantee the possibility
of producing the necessary weapons in the colonies themselves and of training the garrisons established there. The
latter were to be recruited from among the natives. It was
proposed to create, on the pattern of the East India Company,
a contingent in the nature of sepoy colonial troops.

This plan was developed by Shelikhov in a memorandum
addressed to Empress Catherine which he together with his
partner Golikov presented in person as a supplement in
February 1788. We read the following:

"Now, to assist the troops we could profitably employ
up to several thousand of the inhabitants of the islands, a
plucky people, of sound constitution, well fitted to endure
any sort of difficulties, qualified for any enterprise, fearless, and whose obedience to the Russian authorities and
devotion to your Imperial Highness we have already proved
by actual experience on many occasions." The natives
"are not only reliable in the event of internal troubles but
may be trusted, without the slightest doubt, to offer strong
resistance in the event of possible hostile attempts on the
part of foreign powers."[5]

That was the situation with regard to the armed guard for
the future company. As for the labor force, that was to be
recruited in several ways. The company was to be granted
the right "to hire Russians of all classes, even those possessing lapsed passports, upon annual payment of the government taxes for them, for each one in the place where he
is found"; and also to hire men from among those "who have
become insolvent." Simultaneously the company was, according to Shelikhov's plan, to be given fifty convicts who
would be employed primarily in farming. In this way the

Russian labor force was to be recruited from people with
lapsed passports, insolvent debtors, and convicts, that is,
from classes that could be exploited without any trouble, and
who would never have the opportunity to break with the company.

The nucleus, however, of the labor force in the hunting-
posts was to consist of natives. According to Shelikhov's
ideas, the company was to obtain the necessary contingent
of native laborers by buying "from the Americans a number
of men they have taken prisoner and who have belonged to
them for a long time and of whom the Americans have an
abundance." These slaves, called "kalgi," were to become
the absolute property of the Company. As to the Aleuts and
the people of the Kuriles, the Company demanded the right
"to exercise the freedom of hiring them for naval posts, or
for other exigencies that might arise in the present enterprises of the company."[6]

The remaining points of Shelikhov's plan provided for the
granting to the company of the privilege of building its own
port on the Uda River, since the port of Okhotsk was quite
unsuited for handling ships; and the right to establish commercial relations with "Japan, China, Korea, India, the
Philippine Islands and other islands, and in America with
the Spaniards and the Americans." In addition to all this,
on account of the losses incurred as a result of the continued
stoppage of the Kiakhta trade, the Company was to receive
a 20-year loan of 500,000 rubles and a ship from the port of
Okhotsk. Finally, the ninth and last point required that "in
order to encourage the people serving with the Company, who
are exercising their duties under the direction of the officials
placed over them and under the supervision of the company,
it would be necessary to assure every one who deserves it
of recognition and distinction."[7]

The question of the monopoly was formulated by Shelikhov
with complete frankness only some time later, a few months
after he had submitted his plan to the Governor-General in
the petition to Empress Catherine. Evidently Shelikhov had
had time to satisfy himself that it would be all right to come
out openly with a request for a monopoly and that his plans
would not meet with any opposition in government circles.

"Furthermore we beg most humbly," wrote Shelikhov,
"to be protected, ourselves and our property, from danger
on the part of other people who might want to make use of

our discoveries and, in the very same places that we have
acquired, supplied, and constructed at our expense and by
our labor, attack and assail our hunting-posts, and bring
ruin and destruction upon everything that we have already
built and that we plan to build in the future."[8]

At the same time Shelikhov prudently reduced the amount
of the subvention he had requested from 500,000 to 200,000
rubles.

The plans of Shelikhov and of his partner Golikov were
submitted for examination to the Commerce Commission
which, in March 1788, recognized them as worthy of consideration and gave them its approval. Catherine, however,
did not agree with the Commission's decision. In the words
of a Senate decree of September 12, 1788, "it has pleased
Her Imperial Highness to order: 1) that the request of these
merchants, in a petition for a subsidy of 200,000 rubles
from the Treasury for the strengthening of their new establishments therein mentioned and for further activities be
denied; 2) that Her Highness does not regard it right to
give them the exclusive concession to those voyages and to
that trade, since the granting of such a concession would not
be at all in agreement with the principles adopted by Her
Highness for abolishing monopolies of no matter what kind;
3) that it was impossible to provide them with an armed
contingent of some one hundred men and with artillery crews,
considering the otherwise existing need of troops in that
region, where it is hardly possible to bring them in to meet
the need."[9]   Of the whole plan only point 9 was approved,
that of rewarding the members of the Company. Shelikhov
and Golikov were presented with swords and medals "to
wear around their necks, with the portrait of Her Highness
on one side and with an explanation of the award on the other."

Shelikhov's failure, however, cannot be explained by
Catherine's opposition to monopolies. As early as 1764 she
had granted to the two companies of the merchants Yugov and
Trapeznikov exclusive hunting privileges, with the stipulation
that one tenth of all the peltry which they obtained besides
the fur-tribute collected by them, be handed over to the
Treasury. However, the loss of a number of ships belonging
to those companies rendered it impossible for them to make
use of the privileges they had been granted. Two years later,
in a ukase dated March 2, 1766, and addressed to Governor
Chicherin of Siberia, Catherine approved the granting of

monopoly rights to the merchant Adrian of the Tolstoys in the
following words:

> "I hereby confirm your promise to the merchant Tolstoy
> that I will grant certain privileges to the company which
> had previously withdrawn from such a sea voyage, and
> return to him the tenth part of the fur-tribute collected
> from these islands and originally taken from him."[10]

But this company was also unable to realize the privileges
granted to it, because it was economically weak.

Therefore, the assertion that the refusal to grant monopoly privileges to Shelikhov's company was motivated by
the consideration that such a grant "would not be in agreement with the principles adopted by Her Imperial Highness"
hardly conformed to the truth. It is evident that Catherine
refused the request of Shelikhov's company on account of the
general political situation of Russia at that time. The war
with Turkey began in 1787, and the war with Sweden broke
out in 1788. It was necessary again to center all attention
on the European continent. During that period, too, the
alliance between England and Tsarist Russia assumes a
more definite form, an alliance which was finally consolidated in 1791 by their joint action against the middle class
revolution in France. The desire to preserve friendly relations with England was, furthermore, intensified by the
circumstance that the outcome of the two wars in which
Russia was engaged depended, to a large extent, upon the
position of the English government with relation to Turkey
and Sweden. The tsarist government considered it simply
impossible to grant at that time any franchises to any
trading company whatsoever that was active in America. It
would have meant giving official sanction to activities which
would encroach upon the interests of England. That was apparently the decisive reason that prompted Catherine to
postpone for a time the plan for creating a monopolistic
company.

Shelikhov and Golikov, the two aspirants to a monopoly,
were compelled in spite of royal favors, to fortify themselves with a great deal of patience, and in the meantime, to
preserve their predominance in the trading-posts on the
American continent and to nurse their contacts in Court; for,

otherwise, their privileges might fall into the hands of others
the moment it should become possible to grant them.   Utilizi:
the patronage of Zubov, Catherine's favorite, Shelikhov tried
to attract the Empress' attention by his activity.   Smitten
with unusual zeal for the Greek Orthodox Church, he swamps
her with requests for permission to erect churches in the
colonies, since the appearance of the Russians in those parts
"kindles in...those peoples who have no law of any kind the
eagerness to become Christians." Simultaneously, Shelikhov
partner Golikov besieges the houses of the Synod authorities
in St. Petersburg, entreating them to send a clerical mission
to America at the company's expense, since close to 100,000
natives are waiting there "for God's enlightenment." The per
severance of the merchants from Rylsk and Kursk had its
results; Catherine ordered the Synod to assist Shelikhov and
Golikov "in establishing and propagating the Orthodox faith
among the peoples of North America."[11]

The real attitude, however, of these experienced business-
men towards "the ministers of religion" finds expression in
one of G.I. Shelikhov's letters to A.A. Baranov, General
Manager of the Company's colony in America. That letter,
superconfidential in character, was sent out at the same
time as was another letter dealing with the same questions
but in an official capacity. "We consider it necessary,"
wrote Shelikhov on August 9, 1794, "to write to you hereby,
strictly for your own consumption, the following things concerning the business of the Company, because our letter to
you about the new settlement is to be presented to the government which is not supposed to know our internal affairs."
Telling of the coming arrival of the clerical mission in the
colony, Shelikhov orders the construction of a monastery in
the village for the use of the mission, and adds, not without
malice, that it should be "so built together with the church
that the monks should be unable to see what the lay brothers
are doing, and the lay brothers should be unable to see what
the monks are doing."[12]

At the same time Grigory Shelikhov did not neglect the
expansion of his commercial operations on the American
continent. His plans were distinguished by breadth of scope,
revealing him as a man of great ability, endowed with the
spirit of enterprise, and far in advance of his contemporaries.
In his representation of February 11, 1790, to Governor-
General Pil of Irkutsk, Shelikhov, "for the purpose of learning

about the shores of the American continent that extend toward
the North Pole," proposes a plan for an expedition to the Arctic, "in order to dispatch ships directly from the mouth of
Lena, Indigirka or Kolyma to the opposite American shores,
for measuring the width at that point and for studying the
routes in that part of the Arctic Sea and the Bering Strait."
Simultaneously with this expedition, another expedition was
to explore the whole expanse between Okhotsk and north of
the Bering Strait, proceeding along the Aleutian chain. In
the same representation Shelikhov returns anew to the question of granting his company certain privileges, although he
now renounces his claim to a government loan in these words:

"As to our request at that time for a loan in the form of a
sum of money, that we now waive."[13]

Notwithstanding the concessions which the company was
ready to make, the question of the privileges was not yet
ripe for a positive solution; for Shelikhov's failure in his
negotiations was, as we have noted, by no means caused by
financial considerations. Still, while refusing to grant to
the Shelikhov company the privileges it requested, the government was at the same time carefully considering that company as a possible nucleus for a monopoly organization which
would in time be charged with the exploitation and defense
of the Russian colonies in America.

"I believe," wrote Governor-General Pil of Irkutsk to
Catherine in 1790, "that if the ships that the Shelikhov company has on hand were to be combined with the other Russian
trading vessels that are plying the waters of those regions,
and if all of them were generally to agree on regarding as
their main object not the mere protection of their own benefit, but would willingly participate in the curbing of foreign
hunters and traders, only then, it seems to me, it may be
expected, though not directly, that, through their efforts,
the audacity of the Europeans in pilfering the treasures belonging to Russia will diminish."[14]

But, if it was possible, to a certain degree, to count on
the company fleet in the event of a clash with foreign trap pers,
that fleet was, of course, incapable of playing any part whatsoever in the event of armed resistance on the part of some
foreign power. The granting of a franchise had to be postponed until such time as a secure military base had been
created in the Pacific. This thought is very clearly expressed in one of the reports to Catherine by the same Governor-

General Pil of Irkutsk. While giving his full approval to the
activities of the Shelikhov-Golikov Company, Pil believed
that "the profitable advance of the Company along the American coast" would be possible only when "the port on the Uda
had been established and our military forces had been increased."[15]

In the expectation of a favorable situation Shelikhov aimed
to put the colonies in "proper" shape, since they would, in
the near future, be supposed to attain the same condition as
the English colonies in the East Indies. He worked out a
series of measures, all approved by the Governor-General
of Irkutsk, the realization of which was to begin in 1795.
Shelikhov ordered Baranov, administrator of the Company's
affairs on the islands and in America, to find a place suitable for the establishment of a colonial center. "I find," wrot
Shelikhov to him, "that it is incomparably better to establish
a permanent Russian settlement on the mainland than on an
island where foreigners can always come, from whom, in
case of necessity, it is also easier to find refuge on the
mainland; and in general, for the political reasons known to
you, greater efforts should be made to occupy the mainland
rather than the islands."[16]

Shelikhov paid especial attention to the external planning
of this center of Russian colonies on the American continent,
emphasizing repeatedly that "the settlement should, as far
as possible, be built in good taste, and with the necessary
comforts, so that it might, from the very beginning, have
the character of a city and not of a village, in order that
when a foreign vessel arrives, and it should be impossible
to get rid of it, it would be possible to boast that the Russians
live in good order and that the foreigners should not think
that the Russians live just as abominably in America as they
do in Okhotsk where the air is foul and all the necessities are
lacking."[17]

Shelikhov's proposed plan for this new city which was to
be called "Slavorossiya" (Glory of Russia)--a name which
was to be applied to the whole region--included the laying
out of wide streets with identical houses, broad squares
where the public buildings would be concentrated and where,
in time, a series of obelisks would be raised in "honor of
the Russian patriots." "And big strong gates should be erected for the entry and exit," Shelikhov ordered Baranov, "and
they should appropriately be called 'Russian Gates,' or

'Chugach Gates,' or 'Kinai Gates,' or else something like
'Glory of Russia' or 'Glory of America.' And they should always be bolted, and people should be allowed in and out only
upon your orders....The redoubts too, should be named in
honor of our great hereditary reigning sovereigns. These
forts should each have as many as twenty cannon, so that
they could operate in all directions, and one cannon should
be mounted inside the settlement, by the main guard, in case
of necessity." In the morning at the flag-raising ceremony,
boys "instructed in music" should beat the drum, and in the
evening there should be "music sometimes in the fortress or
on the redoubts." "Now in order to lend greater importance
to the settlement in case of a visit from foreign or native
visitors, you would do well to put nice jackets, like those
worn by military men, on the trappers you brought over to
the settlement to become skilled workers, and give them
arms when necessary, only they should wear their bayonets
at their side."[18]

About 1794 Baranov had 149 men under his command on
Kodiak. During 1794, another 123 men were sent to him by
boat from Okhotsk, including some artisans and peasants
from among the convicts, who were being sent to Kodiak by
order of Catherine. Adding to them the Aleuts and Indians,
Baranov had at his disposal certain forces that he could already use in attempting to realize the plan outlined for establishing "Slavorossiya."

The plan was to extend two types of inducements to the
natives to settle in "Slavorossiya." On the one hand, there
were the natives who worked for the Company and who were,
apparently, to be colonized independently; on the other hand
there were the "kalgi", or slaves, a part of whom had been
handed over to the Russian settlers in direct vassalage. "You
should be figuring out ways," Shelikhov points out to Baranov,
"to induce an increasing number of Americans, both men and
women, to settle in the new colony, so that it may be possible
with a great many people to till and sow everything more
speedily and more easily. In this way, too, the American
will more speedily and more easily become accustomed to
our way of life. In particular it is possible to utilize for
this purpose the ransomed prisoners and those who are yet
to be ransomed and who, by right of ransom, may be relied
upon to a greater degree than the others to obey the settlers
to whom they would be handed over to help with the work and

who would be under strict notice to try, by kind treatment, to win their attachment."[19]

By distributing the slaves among the Russian settlers, Shelikhov wanted to create a class of permanently "well-to-do" colonists who would be completely bound up economically with the American settlements.

Everything had thus been provided for, so that when the time came to transform the trade associations belonging to the Shelikhov-Golikov Company into a monopolistic organization, the new company would at once be able to develop its activity. In 1794 Shelikhov organized the new "Northern Company," not as a temporary association but as a permanently active company. Article 2 of the over-all contract of the Northern Company reads as follows:

> "This company is not to be regarded as consisting of just one vessel which we will send out from this time forward, and be like the other companies that have a definite term for dispatching ships with freight; it is, on the contrary, to be regarded as a permanent company, one that does not change in accordance with the number of vessels it has, for the increase or decrease in their number for the purposes of transportation and exploration will depend upon us, in proportion to the success we shall have achieved."[20]

Parallel with the establishment of a settlement in America Shelikhov was preoccupied in those years with numerous plans for opening up new markets for Russian trade. He was busy negotiating for permission to send "merchant ships to Canton, Macao, Batavia, the Philippines and the Marianas with products and manufactured articles obtainable in America and partly in Russia, and to bring back to America from those places all that the Russians settling there and the native inhabitants need."[21]

His plan to explore the mouth of the Amur, a project which was to be undertaken by the Tsarist government only in the 1840's and 1850's is also of extraordinary interest. Shelikhov proposed that the expedition "should proceed along the crest of the broken mountain range which has its inception in the Irkutsk Government, near Lake Baikal, then sweeps on eastward and terminates at the shore of the sea into which flow the famous Amur River and that other river the Uda...."

Coming down to the sea, the expedition should search for a
site where company vessels might find a safe landing place."[22]

Grigory Shelikhov did not live to see the day, however,
when the company created by him received franchises similar to those enjoyed by the East India Company. In 1795,
"in the midst of his exploits, he departed from this world,
leaving to his bereaved widow and children the management
of all affairs relating to America."[23]

It was during that period that the struggle between the
competing companies reached its climax. In the colonies
this struggle had almost assumed the form of open warfare
between the trappers of the rival associations. The situation of the Shelikhov Company became more and more difficult. Here is what Baranov, General Manager of the
Shelikhov Company, writes to his employers from the port
of Pavlovsk in May 1795:

"The 'Lebedevskys' [i.e. the fur-hunters of Lebedev-
Lastochkin Company.--Au:] have occupied all...the suitable
places. We should have flown into a rage, but we are power-
less,--we are cut off from all the feeding places."[24]

Even before this, Baranov had reported attacks made by
the "Lebedevskys" both on the natives working on company
projects and on regular Shelikhov workers:

"Now I am going to tell you about the 'Lebedevskys,'
and how they...joining together in the two vessels, the
'John' and the 'George,' made it a habit to do harm to our
company and have indeed begun to force us out of here.
First they seized the Bay of Kachikmat along the Gulf of
Kenai and established a large artel there, and would not
let us engage in fox-hunting, even where we proved to
them that we had been the original occupants of the winter
cabin we had built.... And finally, by way of confirmation,
I also received bad news from Malakhov[25] amd from the
Gulf of Kenai, that they had actually stopped at our artel--
sixty of them, including Russians and a few dissenters--
and already begun to act in a hostile manner. While
some of them put our Russian worker Kotelnikov under
guard, a few of the dissenters seized our canoes and
removed the gun-carriages, and so forth from those that
had them, beating and mutilating the workers, tying up
those unable to save themselves in flight, throwing them
into the canoes, and carrying them off."[26]

The further commercial independence of all the other
merchants was contingent upon the struggle with the Shelikhov Company which claimed the exclusive right to the exploi
tation of the American fur-trade. The death of Shelikhov
and Golikov's retirement from the directorship of the Company made the task of the other merchants considerably
easier. "Many Irkutsk merchants," we read in a memorandum presented by Shelikhov's heirs to the Board of Commerce, "have for many years been nursing a grudge against
the activities of the late Shelikhov, accusing him of having
been the one to take away their trade on the Pacific (Eastern)
Sea and enriching himself in the very area where it was
proper only for them to enrich themselves. They began to
plot in various ways against Shelikhov's widow, now bringing
paper lawsuits against her, now slandering her before the
authorities--and, most important of all, working dishonor-
ably to undermine her credit."27

The company of Shelikhov's heirs was threatened with decline, and only by securing for itself the right of monopoly to
the exploitation of the Russian colonies in America would it
have had the opportunity to free itself of its rivals and to
maintain its predominant position in hunting and trading in
the Pacific.

The ferocious competitive struggle among the Russian
hunting companies which was more and more assuming the
form of open combat, presented new opportunities to the
merchants from other lands. Taking advantage of the weakness of the Russian fur-hunters, the foreign merchants, especially the English, started to make more frequent maraud-
ing expeditions for furs on the American continent. The
situation in the Russian colonies in America and on the islands had, by the end of the 1790's, become a question of their
very existence.

As Karl Marx wrote in his essay on "The Administration
of India": "When the company of English adventurer-mer-
chants, who conquered India for the purpose of whipping
some money out of it, began to expand the network of its
trading-posts and convert them into a real government organization, its competition with the Dutch and French private
merchants began to assume the character of national rivalry,
and the English government could not, of course, help taking
a hand in the affairs of the East India Company...."28 So
that when the rivalry between the Russian adventurer mer-

chants and the English, like the competition between the English and the Dutch and the English and the French, also assumed the character of national rivalry, the Russian government intervened decisively in the affairs of the hunting companies.

This intervention became possible, however, only in the
last years of the eighteenth century, when as a result of
England's active opposition to new Russian attempts to infiltrate into Turkey, relations between the two countries became
strained. It was this rupture with England that presented
Russia with the opportunity to realize the plans which were
impossible of achievement in the preceding period of friendship with the English government, a friendship which had
been fortified by the necessity of forming a united front
against the middle class revolution in France. Emperor
Paul followed substantially the path already marked out in
the reign of Catherine. He aimed to create an organization
that would firmly carry out the policy of forcing the English
trading companies out of Alaska, the Aleutians, and China,
and would, at the same time, proceed with further expansion.

On June 9, 1797, Paul, at the instance of Governor Nagel
of Irkutsk, promulgated a decision in connection with the
newly created company, headed by the merchant Mylnikov,
in which he ordered "that approval be given in this matter
without harming the already established company of the first
acquisitor Shelikhov, and that the proper measures be taken
to gather...information from those participating in that
company."[29]

According to collected information, the capital of the
Mylnikov Company, notwithstanding the great number of co-
partners, slightly exceeded 100,000 rubles. It becomes
clear from the correspondence on the ban on the company's
operations that the reasons for the ban did not by any means
lie in the necessity of defending the interests of "the first
acquisitor" Shelikhov, but in that apprehension that a company with such meager resources might not be able to prevent "the American acquisitions from falling a prey to those
powers that have long looked with envious eyes at the infant
companies in this field."[30]

The opinion of the Board of Commerce that it was necessary to limit the number of companies doing business on the
islands and on the American continent and to give preferential
treatment to Shelikhov's company had, apparently, become

known in Irkutsk prior to the official decision. This information caused the group of Irkutsk merchants who joined
Mylnikov's company to change their tactics slightly and to
try, by uniting with the company of Shelikhov's and Golikov's
heirs, to obtain the right to operate in the American colonies.

On June 20, 1797, the so-called union between the Shelikhov-Golikov Company and the one headed by Mylnikov was
consummated--the latter company having actually been organized before it had received permission to do so from the
Board of Commerce. The new company received the name
of "Soyedinennaya Amerikanskaya Kompaniya" (United American Company). But in joining with Shelikhov's heirs to help
establish the United American Company, the organizers of
the "Irkutskaya Kommercheskaya Mylnikova s tovarishchami
kompaniya" (Commercial Company of Mylnikov and Associ-
ates of Irkutsk) had no intention to undertake any joint action,
but only to evade the barriers which had been raised against
all newly created companies as a result of Paul's decision.

In this intricate commercial combination Mylnikov operated with the aid of Golikov who, although he was regarded
as a partner of Shelikhov's, had in fact withdrawn from all
direct management of the affairs of the Company. Threatening to leave the Company completely and to withdraw his investment, Golikov, whom Mylnikov had paid a certain sum
for this, obtained the consent of Shelikhov's widow to the
union with Mylnikov. The latter, however, was unsuccessful in his desire to keep the union fictitious, for the Board
of Commerce did not stop half-way, but, having adopted the
firm policy of establishing a single powerful monopolistic
company in the Russian colonies in America, it insisted on
an actual union, and not only of the two companies in question
but of all existing companies. It was no longer a question
of granting exclusive rights to any one company, even as
strong a one as the Shelikhov Company, but of creating a
truly powerful monopolistic association which would be in a
position to compete successfully with the foreign merchants
and to counteract British expansion. Even leaving out of
consideration the magnitude of the resources which a company of that type would have to have at its disposal, it would
still have to be wholly subjected to government control, lest
the commercial interests force into the background the political aim of the company--the gaining possession of the Pacific
coastal region.

The government consequently took the following step: it forced the amalgamation of all the companies operating in the colonies and then brought their activity under government control. These questions were clearly formulated in the memorandum entitled "O vrednosti mnogikh v Amerike kompanii i pol'ze ot soyedineniya ikh voyedino" (On the Harmfulness of Many Companies in America and the Advantages of Combining Them Into One), which the Board of Commerce presented to Paul on August 5, 1797. In it the Board proposed that the following measures be put into effect:

"1. Putting all the companies under one office or person upon whom would be conferred the title of Protector of the American Companies, and who would intercede with Your Royal Highness for them with a view to filling the needs of the Company, as, for example, supplying them with seamen, shipmates, manufactured goods, and other necessities; who would personally receive the report of the Company and would in turn report to Your Majesty about the progress of the Company and would see whether the Company's operations are in accord with our political aims. This is necessary because the reports prepared by the governments established by the Company in the several states might sometimes include certain matters which should not become known in places of litigation.

"2. Uniting all the traders in one body which, on the model of the East and the West India Companies would be governed by directors chosen from among the stockholders. To them would be assigned one representative of the Crown, who would not meddle in business matters in any way, but whose duty it would be to observe to what extent the regulations prescribed for the Company by the government were being carried out; otherwise, he would report to the office or to the official whom your Imperial Highness would deign to entrust with the responsibility."[31]

It was especially emphasized in the memorandum of the Board of Commerce that the joint company, "by intensifying the building of ships, will within a short time, raise a whole fleet in the East that will render our American possessions completely secure."

According to the decision made by Paul, who was in agreement with the proposal submitted by the Board of Commerce,

the company was to be under the "directorship" of the Board
of Commerce itself and the establishment of new companies
"will not be allowed henceforth except with the consent of
the original founders themselves."[32]

It remained only to bring the matter to a conclusion, that
is to effectuate the union of all the companies.

The only trading company that was interested in the realization of the plan as formulated by the Board of Commerce
was that belonging to Shelikhov's heirs. In the unification to
be accomplished, Shelikhov's heirs, who at that time were
already in possession of a vast capital, were indisputably
destined to occupy a preeminent position. This fact, in conjunction with the manifest protection extended to Shelikhov's
heirs in court circles, made it possible for them to swallow
up their rivals and to become complete masters of the new
association. For this reason the other Irkutsk merchants
were violently opposed to the plan of the Board of Commerce.

On July 12, 1798, Treiden, the Civil Governor of Irkutsk,
informed the Board of Commerce that the future stockholders,
though "they led his predecessor to hope that they would give
the proper response to the proposal of the Board of Commerce
on the unification of the separate companies into one," not
one of them had until then presented his reply, except the
merchant Lebedev-Lastochkin, who refused categorically to
join the company, and the merchant Kiselev who handed in a
petition for protection against "possible pressure on his
business on the part of the company." Moreover, "the original partners, Golikov, Mylnikov and the agent of Shelikhov's
widow," as the Governor reported, "began to enter complaints
against each other for vaious supposed failures to perform."
The Board, seeing in such an attitude on the part of "voluntarily uniting" stockholders "only a waste of time, " decided
"to renew its demand...to the aforementioned governor,
explaining to him that, since it cannot waste any more time
in vain expectation of a public, unanimous decision by the
partners themselves, it considers it necessary to set about
the realization of the directive applicable to them."[33]

The opponents of the Shelikhov Company did not, however,
limit their efforts to fighting the new company in Irkutsk; they
had previously carried on a campaign in court circles against
the granting of a franchise to the future Russian-American
Company. In their attack on the granting of monopoly rights
to the united company, the rivals of Shelikhov's heirs brought

forth a plan for the administration of the American colonies
by the Crown that would obviate the creation of a monopolistic company. The whole administration of the colonies would
be entrusted to a state-appointed commissar. The plan for
a crown administration read, among other things:

> "It is necessary, in the meantime, both in order to
> protect the natives against abuses on the part of the fur-
> hunters and in order to bring about a change in the cus-
> toms of the inhabitants and train them to obedience and
> acceptance of the laws, to institute in America the form
> of a crown administration for that region."[34]

The government offices in St. Petersburg swarmed with
lobbyists of the Irkutsk merchants who employed persuasion
and even graft in an attempt to avert the threatening loss of
their commercial independence. The granting of privileges
to the United Company was fought not only by the merchants
who were not included in it, but even by some of the stockholders of the Company, including Golikov who acted in con-
cert with Mylnikov.

The agent for Shelikhov's heirs, in a private letter to a
correspondent in Irkutsk, wrote as follows about the complete failure of his rivals' efforts:

"Golikov's agents poked about everywhere, but didn't hit
the right track. Neither were Kiselev's scribblings of any
avail."[35]

The merchant Kiselev attempted to bring an accusation
against the Shelikhov Company of employing harsh methods
in its exploitation of the Aleuts. But this attempt to arouse
opposition to Shelikhov's heirs in official circles was also
unsuccessful. Two of the three Aleutian "toyons" (elders),
who had managed to escape with the aid of Kiselev's agents,
reached St. Petersburg and even obtained an audience with
Paul in 1798. The petitions of the Aleuts, which described
the shocking facts of the hunters' shameless carryings-on
on the islands and their dealings with the natives, did not,
however, produce any results. The Aleuts were rewarded
with gala dress and sent back empty-handed. The priest
Makary, who accompanied them, came within an inch of paying the penalty for his willful absentation from the islands.

The interests of Shelikhov's heirs were upheld in St. Petersburg by Shelikhov's brother-in-law Rezanov, Head-Procurator

of the First Department of the Senate. The "scribblings" of
the merchant Kiselev and others could not, of course, make
any headway against the papers which Rezanov composed
over the widow Shelikhov's signature and presented to various departments. Being close to government circles Rezanov knew what arguments would be the most effective at the
moment.

In one of the representations submitted to Soymonov in
1798 even the problems of combatting a revolution were advanced to prove the necessity for granting certain privileges
to the Company. Beginning with the statement that "the history of the past centuries shows clearly what great sacrifices
Spain and Portugal have had to pay in their rapid, strenuous,
and more military operations, and how harmful have been
the violent actions against the Americans," Rezanov states
that only "commerce" is capable "of softening the manners"
of the American natives. "Commerce is necessary," he
continues, "because once it has softened the manners of the
savages by bringing them into continuous contact with the
Russians, it can painlessly lay the foundation for all kinds of
comforts derived from agriculture and the handicrafts, and
gradually accustom those peoples to the Russian way of looking at things, a way which ascribes the people's well-being
to the monarchistic system and, therefore, holds out the
promise of turning the natives, too, in time into loyal and
decent subjects. Otherwise," we read further, "the trading
nations that are envious of us and often take a peep into
those regions, may, especially in view of the present unrest
in Europe, lead those natives astray, gullible as they are,
and infuse them with the spirit of republicanism. Most to be
feared in this connection are our English neighbors who have
settled in Nutka and on Hudson Bay and who are secretly envious of our American possessions."[36] Apparently even an
argument of this nature sounded convincing to Paul.

In the same memorandum are also expressed the Company's objections to the introduction of a crown administration in the American colonies:

> "A military or a civil administration might, at this
> time, intimidate those semi-savages, lead them to adopt
> an opinion of us that is contrary to the one they now hold,
> and destroy trade, --the only source of any future benefits
> to the state. The proper time for the establishment of a

government in those regions will come when the old men, steeped in prejudices, have reached the common limit of human life and the young people, having gone through a transformation and having perceived the advantages of education, will become trustworthy members of the fatherland."[37]

Shelikhov's heirs, however, counted on something more than the persuasiveness of their representations. Judging by the correspondence, which has been preserved, between Rezanov's wife and her sister, Madame Buldakov, the main supporter of Rezanov was one of the most influential courtiers of the period of Emperor Paul, the Governor-General of St. Petersburg Count P.A. Pahlen. Informing her sister that Rezanov wants to resign, Anna Rezanov writes that "they won't let him resign, especially Count Pahlen who wouldn't part with him under any conditions and who loves him truly as one loves one's sweetheart, to such an extent has he become more and more attached to him every day. He says that as long as he is military governor, Rezanov will not be allowed to resign."[38]

The party of the opposition worked, apparently, through P.V. Lopukhin, Procurator-General of the Senate and father of the Emperor's favorite. To Madame Rezanov's letter of June 22, 1799, that is two weeks before the franchise was approved, and dispatched not through the mails but with an officer of his acquaintance, Rezanov added the following postscript:

"And we, I think, will soon have a great deal of news to write you about. The crimson is fading. For God's sake destroy our letters."[39]

In a letter of July 13, of the same year, in which Rezanov's wife tells him of the successful result of the negotiations and says that "although we waited a long time, it was well worth waiting for," she also mentions crimson: "crimson is not fashionable here, but is sometimes worn."[40]

Now, in the eyes of the contemporaries, crimson or red was associated with the Lopukhin family. According to Kotzebue[41] even the Mikhailovsk palace was painted crimson in view of Paul's "knightly" kindness toward Lopukhin's wife who once appeared at a ball wearing crimson gloves. Many residents of the capital in order to flatter the object of the

Emperor's affection, also painted their houses in red tints.
So that the expression "the crimson is fading" may be de-
ciphered as indicating the failure of the persons acting throug.
Lopukhin, and the words "crimson is not fashionable" as reporting that Lopukhin had fallen out of grace with the Emper-
or, a circumstance apparently utilized by Rezanov with Count
Pahlen's assistance. The question of granting a franchise to
the Company was favorably decided on the day following the
resignation of Madame Lopukhin's father, who was dismissed
from his post as Procurator-General of the Senate on July 7,
1799.

The newly formed company, approved July 8, 1799, was
designated as "being under the supreme patronage of the
Russian-American Company." At the same time its franchise
and statutes were confirmed for a period of twenty years. The
Russian-American Company was granted a monopoly to all
the hunting and mining "on the north-east coast of America
from...latitude 55° to Bering Strait and beyond it, also on
the Aleutian Islands, the Kuriles, and others situated in the
North-Eastern Sea." (§ 1). The Company was also granted
the right to make "new discoveries, and not only above latitude 55°N. but beyond it, farther south, and to occupy the
lands it discovers as Russian possessions, according to the
rules previously prescribed." (§ 2). The Company was also
permitted to carry on trade will all "the nearby powers" (§ 5),
cut the state forests (§ 7), obtain from the government gunpowder and lead (§ 8), and so forth. A special paragraph
stipulated that the Company was granted the exclusive right
to all the hunting, trade, and navigation in that region and
that "not only those who might themselves desire to undertake a sea-voyage thither were forbidden to take advantage
of these privileges, but also all former fur-hunters who are
engaged in this trade and possess in those regions their own
vessels and trading-posts, and others, who, being partners
in the United Company, would not enter this one." (§ 10).

The propositions worked out by Shelikhov's heirs were
assumed as the basis of the privileges and statutes. The
article subjected to the greatest change was the one dealing
with the number of shares necessary to vote in the general
stockholders' meeting. According to § 8 of the Charter of
the United American Company each share corresponded to
one vote. "As many shares as a person has just so many
voices should he have in the meetings and councils of the

Company." This provision was aimed at Shelikhov's heirs
and was intended to weaken their influence on the affairs of
the Company. Although almost one third of the shares belonged to Shelikhov's heirs (out of 724,000 rubles comprising
the Company's capital 239,000 had been invested by them),
still the numerous group of merchants who were hostile to
Shelikhov were always able, under such an arrangement, to
pass with an absolute majority all the decisions they considered suitable.

Shelikhov's heirs, in their own plan for the franchises to
be granted and the statutes to be formulated, a plan which,
as we have seen, was based on the principle of a united company, brought out another version of the article dealing with
voting. Their proposal amounted to this:

"Every stockholder owning fewer than twenty-five shares
would not have a voice in the Company himself, but would
come under the voice of any of the stockholders owning
twenty-five shares whom he would trust the most. At the
same time, every twenty-five shares would have a full
vote, even though owned by one individual, no matter to
whom of the stockholders that right might belong."[42]

In the statutes as they were finally approved, however,
the question of voting was solved somewhat differently. § 18
of the statutes approved by Emperor Paul read as follows:

"No one has the right to participate in the election of
directors or to vote at general meetings who does not own
ten shares; the votes at meetings are to be counted not by
the number of shares owned but by the number of stockholders present at the meeting."[43]

The decision of the government was of great importance,
since the right to vote and the order of voting at stockholders'
meetings opened the way to the directorship of the Company
not only to merchants but to members of the nobility as well.
In their representations Shelikhov's heirs hypocritically requested more than once that "the Board of Commerce should
be gracious enough to make representations to permit the
well-born nobility to enter the company, after the example
of the English and Danish kingdoms."[44] However, "the well-
born nobility" would, upon entering the company, inevitably

have come under the complete domination of the merchants
and would not have been able to participate in the direction
of the company. At the existing high price of shares it was
rather difficult for "the well-born nobility" to acquire twenty-
five shares. But even after overcoming this obstacle, a
stockholders belonging to the nobility would not be in a positic
to exert any influence on the affairs of the company, since by
the terms of the Shelikhov plan, the votes were counted not
according to the number of those present but according to the
number of shares represented, with Shelikhov's heirs holding
the principal block of shares.

The government, by its very lowering of the requirements
on the number of shares that entitled a stockholder to vote and
by making the voting contingent upon the number of stockholders present at a meeting, strengthened the influence of
the new stockholders, "the well-born nobility."

In order to observe "the actual execution by the Company
of the regulations prescribed for it by the government" there
was established towards the end of 1799 the office of Correspondent of the Russian-American Company, a position which
was equivalent to that of "Protector" proposed by the Board
of Commerce. N.P. Rezanov was appointed correspondent.

The fierce competitors of the Company who, by a simple
stroke of the pen, had been transformed into partners, received the government's solution with a good deal of animosity. The stockholders, as we learn from M.M. Buldakov, the
brother-in-law of Grigory Shelikhov and one of the directors
of the Company, grumbled because, according to the new
statutes, participation in the Company was open to all Russian
subjects, and, secondly, because the Company was not given
any government subsidies. As the same Buldakov reports,
"on the opening day of the main office of the Company the
same untoward incidents were repeated, and they were
brought to an end only by the intervention of the military governor who had been a most highly esteemed spectator of the
events of that period in the Company's history."[45] Order was
restored with the aid of the governor, and the elected directors were able to enter upon their duties.

Shelikhov's heirs, fearing that they might be forced out of
the management of the affairs of the Company, took the pre-
caution to obtain a royal decree appointing Buldakov "Prime
Director." In addition to Buldakov they succeeded in electing
as director Ivan Shelikhov, Grigory Shelikhov's brother.

However, Mylnikov's party also elected two of its men, Mylnikov himself and the merchant Startsev who worked hand-in-
hand with him.

In vain did Rezanov attempt in his letters from St. Petersburg to teach the Irkutsk merchants, who had now become directors, the rules of good breeding. Endless intrigues and
mutual plotting developed even more vigorously after the
Russian-American Company had been created. "The directors are now highly esteemed persons in the government
service," Rezanov observed in one of his letters to Buldakov,
"may God only show them the right way. Suggest to them to
try and put an end to their litigations and pettifoggery and to
preoccupy themselves with the interests of the government,
if they want the seats under them to be steady."[46]

Rezanov, as an experienced administrator, wanted to take
upon himself the direction of the newly hatched "statesmen"
by intervening in all the affairs of the Company, whether it
be the external formulation of the company reports or the
expression of loyalty to the tsar. But the merchants would
not listen to his advice. Even his suggestion that the Company mark "the happy day of July 8 by some token of loyal
thankfulness," particularly by building stone barracks for
the Irkutsk regiment,--an action that "would be most pleasing
to his Majesty,"--or, at least, an old soldiers' home, aroused
the bitter opposition of Mylnikov and others. Except for the
expenditures, the merchants declared, they have not yet seen
any results from the new company, and they did not intend to
incur any more losses.

Aiming to seize the direction of the Company, Mylnikov's
party swamped the courts with charges against Shelikhov's
heirs, and then forced Buldakov out completely. Mylnikov
and his partisans "took the office into their own hands, did
not show Director Buldakov anything concerning its operation, and pushed him away so that he felt compelled to report
about it to the military governor and having no means to combat their insolence, decided to go to St. Petersburg in order
to present his just complaint to His Majesty."[47]

When it became apparent, however, that Shelikhov's heirs,
because of their connections in court circles, were not to be
broken by such methods, some of the stockholders and even
some of the directors, not wishing to invest their capital in
a government-controlled enterprise, simply decided to divest
themselves of the Company's shares.

In 1800 the par value of one share--at one thousand rubles
--rose to more than 3,500 rubles. This tremendous jump in
the value of the shares is attributed by P. Tikhmenev exclusively to the great quantity of merchandise imported from the
colonies during that period, and to the successes scored by
Russian trade in Kamchatka, Yakutsk, and other places.[48]
Tikhmenev would not be expected to give a different explanation of the situation, since he wrote his "Historical Survey" by order of the Russian-American Company for the
purpose of justifying all of its operations and was, therefore,
unable to tell about the backstage intrigues carried on by som
of the directors.

The real secret, though, of such a considerable rise in the
value of the shares was of quite a different character. As
Correspondent Rezanov reported in 1800, the value of the
shares was raised by the Directors artificially: "They
raised the value of the shares in order to profit from them.
One of the directors, Mylnikov, during the whole time prescribed by His Majesty for the sale of the shares, lived in
Moscow at the Company's expense, under the pretense of being preoccupied with its affairs. Instead of that, he was
actually doing harm to the Company, for he sold his own
sixty shares at a little over 2,500 rubles each. Consequently he not only stopped the increase in capital but contributed
to shaking the confidence of the public in the credit of the
Company."[49]

In a personal letter to Obolyaninov, Procurator-General
of the Senate, Rezanov again reports that "they [the directors.--Au.] have raised the value of the shares, setting it
at over 3,600 rubles, and instead of attracting new stockholders to the Company, have been selling their own shares
at a discount, at a little over 2,500 rubles a share."[50]
Rezanov was compelled to ask "that strong measures be
taken to prevent them from selling the rest of the shares."

The fierce battle that had flamed up among the stockholders
forced Shelikhov's heirs, in the interest of self-preservation,
to work for the transfer of the administration of the Company
from Irkutsk to St. Petersburg; in the latter city, they thought
it would be easier for them, in view of the protection they enjoyed on the part of some of the higher officials, to cope with
the obstreperous Irkutsk merchants.

The government was also interested in this transfer, since
the political aims set before the Russian-American Company

required its transformation from an organization regional in character into one of All-Russian significance. The transfer of the administration to St. Petersburg brought it closer to the several departments of the government and, by this very token, tended to facilitate the direction of the operations of the Company and to render its supervision more practicable. In his request to have the administration transferred from Irkutsk to St. Petersburg or to Moscow, Rezanov insinuated unequivocally that, as a result of the transfer, some of the stockholders "would be more useful to the Company because of their knowledge and experience than by investing more money."[51]

On October 19, 1800, the question of transferring the administration of the Russian-American Company to the capital and of leaving only an office force in Irkutsk was approved. Henceforth the strife among the various groups of Irkutsk merchants within the administration came to an end, and Mylnikov and his supporters were forced to resign from the board of directors.

Chapter III

THE EARLY ACTIVITIES OF THE RUSSIAN- AMERICAN COMPANY

THE TSARIST GOVERNMENT set before the Russian-American Company certain tasks of great political importance. It was to be the aim of the Company to realize the grandiose plan of expansion as a result of which the northern part of the Pacific would become "an inland sea" of the Russian empire.

This plan presupposed the further entrenchment of Russia along the west coast of North America, including California, the Hawaiian Islands, the southern part of Sakhalin and the mouth of the Amur. These colonies, together with Kamchatka, Alaska, and the Aleutians, which already belonged to Russia, were to make that country the all-powerful master of the whole northern Pacific. California, apart from its strategic importance, was also to serve as an agricultural base for the Russian colonies in America. The Hawaiian Islands, which constitute the principal naval base for all vessels plying between American and Asiatic ports, would, in case they came into the hands of Tsarist Russia, bring under its control all the seaborn trade with China. Furthermore, it was proposed to establish cotton plantations on the Hawaiian Islands and to export all kinds of spices from there.

It was, in short, a plan for direct colonial conquest. It was tied up with a simultaneous, broad economic offensive against China, by way of the sea through Canton, and with exploratory steps in the direction of the English, Spanish, and Dutch colonies in Asia.

The penetration into Canton, even considering the extensive barter operations of Kiakhta, was of very great importance to Tsarist Russia. The Russian peltry that was being shipped through Kiakhta was able to satisfy only a small part of the Chinese market. Englishmen and Americans supplied China with the identical peltry by reselling the furs they had bought up at very low cost in the Russian colonies themselves. It was impossible even to think of making wide inroads into the Chinese market without forcing out the English and American exporters from Canton. Meanwhile the Russian ships did not even enjoy the right of entry into open Chinese ports, and the Company was compelled to resort to the assistance of foreign intermediaries.

At the beginning of 1803 the Minister of Commerce, Count N.P. Rumyantsev, reported to Alexander I that "no matter how much stronger the Company's establishments may become and no matter how hard it may try to maintain the prices of peltry in Kiakhta, the English and the Boston men, who deliver their stuff from Notka Sound and the Charlotte Islands directly to Canton, will always have the advantage in the business; and this will continue until such time as the Russians themselves have broken their way through to Canton."[1]

It was precisely the trade with China, that, in Rumyantsev's opinion, could assure the rapid development of the Russian colonies in America, which might, in time, be able to extend their influence to the very gates of the East and West Indies. For he wrote the following:

"The Russian-American colonies, seeing the opportunity for marketing in various places furs, fats, fish, and other natural products, would attract people of all kinds, tried in the sciences and arts, and would set about establishing mills and factories for the manufacture of metal objects, leather goods, and so forth. In this way there would gradually develop in the colonies associations of artists and artisans, and cities would finally arise out of the villages, through which the trade with the two Indies would, in time, be established on a firm foundation."[2]

From the drafts of diplomatic notes[3] we learn of the government's desire to infiltrate into Batavia and the Philippines while penetrating into China.

This whole plan of broad expansion by the tsarist government, as it had assumed form by the end of the eighteenth and in the first years of the nineteenth century, and which played a decisive part in the formation of the Russian-American Company, began to be realized, however, just when the political situation rendered its execution most difficult. For the realization of the plan required Russia to make an open break with England--its chief rival in the northern Pacific.

But, in spite of this antagonism, tsarist Russia preferred

not to push the antipathy to the point where a decisive clash
would have become unavoidable. The policy of tsarist Russia
with regard to England in the Pacific was patterned substantially after her policy in the Near East.

Marx and Engels, in analyzing the Near Eastern question
and its importance for tsarist Russia, pointed out more than
once that the question was always subordinated to the problem of combatting a bourgeois revolution in Europe. The
moment the danger of a revolution reared its head on the
continent of Europe, tsarist Russia completely subordinated
to the problem of crushing the revolution all other aspirations
including those she had in the Near East. And it was precisely this circumstance--the problem of combatting a revo-
lution--that, in periods of revolutionary tension, drew
England and Russia together on the European continent, notwithstanding the persisting conflict of interests in the Orient.

The Pacific problem, as well as that of the Near East, was
only of secondary importance. Its subordination was twofold;
on the one hand it was subordinated to the problem of combatting the revolution, and on the other to the problem of the
conflict in the Near East.

The moment the tsarist government came face to face with
the problem of combatting the revolution--and England, consequently, became its faithful ally on the continent of Europe-
Russia would make concessions with respect to the Pacific
problem, striving not to exacerbate in any way her relations
with England. Also, when the tsarist government had reason
to count on a certain degree of sufferance on the part of
England in the Near Eastern question, it again made concessions in the Pacific problem.

The tsarist government adhered to this policy during the
whole first half of the nineteenth century, up to the Crimean
War. Under these conditions, the realization of the plans for
expansion in the Pacific through the medium of the Russian-
American Company which could serve as an excellent disguise for Russia's true designs, presented a number of advantages. And just as the English government "waged war
for two hundred years hiding behind the name of the Company
[i.e., The East India Company--Au.]"[4] so did the tsarist
government wage war for more than half a century for mastery of the Pacific, hiding behind the name of the Russian-
American Company. But this utilization of the Company in
realizing the plan that had been conceived contained certain

negative elements also. In masking its operations under the name of a trading and commercial company, the government was naturally compelled to refrain from broad-guaged aggression. It had to limit its activities, for the time being, to single sorties, undertaken, as it were, in the name of the Russian-American Company. It was, therefore, necessary to execute the plan for expansion formulated by the government without the aid of any sizable armed force. Only in individual cases would a small group of company employees succeed in enlisting the cooperation of men-of-war that would call at the colonies in the course of their round-the-world voyages.

When the Russian-American Company was being organized, there were already in existence a number of settlements of Russian fur-hunters in the Aleutians, on Kodiak, along the littoral of Kenai Bay and Chugatsk Bay, and in the Gulf of Yakutsk. The real activity of the Company in the colonies began when it gained a foothold on the island of Sitka, subsequently to be named in honor of Baranov, the governor of the Russian colonies. The island of Sitka was the strategic point the possession of which, in view of the existence of older Russian settlements, tended to strengthen Russia's position in the north Pacific from the Kuriles down to the west coast of America. The consolidation of Russia's hold on the island of Sitka would, at the same time, signify the creation of a solid base for expansion in the direction of the east Pacific coast.

As to penetration into the interior of the American continent, tsarist Russia did not give any thought to that problem at the time; she limited her efforts, for the time being, to the conquest of a number of points on the coast. In a secret order of April 18, 1802 to Baranov, governor of the colonies, it was stated that "all work in the northern area must cease and that no new efforts should be made there until we have strengthened our possessions adjacent to the English."[5]

But the establishment on Sitka tended, quite unexpectedly, to delay for several years the further advance of tsarist Russia along the shores of the Pacific; for it was here that the Russians were to encounter serious opposition not only on the part of the English but on the part of the natives as well. In 1799 a wooden fortress, called Mikhailovsk, was constructed on that island, and about two hundred Russian

trappers and Aleuts were settled there. In 1802 the Indian
tribe of Tlinkets whom the Russians called Koliuzhams or
Koloshams [Kolushans. -Tr.] suddenly swooped down upon
the settlement, set fire to the fortress and to a Company ship
that was anchored in the port. To judge from the stories of
some of the Russian hunters who survived and were subsequently ransomed from the Tlinkets, English traders also
took part in organizing the attack. It was not by accident
that precisely at the moment of the uprising an English vessel
under Captain Barber was moored in Sitka harbor; the sailors
belonging to that ship led the attack of the Tlinkets.

Only in 1804, when the frigate "Neva" arrived in the Amer-
can colonies from a round-the-world voyage, did Baranov
make a second attempt to gain possession of Sitka. A landing
was effected on Sitka on the eighteenth of September and
siege was laid to the fortress which the natives had, by that
time, managed to build. In the words of the report of this
expedition, "after lengthy but futile negotiations with the
Kolushans in an attempt to induce them to surrender the fortress, conclude a permanent peace and enter upon reciprocal
trade, a second landing was made. After this had been a-
chieved, an assault was made on the fortress under the command of Baranov himself, during which the attacking forces
were subjected to strong cannon and rifle fire that came from
the fortress and from the Kolushans sallying forth from their
stronghold. The Kolushans were supplied with arms and powder that had been previously captured in the ruined fortress or
purchased from the Boston men."[6] Only after a week's siege
did the Tlinkets, "who had suffered many casualties in killed
and wounded, abandon the fortress during the night, leaving
all the stores behind."

After the Mikhailovsk fortress had been taken, it was decided to raze it and to rebuild it on a site that would be inaccessible to attack, a high hill where a Tlinket settlement had
been before. This new fortress, which became the center of
government for the colonies, received the name of
Novoarkhangelsk. Situated at latitude 57°15´N. and longitude
135°18´W., Novoarkhangelsk was to be until 1812 the farthest
point of Russian penetration along the northwest coast of
America; in 1812 the Company succeeded in gaining a foothold in California.

The southward push was conceived at first as a process of
gradual colonization by Russia of the whole west coast of

North America. In a memorandum to the Russian consul-
general in the United States in 1808, the Governing Board of
the Russian-American Company reported that "the Company
had not yet expanded" south of Sitka "for want of time, lack
of opportunity, and especially because of the scarcity of
Russian people who know something about the business; for,
though there are more than six hundred of them, it is still
incumbent upon them to secure the island of Sitka as well as
everything lying behind it along the islands and the coast of
the mainland. As rapidly as time and opportunity will permit,
the Company's hunting activities will move on to the Charlotte
Islands, and then farther on to Columbia, if those lands and
places do not yet belong to any of the European powers."[7]

In Columbia, however, the United States had arrived
ahead of the Russian-American Company. As a result, the
plan for the gradual expansion of the colonies had to be changed,
but the attempt to seize California was carried on at a much
faster tempo.

By the early 1820's, just when the term of the first franchise of the Russian-American Company was drawing to a
close, there were fifteen settlements on the islands and on the
American continent. Included in this number are only the
permanent settlements. As to the temporary ones that were
set up only for the duration of the hunting or fishing season,
they were scattered in many other points along the Pacific
coast.

The Russian settlements, in order of their location east of
Kamchatka, were the following:

The first settlement was situated on the first of the Komandorsky Islands where a small artel of hunters was left to catch
foxes, sea-otters and fur-seals. This was one of the oldest
settlements established during the Shelikhov period;

the second settlement was situated on Atka Island, one of
the Andreanof group of islands, where hunting had also been
carried on for quite a time. This settlement was built on
Korovin Bay. Here, under the direction of a special administrator, there lived about fifty Russian hunters. The jurisdiction of the Atka division comprised also 331 Aleuts, sixty
on Atka proper and 271 on eight tiny islands, subject to the
Atka administration;

the third settlement was in Captain's Harbor on Unalaska,
one of the Fox Islands. Here was the settlement of "Dobroye
Soglasiye" ("Concord") with a population of about thirty Russian

hunters. The Unalaska settlement was the center of all the
hunting settlements on the Andreanof Islands. According to
data for 1805, there were 360 Aleuts on Unalaska. On the
other islands which came within the jurisdiction of the Unalaska
division, including the Cape of Alaska, there were 673 Aleuts
Consequently, the Aleuts in the whole Unalaska division
totaled 1,033;

the fourth and the fifth settlements, situated on the Pribilo
Islands, also came under the jurisdiction of Unalaska. These
settlements were built on St. Paul Island and on St. George
Island. Here there were a small number of Russian hunters
who were engaged in hunting fur-seals (between thirty and
fifty thousand skins annually) and in searching for walrus-
teeth which were exported by the Company to Turkey and
Persia. As much as 200 poods (7,200 lbs. avdp.) of walrus-
teeth were exported from the Pribilof Islands annually.

These five settlements closed in, as it were, the Bering
Sea, converting it into an inland sea of the Russian Empire.

Additional settlements sprang up along the Pacific coast
and on the islands of the Pacific.

The sixth settlement was on Kodiak and was situated, at
first, at the harbor of the Three Saints. For twenty years,
from 1784 to 1804, Kodiak was the center of the Russian
settlements in the Pacific.

Upon the seizure of Sitka and the transfer of the administra
tion of the colonies to Novoarkhangelsk, the settlement at the
harbor of the Three Saints was moved to the harbor at Pavlovs
in the eastern part of the island, where a wooden fortress was
constructed, with earthen fortifications which mounted a number of cannon. There were a shipbuilding yard, two-story
barracks for the hunters, storehouses, and so forth. Accordin
to reports for the year 1817, there were 119 Russian hunters
on Kodiak. Of native Eskimos there were, according to 1804
reports, 3,429 persons of both sexes on Kodiak and in the
thirty-eight settlements on the nearest islands.

A number of settlements on Kenai Bay [i.e., Cook Inlet.-
C.G.] and Chugatsk Gulf came under the jurisdiction of the
Kodiak trading-station. These settlements were located on
the American continent proper and represented small fortresses, though still earthen fortifications. Such were the
fortresses of Pavlovsk, Georgiyevsk, Aleksandrovsk, and
Voskresensk, all on the shores of Kenai Bay. We do not have
at our disposal any information about the Russian population

of these fortresses. As to the native population, it consisted in 1817 of 1,474 souls. There were three settlements on Chugatsk Gulf: "Constantine and Yelena," Nikolayevsk on the Bering Sea at Yakutat Bay, and Simeyonovsk on the Cape of St. Elias. There were also fortresses, with a surrounding population of 1,130 natives in 1817.

The above-enumerated settlements on the islands, together with the fortress of Kenai and Chugatsk, comprised thirteen in all.

The fourteenth settlement was on Baranov Island (Sitka). The port of Novoarkhangelsk comprised the following, at the beginning of the second decade of the nineteenth century: a wooden fortress, a shipbuilding yard, storehouses, barracks, and dwellings. Of the 222 Russians living there, seventy were engaged in guard duty. The native inhabitants numbered about a thousand.

The fifteenth settlement was located in California; it was the colony of "Ross," founded in 1812.

Administratively all these settlements came under the jurisdiction of the governor of the colonies, who had his seat in Novoarkhangelsk. On four of the points, the islands of Sitka, Kodiak, and Unalaska, and in California, branch offices were established to look after the local administration. By the second decade of the nineteenth century two of the settlements had already been liquidated. The settlement at Yakutat Bay on the Bering Sea called "Slavorossiya" was destroyed; it was there that, in Shelikhov's opinion, the experimental cultivation of agricultural products was to be instituted. The settlement was burned by the natives and never rebuilt. After an uprising of the Russian hunters, the settlement on Urup Island was also liquidated. The hunters, who revolted against the beastly treatment meted out to them by the administrator, abandoned the settlement on Urup and the Company never reestablished it.

The main object of all the settlements of the Company was hunting for fur-bearing animals. The most valuable type of furs were the skins of sea-otters. The average selling price of a single otter skin fluctuated between 100 and 300 rubles, and the price of individual specimens of the most costly variety sometimes reached 1,000 rubles. The otters sold by the Company were the best in the international fur market, since the most valuable species of that animal were found along the coast of the Russian colonies in America. A small part of

the sea-otters caught by the Company was exported to China
by way of Kiakhta and was delivered directly to Canton. The
greater part of the otter-skins was sold in Russia.

Quantitatively the most extensive trade was carried on in
fur-seals. These were found in abundance around the island
in the Bering Strait and on the Aleutians. They were also
found in Hudson Bay and in other places that were inaccessib
to Russian hunters. The best types of fur-seals, however,
were found in the region of the Russian colonies. A certain
part of the seals was sold in Russia "for use by the lower
classes of people," another part was bartered for manufactured products with foreign merchants who would visit the
colonies, and the rest was also exported to China by way of
Kiakhta and, whenever possible, by way of Canton.

Then there were other pursuits, of secondary importance
to the Company. Black-brown foxes, reddish grey ones, blu
foxes as well as other varieties, were hunted on almost all o
the Aleutian Islands, on Kodiak, Sitka, and on the American
mainland. The blue foxes were of a lower quality than those
found in Kamchatka, but they still sold rather briskly on the
domestic Russian market and in the foreign markets of China
and Turkey. There was almost no hunting of sables and
gluttons (wolverenes). These animals were found in the interior of the continent, and since, according to a report of th
Company, "the hunters do not go far inland in pursuit of game
for fear of the local population, the hunting of these animals
is of little importance."[9] A small quantity of walrusbone,
whalebone, and castoreum was exported from the colonies.

The Company, in calculating the quantity of animals processed during the first two decades of its operations, started
not with the year 1799, when its privileges were affirmed,
but with 1797, when the United Company was formed. Betwee
1797 and 1818 the Company procured the following quantity of
animals in the two categories in which it was chiefly intereste
namely otters and fur-seals: 80,271 otters and 1,493,626
fur-seals. During the same period the Company received in
all categories of peltry, walrusbone, and so forth at various
prices, the amount of 16,376,695.95 rubles, or an average of
818,835 rubles annually.

The Company sold to foreign merchants in the colonies,
avoiding the payment of Russian customs duties, goods to the
value of 3,647,002 rubles, which was more than 20 per cent
of all the furs it had procured. The greater part of the furs

was sent to Russia, whence they were exported to China through Kiakhta, or sold in the domestic market. The foreign merchants exported to the Hawaiian Islands and to Canton the furs which they had received in the Russian colonies in exchange for victuals. They sometimes even brought to Kamchatka the furs they had bought in the colonies, which was very detrimental to the Company's business; for it was in Kamchatka that the Siberian merchants would usually buy the furs for distribution among the domestic markets. In the interior of the country furs were sold at the Makaryev[10] and Irkutsk fairs and directly in Moscow and St. Petersburg.

In the larger commercial towns and at focal points of transit the Company maintained offices or commission agencies. It opened offices in Moscow, Irkutsk, Yakutsk, Okhotsk, and Kiakhta, and agencies in Kazan, Tiumen, Tomsk, Kamchatka, and Gizhiga.

In the colonies the Company carried on a trade in consumers' goods. The merchandise was sold to the Russian hunters and, by means of all kinds of machinations, was exchanged for peltry with the so-called "independent" natives. This exchange constituted a considerable portion of the income from the Company's operations. Some years the quantity of furs obtained by exchange with the native tribes reached one third of all the peltry obtained in the colonies.[11]

There was such an abundance of fur-bearing animals in the regions belonging to the Company that, with the proper management, the Company might have figured on colossal profits, despite the most unfavorable prospects of the Chinese fur-market at the beginning of the nineteenth century. The rapacious exploitation of the inexhaustible natural resources which fell into the Company's hands very soon undermined its activity, however.

The Russian-American Company made its calculations with a view to exporting furs primarily to those areas, especially China, where there was a ready sale for furs of the medium and lower grades. At the same time, the Company, by the quality of the raw materials, had all the opportunities to capture the European market as well. In order to accomplish this, however, it was necessary to abandon the primitive methods of processing the furs, methods which turned the most valuable raw materials into furs of very low quality. When, towards the end of its existence, the Company did make an attempt to export some peltry to London, it was compelled to send not processed furs but raw skins salted in barrels; the European customer would not buy the furs processed by the Company. But, as long as the lower grade furs sold in the eastern markets, at a profit, the Company gave no thoug to perfecting the methods of their processing.

The peltry, before it was put on sale, was subjected to a single operation, drying in the open air. The skins were dried in the sun by stretching them on poles. This was the method of treating skins which the pioneer-hunters in the Aleutians had used since time immemorial. "This is the wa it was always done, and this is the way it is being done now, wrote the Governing Board of the Company in 1815 in dis- cussing the methods of treating the skins. It was not always possible, however, to dry during the short summer season the whole tremendous quantity of seal-skins that would ac- cumulate in the colonies during the same period. An attempt was made to "rationalize" the process somewhat, on the very spot where it was in operation. This was done by drying the seal-skins in highly heated baths. The result of this new method was that the skins "either firefanged so that the pellicle came off the hide together with the hair, or were burned so that they broke like the bark of a tree when they were bent." In 1802 as many as 800,000 skins were ruined in this way.

The accumulation of a large quantity of spoiled seal skins in the Company storehouses coincided with a sharp drop in the demand for furs in the Chinese market. The management wrote as follows to A.A. Baranov in 1803:

"The Company is the more conscious of the injury in- flicted upon it with respect to the fur-seals when there are on the island about one million ready skins of that animal, and when both here and in Kiakhta such an insignificant quantity is sold of those previously exported that it is a shame to say; and they sell at no more than two rubles instead of at from six to seven rubles which they brought in some four years ago."[12]

Then, as K. Khlebnikov, the later Director of the Company tells in the hitherto unpublished portion of his journal, "the Governing Board, going into the state of affairs, noted the great mistake made in the conduct of the business, namely that the fur-seals lost their value as a result of the exces-

sive supply of them in the Kiakhta market and lost their quality as a result of the hasty processing." Farther on he writes:

> "Any attempt to maintain the price by reducing the quan-
> tity and to revive the confidence of the Chinese by improving
> the quality of the goods, called for a great sacrifice. This
> sacrifice the well-intentioned, honorable directors did not
> hesitate to bring. They ordered several thousand skins
> that had been burned to be delivered to the flames. And
> only by this means were they able to attain their end."[13]

About 700,000 skins were burned in Unalaska alone.
Later on the Company tried in every way to conceal the fact
that one of the reasons which had prompted it to decide upon
the mass destruction of the seal-skins was the desire to raise
the prices in Kiakhta. But the fact that the Company resorted
to the destruction of seal-skins in the following years also,
when the drying in baths had been discontinued, and did it
openly in various towns in Siberia and on the Chinese border,
fully disproves the Company's contentions.
According to reports of the Company itself many seal-skins
were burned in 1810 and 1813. The Company wrote as follows
in 1815:

> "In those years there were burned, in the presence of
> the authorities exactly 79,600 seal-skins in bales and in
> 277 mat-bags in Irkutsk, and 32,199 skins in Okhotsk, but
> not at all in order to reduce the quantity with the view of
> raising prices."[14]

The management, as before, pleaded that the skins it had
burned were damaged skins which it was absolutely impossible
to sell, and that, in order not to overcrowd the warehouses
for nothing, the Company was compelled to get rid of them.
The Company's assertions that no one supposedly wanted
to buy the damaged skins are completely disproved by the
reports of the local administration. Captain Minitsky, Commander of the port of Okhotsk, reported to the Governor-
General of Siberia in 1815 that the Company, "in order not to
show in its books the losses incurred on skins of good quality,
has ordered the burning of large quantities of its fur-skins.
This took place mostly in 1811 and 1812 in Okhotsk and
Irkutsk, where publicly, and under police supervision, several

hundred thousand seal-skins were burned by the Company,
for which, as I remember, a good many merchants offered
to pay cash right there and then according to what they
thought the skins were worth, but such offers were not given
any consideration, and the skins were then burned by the ma
thousands."[15]

The great dependence on the single Chinese market, combined with the wasteful measures taken in an attempt to raise
prices, brought the Company to the verge of bankruptcy in th
very first years of its existence. The capital with which the
Company began its operations was very soon exhausted. In
the words of Prokofyev, Director of the Company, in his report of 1824 to the general stockholders' meeting, "the reaso
for this is demonstrated by the fact that when, subsequently,
the conditions of the Company assumed the aspect of general
prosperity, all the capital which, at that time, served as the
basis for the balance was figured, only for the sake of information, at one ruble, for zeros must sooner or later be reco
nized as zeros."[16]

The basic capital of the United American Company before
was granted the franchise and renamed the Russian-America
Company was supposed to be an even 724,000 rubles, divided
into 724 shares. These shares were not to be offered for sal
to the general public, but were to be distributed only among
the partners. According to the provisions of the charter
approved for the Russian-American Company, another thousand shares, valued at 1,000 rubles each, were added to the
724, to be offered for sale to the general public, with every
Russian subject having the right to purchase them. The shar
were to be sold with the addition of that portion of the profits
that had accumulated since the official union of Shelikhov's
Company with Mylnikov's.

This provision, in view of the inaccurate figuring of the
income (the income from a number of vessels which had not
yet returned from their trips was calculated "on the basis
of information on hand"), provided the management with an
opportunity artificially to inflate the value of the shares while
carrying out, at the same time, a series of speculative transactions. The directors who, according to Rezanov's report,
"made bold...to draw up a false inventory and present it to
His Majesty,"[17] forced up the value of each share in 1799 to
3,638.6125 rubles.

During the first six months following the announcement in

the press of the sale of shares only one share was sold, not counting those belonging to Mylnikov personally that were re-sold below the official price. Rezanov, believing that it would be impossible to dispose of the shares on account of their high nominal value, proposed that beginning with December 1, 1799, shares be issued in denominations of 500 rubles instead of 1,000. In this proposal he was following the practice of the East India and West India companies, the shares of which had a nominal value below 500 rubles (£50 for the East India Company, and 2,000 Livres for the West India Company--in either case below 500 rubles). Not hoping that the shares would be rapidly sold out even in small denominations, Rezanov pro-posed in addition that anyone buying no fewer than fifty shares should be awarded a special order, with the Imperial mono-gram, to wear on a ribbon. "If such an order should be esta-blished," he declared, "the prescribed quota of shares would be filled in a short time."[18]

But these artificial measures were of no avail either. Dur-ing the two years--the term in which the thousand shares an-nounced for sale were to be distributed--only fourteen were sold.

The merchants who had been so eager to take part in the exploitation of the American colonies, now avoided investing their money in shares of the trading company which was under the direct and unremitting control of the government. The nobility, too, watched the Russian-American Company with-out particular interest. The income of that company was still extremely problematical. And in general, the joint-stock form of trade associations was a novelty in Russia, and shares were looked upon with suspicion.

Despite the complete failure of the distribution of the shares, the government approved on August 17, 1801, the issuance of 7,350 shares, each with a par value of 7,500 rubles in paper money. In this way, while during the first two decades the issuance of shares to the amount of one million rubles (1,000 shares at 1,000 rubles each) was au-thorized, during the second two decades shares were issued amounting to 3,675,000 rubles (7,350 shares at 500 rubles each). New steps were now taken to hasten the sale of shares. The purchase of shares of the Russian-American Company was pictured as carrying out a government obligation of com-mon interest. Alexander I personally bought twenty shares and the grand dukes followed suite. The purchase of shares

by members of the Court was to emphasize to the nobility and
the wealthy merchant class the necessity of following the tsar
example. "And in general it was instrumental," wrote the
Governing Board of the Company relative to Alexander's buying of some of its shares, "in bringing about the investment
of more than 500,000 rubles in shares during that one period
by people of all conditions, including not a few of the first
notables of the realm and some of the magnates from among
the merchant class."[19]

In spite of the fact that the shares sold with difficulty and
it was hardly to be supposed that all the shares authorized
for issuance would be sold, the number of paid up shares
figuring in the balance-sheet was considerably higher than
7,350. In 1806, according to the balance-sheet, the Company
had 8,318 shares outstanding. From that time on, however,
we observe a diminution in the number of shares. Those
shares that again came into the possession of the Governing
Board as a result of an expired deposit or were actually bough
by the Company, were not put up for sale again. They were
either written off or, as the balance-sheets put it, were included "in the general allotment." In twenty years, from
1806 to 1826, 834 shares with a nominal value of 417,000
rubles, were put into the general allotment and were thus excluded from participating in the profits. In this way, by 1826
the number of shares had dropped to 7,484.

If we are to judge by the data cited in the report of the
Company over the twenty-year period, then all the 7,713
shares belonging to the Company in 1818 were wholly in the
hands of the stockholders and of 630 "persons in various
places." At the same time we have, however, a silent indi-
cation that a certain number of shares remained in the Company's portfolio. In the new charter of the Company, approve
on September 13, 1821, it is noted in § 2 that of the shares
authorized to be issued there remained a small number that
was not sold, purportedly "only because the Company, as a
result of the favorable situation of its affairs, does not need
any additional capital, having enough of it."

Considering the information given in that same report, it
may be presumed that the shares resting in the Company's
portfolio were not only included in the total number of shares
(7,713) on which the profits were calculated, but that their
number greatly exceeded the number of shares in the hands
of individual holders.

The share capital of the Company, amounting to 4,429,426.35 rubles in 1818, was made up of several components. First, it included 723,000 rubles that had been invested by the founders of the Company not in cash but in the form of the property that these first stockholders had in the colonies when the Company was being organized. Here, too, are included 515,838.78 rubles invested by new stockholders during the first twenty years of the Company's existence. These new stockholders were given the appropriate number of shares. Supposing that they were given their shares at a nominal value of 500 rubles each (actually they paid on them "the increment of the profit," and hence more than 500 rubles), even then the number of shares issued to the new stockholders would not have exceeded one thousand odd. Adding this number of shares to the number given to the founders of the Company on account of the afore-mentioned 723,000 rubles, we are bound to come to the conclusion that actually the number of shares paid up in cash or, at least, in property did not exceed 2,500. The remaining 5,000 shares of those authorized for issuance were in the Company's portfolio and had not been paid up by the stockholders. The profits, however, were figured on these shares, too. Furthermore, these nonexistent shares were substantially instrumental in determining the value of the real, paid-up shares that were in the hands of the stockholders.

There was not quotation of the prices of shares on the stock exchange at that time, and their value was set each year by dividing the whole of the share capital, together with the undivided profits, by the total number of shares belonging to the Company. By 1818 there had accumulated in undivided profits the sum of 3,190,687.50 rubles, which included the statutory 10 per cent deduction from the profits to be added to the share capital. This allowed the value of a share to be set at 574.28 rubles in 1818. By artificially maintaining the value of its shares above the nominal price and by including at the same time in its calculations the fictitious shares that were counted only on paper, the Governing Board of the Company deprived the real stockholders of the lion's share of the profits. Naturally, under such circumstances it was in the interest of the management to have a larger number of fictitious shares and a smaller number of real ones. The first was attained by increasing the number of fictitious shares over and above the total permitted for issuance; the second, by writing off real shares as expenses. The increase was on the account

of the fictitious shares; the reduction, on the account of the
real ones.

True, the offering for sale of more than 5,000 shares
might have brought considerable capital into the coffers of th
Company, capital which, in spite of its declaratory announce
ment, it badly needed. Such additional capital, however,
would have added to the Company's obligations to its stockholders. It was much more profitable to cloak the need for
capital by government subsidies and loans rather than to offer
for sale the shares resting in its portfolio. As early as 1803
the Company received its first loan of 250,000 rubles to enab
it to send out the first round-the-world expedition. By adopt
ing the policy of borrowing, the Company had contracted debt
by 1807 to the amount of 2,394,362.375 rubles, [20] exceeding
by one million rubles the whole share capital of the Company

About that time the Company, in the words of one of its
directors, had "already contracted such heavy debts that, con
sidering its widely scattered and essentially insignificant cap
tal, might have been regarded as non-payable; for, except fo
the hope of a possible change in the situation and for successf
hunting, the debts had no security behind them whatsoever." [2]

The financial condition of the Company was such that "had
the credit of the Company been shaken in the slightest, its
complete collapse would have been inevitable." Until 1807
the management, nevertheless, regularly indicated a profit in
the balance-sheet, but insisted upon adding the profit to the
joint stock. However, for the two-year period of 1808-1809
even the official balance-sheet already showed a loss, and
the nominal value of 500 rubles a share was recorded as
472.38 rubles, and in the following two-year period, 1810-
1811, as 475.475 rubles. This balance-sheet, by the way, wa
brought to the attention of the stockholders only in conjunction
with that for 1812-1813, when the value of a share was raised
to 550 rubles, showing a 10 per cent profit per share.

In the course of twenty years, according to the Company's
reports, the capital of 1,238,738 rubles netted the amount of
6,250,487 rubles in profits, of which 3,059,799 rubles were
purportedly distributed among the stockholders on the 7,713
shares which they held. However, if one were to accept our
supposition that there were no more than 2,500 shares in the
hands of the stockholders, then the amount of profit must be
regarded as considerably smaller.

The balance-sheets drawn up by the management were shee

falsifications. The method of calculating the basic capital is
very instructive in this respect. To the original valuation of
a boat or structure were added, from year to year, the amounts
spent on repairs, while the amortization was not deducted at
all. In line with this method, an old, half-rotted ship would,
after a few years, be evaluated by the Company's calculations,
at twice, and sometimes at several times the value of a new
boat of the same type. To the basic capital, thus inflated,
was added the income for two years, since the Company drew
up its accounts on a biennial basis.

The rise in the earning capacity of the Russian-American
Company at different times in the course of its existence was
contingent not so much upon an increase in its business, or
even upon a favorable market situation, as upon a reduction
in the tremendous company expenditures. The lion's share
of these expenditures went to maintain the administration itself. During the twelve years from 1808 to 1820 the Company spent 2,317,318 rubles on supplying the colonies and on
maintaining them, while the cost of the upkeep of the main
office in St. Petersburg during the same period amounted to
4,696,364 rubles.[23]

Beginning with the year 1812 the administration instituted
the policy of supplying the colonies primarily with merchandise of foreign origin, procured from the foreign merchants who
visited the colonial ports. This barter trade with the foreigners
in the colonies brought about a considerable reduction in the
cost of maintaining the colonies. Furthermore, it freed the
Company of the necessity of fitting out frequent round-the-
world expeditions. Every such expedition absorbed huge
sums of money, amounting, in some cases, to more than a
million rubles.

The first expedition under the command of Lisyansky and
Krusenstern was sent out in 1803, the second in 1806. After
that, there were no expeditions until 1813. This fact, together
with the profitable trade carried on directly with the foreign
merchants in the colonies, gave the Company an opportunity
to strengthen its financial position rather rapidly. The stockholders' dividends began to increase in value. During 1814-
1815 the Company paid the stockholders at the rate of 100.28
rubles per 500-ruble share, during 1816-1817 it paid 150 rubles,
and during 1818-1819 the maximum amount for that period--
155 rubles, totaling altogether 31 per cent for the two-year
period.

The following two-year period, however, brought a drop
in the size of the dividend to 82 rubles, and during 1822-1823
no dividends were paid at all. Though the loss incurred by
the Company was given as 300,000 rubles at the most, one
of the directors made the admission that "the loss actually
exceeded that figure." The policy adopted in the early 1820's
of developing barter trade with the foreigners who were engaged in smuggling activities with the natives, was terminated by the regulations of 1822 which forbade foreign ships
to approach that portion of the coast where the Russian
settlements in America were located. The Company once
more was compelled to resort to the fitting out of round-the-
world expeditions. Three such expeditions were sent out
between 1819 and 1821, at an overall cost of 2,400,000 rubles

These expeditions, ruinous, as we shall see later, to the
stockholders, were very profitable to some of the directors.
As for the colonies, these expeditions were of little benefit
to them, too. The 1820 expedition on the "Kutuzov" for
example, which cost the Company 700,000 rubles brought
back cargo valued only at 200,000 rubles. What was most
detrimental to the Company was the narrow scope of its domestic market, the effects of which it began to feel, when
the barter trade with the foreigners was terminated. Prokofye
director of the Company, in his report for 1824 emphasized
that "under the previous system, especially in the last years,
only such seal-skins were bartered with the foreigners as
would not under any circumstances sell in Russia in the
quantity in which they are annually processed; consequently,
under the new system, a considerable quantity of these skins
must be exported from Russia, if only not to have them lying
about to no purpose in storehouses for years at a time, often
losing their good quality."[24]

The next expedition, originally scheduled for 1822, was
cancelled, and the Company started negotiating for the permission to engage in barter trade with the foreigners. In
other words, the Company was now working for the repeal
of the very same regulations that had been promulgated at its
own initiative.

The failure to pay dividends for several years and the
resulting drop in the value of the shares to below par, together
with the systematic delay in presenting the customary reports,
were all instrumental in convincing the stockholders within a
short time that the Company was one of those enterprises in

which, according to the witty expression of an eighteenth century economist, "it is very fine to be a director, but very dangerous to be a stockholder."[25]

The sanguine expectations of the stockholders who, as Captain V.M. Golovnin sarcastically observed, had but a short time before been preparing, as it were, iron coffers in which to keep their gold, were utterly shattered by the cheerless results of the commercial operations of the Company.

During the period from 1822 to 1826, when the Company suspended the payment of dividends, no one would buy the shares that had been pledged and become subject to sale. It was with the greatest difficulty that the fifty shares pledged by one of the stockholders were disposed of at 350 rubles each, or at 150 rubles below par.

The general meeting of the stockholders, which had always taken place in an atmosphere of the greatest solemnity, now assumed a very tempestuous character. "The general meeting took place on March 18," wrote the Decembrist K.F. Ryleyev, Manager of the Company, to his friend, also a Decembrist, V.I. Steingel in March of 1825, "and, as usual, was quite noisy and did not make much sense. The Lobanov brothers ranted more vociferously than the others, while Politkovsky was plotting on the sly. It was a question of the balance-sheet which had not yet been signed because Kramer would not come to look it over."[26]

But it was not without reason that Director V. Kramer was afraid to appear at a meeting of the stockholders. The abuses of the directors in the conduct of the Company had reached such proportions that it was dangerous business to present the balance-sheet for 1822 and 1823 to the stockholders for their examination.

The directors, with the support of government circles, took certain steps to hush up the growing scandal in one way or another. First they tried to ward off the possibility of any rumors getting into print that would be harmful to the Company. On February 14, 1825, one month before the convocation of the general assembly, Ryleyev presented a petition to the Petersburg Censorship Committee against allowing any information about the Russian colonies in America to be printed without the sanction of the Russian-American Company. The formal excuse for such a request was the publication in "Severnaya Pchela" (the Northern Bee) of a rather inoffensive short description of Novoarkhangelsk. Moreover, the article was not original but had appeared in the press twice, in a German newspaper published in Riga and in the "Journal de Saint-Pétersbourg."

In his memorandum Ryleyev asked the Censorship Committee "not to approve for publication in any of the local papers any articles about that Company or its colonies that do not bear the Company seal and the signature of some member of the chancery, for, otherwise, the secrets of the Company may be revealed, or erroeneous and false information may be given currency; the publication of the former and the groundlessness of the latter may bring harm to the affairs of the Russian-American Company."

The Company's efforts were successful. For the purpose of examining the affairs of the Company a commission was created which was composed of A. Ya. Druzhinin, Director of the Chancery of the Ministry of Finance, and Captain V.M. Golovnin. At a special meeting which listened to the report of the commission, every means at hand was employed to parry the blow from the directors and to preserve the "prestige" of the Company. The abuses of the directors, however, were so incontrovertible that the presiding officer, Count N.S. Mordvinov, was only able to declare that "What is lost is lost" and "It is at home, not in public, one washes dirty linen." Some of the infuriated stockholders not only demanded the removal of all the directors without exception, but wanted to make them financially responsible for their crimes.

One of the stockholders, Lieutenant Lobanov, who had received 299 shares from Golikov's heirs in settlement of an old lawsuit, came out with a sharp attack against Mordvinov for his defense of the directors. Turning to Mordvinov, he said: "It is allright for you, Your Excellency, to say that 'what is lost is lost,' because you have only fifty shares involved, which to you don't mean anything, but I have 300 of them"[28]

Yet, the directors were saved. They were not made to bear any financial responsibility, and the only one to resign was Kramer, who was represented as bearing the entire guilt of all the mishaps that had befallen the Company.

This, however, was not the end of the affair. The ruined Lobanov, whose whole property consisted of stock in the Company, and who was now compelled to resign from his position on account of his debts, was determined to bring his

grievances before the tsar. He addressed to the tsar one
tearful petition after another, with detailed descriptions of
the dark doings of the directors.

As is evident from the material presented by Lobanov, a
considerable part of the expenses of the Company went to
maintain the directors and to provide bonuses for them. They
each received a salary of 15,000 rubles annually except
Buldakov who, according to the Decembrist Steingel had by
that time "worn himself out physically and mentally, especially mentally,"[29] and who was paid, in addition to his salary, an annual pension of 10,000 rubles. The Director
Prokofyev, furthermore, received 12,000 rubles subsistence.
Then there were bonuses. At the very time when the financial condition of the Company was truly catastrophic, each
one of the directors received a bonus of 100,000 rubles.[30]

Another source of income for the Directors was the preparation of round-the-world expeditions. These expeditions
were being organized all the time, though they brought nothing
but losses to the stockholders. When it was decided in 1821
to send out the usual round-the-world expedition, the purchase
of the ship was entrusted to the firm of the Kramer brothers,
at the head of which was the director of the Company V.
Kramer. Upon procuring the "Yelena" for the Company in
the United States, Kramer was, first of all, paid a commission amounting to 6 per cent of the cost of the vessel. Not
only that but, when it had already become known that the
"Yelena" was on its way and would arrive in Kronstadt in the
near future, Kramer purchased another boat for the Company,
the "Yelizaveta," a vessel that was known to be completely
unseaworthy. The "Yelizaveta" had belonged to an insolvent
debtor of Kramer's. The director acquired the half-rotted
ship, for the Company at a cost of 30,000 rubles. Then he put
the amount of the debt in his pocket, and the Company was
forced to spend 70,000 rubles additional in repairs on that
"acquisition." But since it was inconvenient to keep the ship
in Kronstadt idle, it was fitted out for a round-the-world
voyage, together with the "Riurik" which had recently returned
from such a trip. As for the "Yelena" which Kramer had
acquired in the United States, it was left at its moorings in
the Kronstadt roadstead since one expedition had just been
sent out.

The "Yelizaveta," made her way to the Cape of Good Hope
with great difficulty. Here the cargo was sold at a loss, along

with the ship itself. A part of the crew was transferred to
the "Riurik" and the rest was returned to St. Petersburg as
passengers.

It also appears from the data submitted by Lobanov that,
while the management was borrowing money at interest from
the bank, the funds of the Company were at the personal disposal of the directors.

The government, however, had no intention of taking action
on Lobanov's complaints; it, too, no less than the Governing
Board of the Company, was interested in preserving the repu-
tation of the Russian-American Company as an economically
profitable undertaking, which paid considerable dividends to
its stockholders. The prestige of the Company, which was
the spearhead of tsarist expansion in the Pacific, was not to
be undermined at any cost.

Years passed, Lobanov kept up his petitions, but the affair
hardly made any headway. In the meantime the Company resumed the payment of dividends, and the stockholders once
again passed resolutions of gratitude at every general meeting to the very same directors whom they had been trying,
not so long since, to bring to trial, and once again, as before,
they paid the directors large bonuses for their "zeal" in upholding "the glory of the fatherland,"--paying them out of the
income belonging to the holders of the Company's securities.

For the years 1824-1825 the Company's books showed a
profit of a million and a half rubles, and in 1827 the Company
paid the stockholders at the rate of 147 rubles per share.
True, this profit was not figured without some subtle prac-
tices. The dividends were paid out of the income yet to be
obtained from the sale of merchandise in 1826. This practice of paying dividends out of the income for the following
year was continued for a long time, until 1842. It was due
to this system that it was possible to show a profit even for
those years when the business of the Company was definitely
in the red.

Chapter IV

THE RUSSIAN COLONIES IN NORTH AMERICA AND THE CONVENTION OF 1824-1825

THE CHARTER of the Russian-American Company was confirmed by the government for a term of twenty years. That term came to an end on July 8, 1819. A re-examination and a confirmation of the new charter were to decide, first of all, the problem that was most important for the further activity of the Company, that of the boundaries of the Russian colonies in America.

The charter granted by Emperor Paul had assumed the boundary of the Russian possessions to be at latitude 55°N. In spite of the fact that the coastal strip of that territory was not yet in full possession of the Russians, the old boundaries already seemed inadequate. Not without reason had the governor of the Russian colony been enjoined in 1802 to publish, at the proper time, Russia's claims to territory as far as Nutka Sound, that is, to the 51st parallel of north latitude. The new territory which, according to the Company, it was necessary to make the lawful possession of Russia, was to comprise the whole of the coastal region as far as the 45th parallel of north latitude. This would have included Columbia and would have extended the limits of the Russian possessions down to Oregon.

However, as a result of the growing claims to the Pacific coastal regions on the part of the United States, claims which became stronger after the War of 1812, and as a result, too, of the rivalry of England itself, the Company's plans had already become obsolete. The 51st parallel north latitude, that is the northern promontory of Vancouver Island, was recognized as the new boundary. Thus the boundaries of the Russian possessions advanced southward only 4°, in comparison with what they had been under the first charter.

The problem of further progress also became more acute. The old charter had granted the Company the right to expand its possessions beyond the established boundaries whenever the new territories "were not occupied by any of the other

powers and had not become their dependency." At the same
time there was particularly no point in counting on vacant
lands, and had the Company really been guided by these rules
it would have been deprived of the opportunity to occupy any
of the territory settled by natives. The new charter rendered
this problem more acute. The Company was permitted to
seize new territories beyond the designated boundaries, if
those lands "were not occupied by other European nations, or
by citizens of the United States of America, and had not become their dependency."[1]

In the new charter as confirmed by the government article
17 is worthy of notice. This granted the Company the right
to import and export, free of duty, goods of Russian and
foreign origin from the mother country into the colonies. To
the extent, however, that there was no further control over
the transfer of the goods, the right to export from one Russian
port (Kronstadt) to another Russian port (Novoarkhangelsk)
had essentially become the right of free trade.

Article 9 of the new charter was also of great importance.
The employees of the Company had all the rights of persons
in the government service. This enabled the Company to
attract to its service not only civil servants but also members of the armed forces, primarily naval officers.

The new charter was confirmed on September 14, 1821.
On the eve of its promulgation, the problem of combatting
foreign smuggling was also solved. This problem has a long
history behind it.

From the very beginning of the Company's existence, foreign smuggling in the colonies constituted one of the most
burning questions. Foreign merchants, especially Americans
by securing through barter with the Tlinkets and other Indian
tribes, all the skins that these natives had procured, practically limited the sphere of activity of the Russian-American
Company to the hunting-stations manned by natives who were
dependent upon the Company. K. Khlebnikov, subsequently
one of the directors of the Company, in his memoirs dealing
with Russian America (where he lived for a long time) reports
that while the Americans paid the Tlinkets for one skin "five
or six blankets, in addition to molasses, hard tack and groats
we were unable to pay all that, because the cost would have
been twice the fixed price, and sometimes also because we
did not have a sufficient quantity of merchandise."[2] According
to the Company's calculations, an average of fifteen vessels

were plying their trade along the shores of the Russian colonies, exporting between 10,000 and 15,000 otters annually.

The Russian-American Company, not being able through its own efforts to counteract the smuggling activities of the foreigners, plied the government and the tsar himself with requests to defend it against the American merchants. The management of the Company adduced a number of political arguments, asserting that "the citizens of the United States of North America, as a republican nation," were engaged in bartering the animal-skins with the natives for fire-arms and cold steel, "teaching them how to use them, to the detriment of our hunters." The main argument was to the effect that the American merchants set "such low prices" on their merchandise "that the same articles sold by the American company are much more expensive to the Russian company, by reason of the wearisome and expensive transportation through Siberia to Okhotsk."[3]

The Russian men-of-war, which appeared near the American shores once in two or three years, in the course of their round-the-world voyages, presented no obstacle to the foreign merchants. The attempts, begun as early as 1810, to settle the question of smuggling in the Russian colonies through diplomatic negotiations also came to naught. And Count Pahlen, Envoy Extraordinary to the United States, and Dashkov, Consul-General in Philadelphia, declared unanimously that the American government had neither the desire--inasmuch as some members of the government made investments themselves in the expeditions sent off to the Russian shores--nor the ability--inasmuch as there were no American men-of-war off the American shores--to block this type of trade.

The Company posed the problem of taking decisive action against foreign competition with particular sharpness after the Americans had penetrated into Columbia. In its memorandum to Alexander I of December 18, 1811, the Governing Board laid stress on the fact that "it is impossible to ward off this danger except by issuing a determined warning to the North American navigators who, by reason of the spirit of liberty embodied in their constitution and the freedom to sail and do business wherever and however one pleases, will not heed any suggestions."[4]

The Governing Board reported on the intensified competition of the Americans as a result of the penetration of the United States into Columbia, that borders on the Russian

colonies, and on the establishment of an American trading
company there. Then it requested the tsar to take decisive
action against the foreigners:

> "Your Imperial Majesty who has most graciously taken
> the Russian-American Company and the country's com-
> merce in general under his protection will not allow, in
> a way known to his royal fatherly heart, any further inter-
> ference with Russian business on the part of private North
> American hucksters and will not permit the aforementioned
> company, which, having settled at Columbia, is continuing
> with the aid of its other unmanageable fellow countrymen
> to barter arms with the Indians, to crush every opportunity
> for developing more trade and to violate to all intents and
> purposes the tranquillity of the Russian colonies."[5]

The Company posed before the government the problem of
maintaining a permanent patrol of warships in American
waters. But in a period marked by a gathering armed clash
with Napoleon, it was, of course, out of the question to start
anything that might aggravate the relations with the United
States. "I believe," wrote the Minister of the Interior, O.P.
Kozodavlev, to State Chancellor N.P. Rumyantsev, "that any
methods employing force and arms in warding off the attempts
of the North Americans, even though their success be assured
can have no place here for the very good reason that to break
diplomatic relations for the sake of a private company would
not be altogether a sound action."[6]
Kozodavlev knew, of course, very well what the "private"
Russian-American Company represented. But he was indisputably right in declaring that to proceed to break diplomatic
relations with the United States at that juncture "would not be
altogether a sound action"; for, should the United States openl
ally itself with France, the danger threatening the Russian
colonies would be something more than that of the American
merchants.
In the post-Tilsit period, when Russia was compelled to
conclude an alliance with France, the tsarist government
tried to utilize the anti-British tendencies of American policy.
Thus we read in the outline of the instructions given by
Alexander I to Count Pahlen, who was sent as envoy to the
United States in 1809:

> "I see the United States as a particular kind of rival

to England. I believe that the special interests of the
United States will force them to watch more carefully
than the governments on the European continent have
done for an opportunity, if not of restraining the per-
nicious despostism shown by Great Britain on the seas
then   at least of mitigating it."[7]

Still, a few years later, when Russia broke with Napoleon
and allied herself with England, the tsarist government was
compelled to maintain friendly relations with the United States
as it had done before, but for reasons contrary to those that
had operated during the period of Franco-Russian friendship.

The United States attempted to support France whenever
possible. Some idea of the sympathy with Napoleon which was
widespread in the United States may be obtained from the
correspondence between Bashkov, the Russian Consul in Philadelphia, and Nesselrode. In a letter from Philadelphia,
dated March 15, 1815, Dashkov, touching upon the venality
of the American press during the period of the war with
Napoleon, wrote, among other things:

> "The Russian minister has least need of all of employ-
> ing that political weapon [i.e., bribing the newspapers.--
> Au.] and would almost manage without it, if the American
> government, in its blind devotion to Napoleon, did not
> favor the views of the French minister even with regard
> to the estranged relations existing between Russia and
> America."[8]

This friendly attitude of the United States towards France
was brought about, in the first place, by the antagonism between the United States and England which led to the War of
1812 between the two countries. In those conditions, it was
not to Russia's interest to provoke America.

It was suggested to the Company that it compose all the
differences that had arisen between it and the American merchants by peaceful means. Following Dashkov's proposal,
which was supported by the Minister of the Interior, the management of the Russian-American Company signed on May 20,
1812, a four-year agreement with the fur-trading company
that was formed in Columbia under the New York merchant,
Astor. The Columbia company was granted the right to bring
certain fur-skins into Russia free of duty, although the impor-

tation of such skins was prohibited under the regulations then
in force.

Astor's company pledged itself not to engage in trade in the
territory belonging to the Russian-American Company, exclu
sively to supply the Russian colonies with all the provisions
they needed, and to transport the Russian furs to Canton in its
own ships. In the event that any of the American merchants
engaged in hunting or trading in the Russian colonies, Astor
was obliged to act "jointly and in agreement" with the Russian
American Company "to decline such an undertaking." The
Russian company figured on Astor's family connections with
important politicians in the United States. However, the
agreement concluded with Astor did not bring about any change
in the existing situation. Astor imported into the colonies
primarily such goods as the Russian-American Company did
not need. He charged high freight rates on his boats, and the
reports about the influence he allegedly exerted over the
American merchants, an influence that was expected to make
them relinquish their unwarranted trade in the Russian colonies, proved to be false.

In 1817 the Governing Board of the Company submitted to
the tsar for his consideration a draft of the regulations to be
imposed upon foreign vessels touching at the Russian colonies
in America. The draft compared, as to statutes, the colonial
ports with those on the Baltic. But it made no progress, and
smuggling went on in the colonies just as before. The foreign
merchants felt quite at home in the Russian colonies, even in
those that were situated in close proximity to the center of the
colonial administration.

The famous Russian navigator, V. Golovnin, upon returning
from a trip in 1819, in a letter addressed to the directors of
the Russian-American Company imparted a number of facts
which testified to the tremendous proportions that foreign
trade had assumed in Russian America.

He pointed to the necessity for decisive steps by the government in the defense of the Russian territory in America
against Foreign penetration. And, in its day, his letter received wide publicity in government circles. The letter began with the argument that the territory which, according to
the charter granted, was in exclusive possession of the
Company, actually belonged to Russia both by right of first
discovery and of first settlement, without which letter, in
Golovnin's opinion, the former had no validity whatsoever.

Citing the results of the voyages of Bering, Chirikov, and of other Russian navigators, Golovnin argued that the subsequent "re-discovery" by foreign travelers of a number of places on the American continent where they found Russian settlers, amounts to nothing more than the assigning of new names to those places in honor of some dignitaries--something which neither Bering nor Chirikov had ever done.

Golovnin wrote as follows:

"Were a modern navigator to succeed in making discoveries such as those made by Bering and Chirikov, he would not only assign names of princes and counts to all the American promontories, islands, and bays, but would even have seated all the ministers and all the nobility on bare stones and proclaimed his compliments to the whole world."[9] As for the colony of Ross, while the right of first discovery did not in this case belong to Russia, the right of first settlement justified Russia in taking possession of that region, since it is the first settlement and not "the first discovery," as Golovnin points out, that bestows the right to possession. "That not mere discovery," writes Golovnin, "but actual occupation gives the right to possession, of that we have instances even in the olden days. For example, under Queen Elizabeth of England the Spanish court demanded of her ministers that they order the Englishmen who had occupied a certain place in America to leave that place because it belonged to Spain by right of discovery. Elizabeth, however, had the following reply given to the demand, namely that mere discovery without actual occupation does not give the right to possession, and that the Spaniards had discovered that place when there were no cannon there, and that now they will have to discover it anew."[10]

Golovnin points out further that "His Majesty, having granted to the Company certain rights and privileges to the exclusion of all his other subjects, did not, of course, intend to allow foreigners to profit, in the areas belonging to Him, by the advantage granted only to the Company and appurtenant to it."[11]

In the meantime the territory from latitude 42° to $54^{\circ}40'$N. was, according to the agreement of 1818, occupied jointly by England and the United States. This circumstance contributed to enhance the interest of American business circles in the Russian possessions that abounded in fur-bearing animals.

From that time on, reports Poletika, the Russian envoy in America, to the Minister of Foreign Affairs, Nesselrode, "the curiosity of the Americans about the northwest coast of America and about our settlements in that wild region attaine a degree of intensity that truly amazed me."[12] In the same report, dated January 21, 1821, Poletika relates:

> "It often happened that private individuals would imper-tinently--and even in my own house--demand information of me concerning the activities of the Russians along the shores of northwestern America.... I have refrained until now from submitting a report to Your Excellency on these instances of political madness, because I noticed no dis-position on the part of the American government to pre-occupy itself seriously with the settlements on the shores of the Pacific. But all this may radically change, es-pecially now when Congress is preoccupied with those settlements."[13]

The question of the Russian colonies was raised in Con-gress in connection with the occupation by the United States of the Columbia Riber basin, which brought the boundaries of the American possessions closer to the Russian settlements on the northwest coast.

On January 9, (21, New Style) 1821, Congress heard a report by a special committee which had been charged with investigating the results of the expedition sent by the United States to effect the occupation of the territory along the Columbia River.

With regard to the pursuits of fur-hunting and whaling in which American citizens were interested, the committee noted that the United States missed the opportunity to gain full possession of that region, while "all nations, whether or not they have any rights to that region, are taking care to occupy some place therein and do not want to be reimbursed for their expenditures, if they can only share in the income therefrom." By way of illustration the committee cited the case of Russia:

> "Russia, which, by her possessions in the Asiatic area, occupies a position similar to that occupied by our possessions here, has long realized the importance of commerce there and the profits thereof.... The European powers did not even take notice of Russia until she started to engage in novel undertakings, sparing neither toil,

trouble, nor expense in trying to make the four parts of
the globe her vassals."[14]

The congressional committee examined the Russian colonies in America within the framework of tsarist Russia's
general plan for expansion. The committee pictured Russia
as a mighty power whose aim was world domination: "Fortresses, storehouses, cities, trade--all have sprung up in
that region as though by magic. With an armed force of one
million men at her disposal she is not only defending her
obligation with the grandeur in which Europe regards her,
and is threatening the Turk, the Persian, Japan and China,
but even the possessions of the King of Spain in North America
are not safe from her terrible might."

In the opinion of the committee, Russia's activity was increasing from day to day: "Her alertness in opening up suitable routes for profitable trade is growing more intense by
the hour. In the midst of all her difficult undertakings she
did not miss the opportunity of occupying two important posts
on the American coast of the Pacific, one at a place called
Arkhangelsk, at about latitude 57°N., and the other in Bodega
Bay at latitude $38^\circ34'$N." After a brief description of the
Russian fortifications and the methods used to supply the
Russian colonies by land as far as Petropavlovsk and from
there by sea to Novoarkhangelsk, the congressional committee wrote in conclusion that "a nation which undertakes such
voyages, often over frozen seas, in tempests and snowstorms
which make it impossible to see an object a few feet away,
in order to hold on to some branch of trade, must well and
thoroughly understand all its importance, so that the objec-
tives it has in view are not, in some way, taken away from
it. By overcoming such extraordinary difficulties, Russia
has found a way to occupy one of the Sandwich Islands, which
not only enables her to maintain her positions, but to have
command of the whole northern part of the Pacific."[15]

The congressional committee, as we have seen, posed the
question of the Russian colonies in America very sharply.
This attitude was the result not only of the generally intensified interest of the United States in the Pacific coastal region,
but also of the opposition that American trade had encountered
in the Russian colonies on the part of the Russian-American
Company.

In August, 1820, the management forbade the colonial administration to carry on any barter trade with foreigners. One year later this prohibition received government sanction. On September 4, 1821, simultaneously with the approval of the new charter of the Russian-American Company, an ukase was issued absolutely forbidding all foreign vessels, without exception, to put in at the Russian colonies.

The right to trade and to engage in fishing and whaling along the whole northwest coast of America, from the Bering Strait to latitude 50°N., and in the waters around the Aleutian and the Kuriles, was by the terms of that ukase granted to Russian subjects exclusively. The ukase forbade "all foreign vessels not only to put in at the shores and islands subject to Russia as specified in the preceding article, but to approach them within less than 100 Italian miles."[16] Vessels caught trading with the natives or entering the prohibited zone, would be subject to confiscation by men-of-war, which it was proposed to send cruising along the American coast. In October of the same year the frigate "Apollo" sailed from Kronstadt. Exactly one year later, in October, 1822, it started cruising along the shores of the Russian colonies in America.

These decisive measures, however, resulted only in the suspension of the purchasing of goods from foreign merchants for the colonies; the smuggling trade of the foreigners with the native population continued at full blast.

The prohibition imposed upon foreign ships from approaching the Russian colonies in America, evoked a sharp protest not only from the United States but also from Great Britain. On June 3, 1822, K. V. Nesselrode wrote as follows to Count D.A. Guryev, Minister of Finance, concerning the protest of the American and English governments against the extension of the boundaries of the Russian colonies in America, as proclaimed in the new charter of the Company, and also against the ukase of September 4:

"The American government has protested against what it calls the expansion of our possessions and against the degree of power granted by us to our naval tribunal." The English government, wrote Nesselrode in the same letter, "has likewise made a representation to us which is based on the same grounds."[17]

This was at a time when the tsarist government was not in a position to disregard these protests, especially that of England. The tsarist government had just presented a note

to the member powers of the Holy Alliance urging that Russia
be entrusted with "the restoration of order in the Balkan Peninsula" in connection with the Greek Revolution which had
broken out in 1821 under Ypsilanti's leadership. England and
Austria, more than any of the other powers, tried to prevent
this "restoration of order in the Balkan Peninsula" which
Alexander conceived as a pretext for the partition of Turkey.
The Greek problem, which was essentially the problem of
the Straits, was the crux of Russia's foreign policy. Preparing
himself for a campaign in "aid" of the Greeks, Alexander had
to disguise his interventionist designs in every way possible.
It was manifestly disadvantageous to the tsarist government
to come into conflict, at that time, with England and the
United States over the Russian possessions in America. It
was not worthwhile to allow the relations with the powers to
deteriorate over an acquisition such as the American colonies,
while those powers were also opposed to Russian intervention
in the Greek affair. In the letter of June 3, 1822, which we
have quoted, Nesselrode informed Guryev that Alexander had
ordered all vessels cruising off the shores of Russian America
"to conduct their observations as close to dry land as possible
and not to extend them beyond the latitude in which the American company actually enjoyed its prerogatives in hunting and
fishing, both at the time of its establishment and when its
charter was renewed in 1799."[18]
    Thus, the declaration of September 4 relating to the ex-
tension of the Russian border clear up to latitude 50°N. was
practically annulled, though without the benefit of a formal
announcement. As for the ban on foreigners to land on the
shores of Russian America, that question, too, according
to Alexander's order cited above, was really not considered
definitively solved. It was suggested in Washington to Baron
Tyuil, the new ambassador to the United States who had replaced Poletika, that "an agreement be concluded on the
measures to be accepted by common consent to avert all
further controversy with regard to the extent of the respective possessions on the northwest coast of America, to eliminate all such complaints as have heretofore come from the
American company against the undertakings of certain citizens
of the United States, and finally, to avoid the duty of putting
into effect the declaration of September 4, a step we should
be obliged to take under any other arrangement."[19]
    The question of the right to do business in the Russian

colonies was of prime interest to the United States, since it
was chiefly American merchants who were engaged in supply
ing the colonies and in smuggling goods to the natives. The
question of the boundaries of the Russian possessions, howev
was of equal concern to England and to the United States. A
common stand by these two powers, which had only recently
been at war with each other, against the declaration of
September 4 was assured complete success.

The French historian Barral-Monferrat notes that "Lord
Castlereagh, [20] without the slightest hesitation, began to back
up the rights of the United States with as much energy as he
would have upheld those of his own country." "R ussia," write
Barral-Montferrat farther on, "which still affected treating
Americans as one would a second-rate people, towards
whom one could permit oneself to be somewhat unceremoni-
ous, radically changed her attitude when she felt that Englanc
backed them up. She took the initiative in proposing that the
regulation of the boundaries, a question which she had but
lately maintained to be able to settle unilaterally of her own
prerogative, be entrusted to a conference to be called in
St. Petersburg. She gave her delegates the most concilia-
tory instructions and hastened to extricate herself in this
way from a needless conflict over Alaska. The St. Petersburg conference gave complete satisfaction to the Washington
government both juridically and practically, and the material
interests of the United States were fully safeguarded."[21]

The conflict over Alaska was indeed "unnecessary" for
Russia, since at that time problems of great import to her
were being settled on the Balkan Peninsula.

On November 20 (December 2, New Style), 1823, President Monroe sent a message to Congress in which it was
stated for the first time that "the American continents, by
the free and independent condition which they have assumed
and maintained, are henceforth not to be considered as subjects for future colonization of any European powers." The
direct cause of this declaration was the continuing expansion
of the Russians on the North American continent and, in part,
the declaration of September 4, 1831. In this message, whicl
laid the foundation of what came to be known as the "Monroe
Doctrine," it was clearly noted that the president thought it
proper to enunciate the above principles precisely at the time
that, at the suggestion of the Russian government, the representative of the United States in St. Petersburg was given the

authority to determine, through peaceful negotiations, the mutual rights of the two countries on the northwest coast of the American continent.

It was at the St. Petersburg conference, which considered the boundaries of the Russian colonies in America, that the Monroe Doctrine won its first victory. But this victory was won mainly as a result of the common stand with England which, in turn, was the result of the opposition manifested by that country to the interests of tsarist Russia in the Near East.

The convention regulating the relations between Russia and the United States on the American continent was concluded on April 5 (17), 1824. A similar convention was concluded with England on February 16 (28), 1825. When all the "American" problems had been settled in February, 1825, negotiations with England and Austria began in St. Petersburg on the question of the Greek Revolution. It became apparent at once that all the negotiations that had taken place previously were only in the nature of deliberate procrastination, and that neither England nor Austria would allow Alexander to use the Greek Revolution as a pretext for meddling in Turkish affairs.

The tenor of these conventions, concluded, as they were, at a time that was most propitious for exerting pressure on the tsarist government, was in direct contradiction to the ukase of September 4, 1821. The two conventions were perfectly identical in their main provisions. Article 3 of both conventions fixed as the boundary of the Russian colonies latitude 54°40′N., that is 3°40′ short of the boundary indicated both in the ukase of September 4 and in the new charter of the Company. As to the colony of Ross, that question was simply ignored in the agreement.

Article 4 of the convention with the United States and Article 7 of the convention with Great Britain granted to the citizens of the two countries the right of unimpeded entry to all the inland waters of the Russian possessions in America, both for the purpose of fishing and for trading with the native population. A similar right of entry to the inland waters of the American and English settlements in America was granted to Russian nationals. Only those places were excluded from the terms of the convention that were considered not only the territory of a power that was a signatory to the agreement but were actually settled by its nationals, Russians in the first case and Americans or Englishmen in the second case.

However, it was clear to both sides, even while the agreement was being signed, that, since the Russian merchants
were in no position to compete with their English and American rivals, this formally reciprocal obligation would actually
assume the character of a special privilege extended to
American and English merchants.

The convention signed with England ten months after that
with the United States made more acute the problem of the
boundaries, not only from the direction of the American west
coast but from the East as well. Furthermore, the convention established, with relation to England, the condition of
the most favored nation, meaning that in the event any nation
was granted the right of free trade in the Russian colonies
for more than ten years, that right would also be granted to
England.

The two conventions placed the commercial activity of the
Russian-American Company in an extremely difficult position.
The attempt through government measures to eradicate smug
gling on the coastline belonging to the Russian colonies ended
in failure. What was more, that type of trade was now legiti-
matized, not only in the coastal zone but in the inland waters
as well, not to mention the fact that the conventions had set
up serious obstacles in the way of any territorial expansion
on the American continent.

It did not prove so easy to forswear completely all trade
relations with foreigners, as the management had wanted to
do at first when it secured the ban on foreign vessels. Even
before the signing of the convention with the United States, the
Company was forced to appeal to the government for permission to renew its trade with the foreigners in the colonial
center of Novoarkhangelsk, so it might be able to supply the
colonies with food and other necessities. Count N.S. Mordvinov in a private letter to K.V. Nesselrode, dated January 8
1824, pointed out that "the interruption of trade with the foreigners has placed the Company in a very difficult position.
The delay in negotiating a permanent agreement with England
and the United States on questions of boundaries and commercial relations, may, in the meantime, contribute to the
exhaustion of the Company's funds, reduce the fur-hunters to
ruin, and arouse the indignation of the natives who have been
receiving all their necessities from the Company."[22] The
council of the Company, for its part, in its memorandum to
the Minister of Finance urged him most strenuously to solve
this problem.

There was one other factor which prompted the Company to insist on a partial abrogation of the very same regulations for the promulgation of which it had vigorously fought. The ban on foreigners against trading in the territory belonging to the Russian colonies aroused the anger of the natives, especially of the Tlinket tribes; for the colonial administration was unable to supply them with the merchandise which they were accustomed to buy from the foreign merchants. A revolt of the Tlinket was always a real threat to the Russian colonies in America. Now, according to the report of the governor of the colonies, Muravyov, that threat was to become even more imminent as a result of the scarcity of goods. Rumors, highly exaggerated to be sure, that the Tlinket were arming and that the Americans were exercising undue influence over them also played a part in confusing the situation. "It is well known," reported the frightened Muravyov, "that cannon may be found in many of the sections inhabited by the Kolosh. Members of the crew of the royal frigate 'Apollo,' which is cruising along the coast of the colonies, have reported that during their stay in the Kaigani, they had seen a small fortress with cannon, under the American flag, and that every day they fire a cannon at sunset and raise the flag. Exceedingly large stores of rifles and gunpowder may be seen in that fortress."[23]

Muravyov requested the immediate delivery of the merchandise needed by the natives and the dispatch of men "as reinforcements," declaring that otherwise "he does not know what to do." "Considering that they see in us alone," wrote the management of the Company in regard to the Tlinkets, on the basis of reports received from the colonies, "the only obstacle both to the selling of their furs and to the easy acquisition of those things that have become indispensable to them, we cannot expect a friendly attitude on their part nor any mercy from them when they have become strong. Consequently, the danger to us from them will increase as we set up more obstacles in their way dealing with foreign seamen."[24]

On March 27, 1824, ten days before the signing of the convention with the United States, Alexander I allowed the Russian-American Company to resume trading with foreigners at Novoarkhangelsk. In ratifying this permission, however, the convention went considerably farther. By giving the opportunity to the Americans, and later also to the English, to carry on their trade, with the consent of the

Company, wherever there were Russian settlements, the
convention gave to the foreign merchants the right of unimpeded trade in the Company's territory that was not settled
by Russians. This meant that the Company had deprived itself of any perspectives of expanding its operations even
within the limits of the territory formally belonging to it. To
its own surprise, the Russian-American Company encountere
powerful and enterprising rivals on its own territory.

The management of the Russian-American Company, knew
of course, even before the convention was signed which way
the negotiations were going.

The interests both of the stockholders and of the directors
were at complete variance with the appeasement policy pursued by the tsarist government on the American continent.
In his reminiscences of Ryleyev, who, at that time, was the
manager of the Company, Ye. P. Obolensky says that "he
was seriously distrubed by the surrender, forced by virtue
of the agreement with the North American Union, to the
North Americans of the colony of Ross which we had established in California. This colony might have become a strong
base for us from which we would have been able to participate
in the rich gold discoveries which were subsequently to become so famous."[25]

Ryleyev was indeed very much disturbed by the terms of
the agreement, but not on account of the surrender of Cali-
fornia--the agreement did not provide for that at all--but
because he had an apprehension that the ratification of the
convention would deal a heavy blow to the whole activity of
the Company.

Not only the management of the Company but also some of
the most influential individual stockholders tried to bring
pressure upon the government in one way or another, in an
attempt to keep it from making concessions to the United
States.

"However useless the extensive possession of desert land
may seem at present," wrote Count N.S. Mordvinov to K.V.
Nesselrode in February, 1824, "we cannot forget the cession
by Russia of the border region between the Yablonoi Mountains
and the Amur to the Chinese. At the time we ceded that regio
we were content with the vast expanse of Siberia and we de-
spised the wildness of the lands we were about to yield. Now,
however, we regret that Amur, the only Siberian river flowing into a sea that is open to our navigation, no longer flows

within our boundaries, and that we cannot recover these great losses."[26]

The management of the company placed great hope in N.S. Mordvinov's authority. But events as they developed were not propitious to the Company. Nesselrode, in informing Mordvinov after the convention with the United States had been signed, that his letter had been presented directly to the emperor who, "accepting it graciously, deigned to consider it worthy...of His Majesty's attention," gives the following interpretation of the convention just signed:

> "In Article IV we allow the United States to trade and to fish, but only for a period not exceeding ten years, in all places under our jurisdiction. Our cabinet was compelled to agree to this provision favorable to them--for two reasons, both equally worthy of consideration: first, because the government of the North American Republic has, not without foundation, demanded compensation for the considerable advantages accruing to us from the other provisions of the agreement, especially from those in Article V [the ban on the sale of spirits and arms throughout the territory of the Russian colonies.--Au.]; secondly, because the Americans had been carrying on their trade and fishing for a long time and the Company had until now not found the means to stop them, and it is, of course, a great deal more injurious to the Company to allow them to continue to enjoy their pursuits by what had come to be regarded as a natural and inalienable right than by our permission, given by us in solemn agreement; for, by signing this agreement the Americans have just as solemnly admitted that, at the expiration of a few stipulated years, we shall have the legal power to forbid them absolutely to trade or fish in that whole area."[27]

Further Nesselrode expresses the thought that "by this agreement our colonies stand to gain even more; in a certain sense it marks the beginning of their political existence and of their freedom from danger, since now, for the first time, their relations with foreign governments are being determined. The importance of this is obvious, and the honorable members of the Russian-American Company will, no doubt, feel the full measure of this great new favor bestowed upon them by their most august protector."

The conventions just concluded were, in fact, the first mutual international agreements in which Russian possession no
only of the Aleutians but also of a clearly defined territory o
the American continent itself was duly recorded. However,
"the honorable members of the Russian-American Company"
still evaluated these agreements not at all as "a great new
favor bestowed upon them by their most august protector,"
but as a great new calamity which placed in jeopardy the ver
existence of the Company.

In spite of the fact that Article IV of the agreement, to jud
by the Russian translation, allowed the Americans in Russia
territory only "to engage in fishing and trade with the natives
thereof," it was clear that it also included the right to engag
in the hunting of sea-animals. Mordvinov was quick to call
Nesselrode's attention to the fact that the word "pêche" trans
lated in the Russian text of the convention by the word
"rybolobstvo" (fishing) lent itself to a very broad interpretation, including the hunting of sea-animals. Nesselrode explained to Mordvinov that he had provided for the broad interpretation of the term "pêche." "I hasten to reply to you,
with the approval of His Majesty," he wrote, "that, by the
Russian word 'rybolovstvo,' which I used in my letter, and
the French word 'pêche,' which is used in our convention
with the North American Republic, we, for lack of other mor
precise words in the two languages, understood, as is custom
ary, the catching of all aquatic animals and, in general, all
the creatures of the sea."[28]

During the short period which separated the signing of the
convention from its ratification--April 5 to May 10, 1824--
the Company was still making attempts to avert the approaching catastrophe.

There has been preserved in the archives of the Ministry
of Foreign Affairs a copy of a second representation made by
the Company to Ye. F. Kankrin, Minister of Finance, copied
in K.F. Ryleyev's own hand and apparently written by him,
with regard to the Russian-American convention of April 5,
1824. In this memorandum to the Minister of Finance the
management pictures the future of the Company, in the event
the agreement is ratified, in very dark colors. "As soon as
the foreigners," writes the management, "have received the
legal right to enter into competition with the Company in its
own hunting-posts--which constitute the only source of its
wealth--then not only would those who used to frequent our

shores and sail our waters flock there but so also would those who had never given a thought to such an enterprise. The latter would not, of course, miss the opportunity to combine with the former in intensifying the hunting of animals and the direct trade with the inhabitants of the coast within the confines of our colonies.

Furthermore, the foreigners, spurred on by commercial gains, will, as may affirmatively be supposed, inspire the savages, who are attached to Russia, with a distaste for their former state of dependence on the Company and will not need to trade with the Company in its main colony; for, whatever they are able to obtain from the Company in exchange for necessities they will supply through their own trading-posts, and by direct contact with the inhabitants. Thus our colonies will remain without immediate means of subsistence, just as they were during the time when trade was prohibited, and it will, therefore, be necessary to keep them supplied from Russia, through round-the-world expeditions. The tremendous expense that these expeditions entail and the undermining, at the same time, in the Company's own trading-posts of the only source and means of its existence, hold out no other promise for the future, of course, than inevitable disaster."[29]

Computing the losses that the Company would incur in the ten years during which foreigners would be allowed to trade freely in the Russian colonies, the author of the memorandum writes:

"The Company has every reason to fear that not alone within ten years but within a much shorter period the foreigners, with the incalculable resources at their disposal and in view of the advantages they will have obtained, will bring the Company to a state of complete destruction."[30]

The Decembrist D.I. Zavalishin, who, like Ryleyev, took a direct part in the affairs of the Company, also came out with sharp criticism of the agreement that had just been concluded. His memorandum, "Concerning the Ban on American Citizens to Visit the North-West Coast of North America," was also devoted to a criticism of the Convention of April 5, 1824. He regarded the permission granted to the Americans to visit the Russian colonies, Sitka in particular, as marking the end of Russian rule in those areas. He wrote as follows:

"Only one thing could assure the security of Sitka, the complete removal of citizens of the United States from its shores. Otherwise, I believe, it would be more advantageous to the Russian-American Company to abandon that fortress altogether."[31]

Zavalishin came out with even sharper criticism of the Anglo-Russian convention of February 16, 1825. The establishment of the boundary along the 141st meridian west of Greenwich he considered a useless concession. The right of foreigners freely to navigate in the inland waters he regarded as equivalent to Russian's renunciation of control over her colonies. "Article VI," he wrote, "renders the domination of the continent perfectly useless; by allowing foreigners to navigate the rivers freely and in perpetuity, it makes them the real masters of the land, leaving to us only the empty form of domination."[32]

But inasmuch as the Convention had already been conclude Zavalishin proposed a number of measures which might neutralize, to some degree, the serious consequences of the Convention for the Russian-American Company. Since Article II of the Convention forbade foreigners to put in ashore for the purpose of barter only in those places in the Russian colonies where there were Company settlements, Zavalishin, "always thinking of how to block the trade by foreigners," proposed that Company trading-stations be established in all places suitable for commerce. To neutralize Article VII, which gave the English the right for ten years freely to navigate in Russian inland waters, Zavalishin insisted that the Company take advantage of the dual nature of that Article:

"The Company should by all means send there [i.e., in to English territorial waters.--Au.] all the merchandise it can give away at lower prices than the English, and so try to undermine their trade and compel them to return home leaving the places in question to us."[33]

But despite all the efforts of the Russian-American Company the two conventions were signed and some time later ratified.

For the sake of its interests on the European continent the tsarist government made important concessions on the

American continent. K.V. Nesselrode in one of his letters to
Count N.S. Mordvinov emphasized with great clarity the necessity for subordinating Russian interests on the American continent to the more important problems facing the government:

> "While trying to preserve the gains we have made by
> dint of hard labor, and even aiming to make new ones by
> all legitimate means, we must not forget that there may
> be other most important government needs and advantages
> which involve very important government obligations. I
> consider it unnecessary to explain to you, Sir, a man who
> is well versed in all branches of the science of govern-
> ment, that the degree of usefulness of the desired acqui-
> sitions should not serve as a guide in political negoti-
> ations."[34]

Chapter V

THE COMMERCIAL COMPANY BECOMES A
GOVERNMENT INSTITUTION

CONTEMPORARIES were often under the impression that
the Russian-American Company acted independently and was
not subject to any government control, being, as it were, a
"state within a state."

The physician Langsdorf, who was a member of I.F.
Krusentern's expedition, wrote as follows:

> "I was often surprised by the fact that it was possible
> for a free trading company to develop under a monarchi-
> cal government, without being subject to any administra-
> tive control, and to be able to exercise its rule, auto-
> cratically with unlimited power and with impunity, over
> vast new territories."[1]

Such a notion could have arisen only in the mind of one
who had only a very superficial knowledge of the true state
of affairs. All the activities of the management, from the
first day of the founding of this formally private company,
were controlled and directed by the government.

By the provisions of the charter approved in 1799 the
Russian-American Company was comparable with regard to
its subordination to the power of the state, to an independent
government department. In conformity with § 12 of the
charter of 1799, the management "was under obligation to
report directly to His Majesty about everything relating to
the affairs of the Company, about its dispositions and the
progress resulting therefrom."

For the purpose of guiding the activities of the management and of exercising the necessary control over it, the
office of "correspondent" or "protector" of the Company
was created. But N.P. Rezanov, who was appointed correspondent of the Company in 1799, was not only a high government official--Chief Prosecutor of the First Department of
the Senate--but a close relative of M. Buldakov, Director or
Company, and the owner of a considerable block of shares.

94

By virtue of his position, then, Rezanov was not so much "the eye of His Majesty," looking after the Company, as its agent acting for it in the most diverse matters. At the same time the growth of the importance of the Company and the necessity for coordinating its activity with that of various government departments--the Ministry of Foreign Affairs, the Navy Department, and others--posed the question of transferring the Company from the one-man control by the "correspondent" to control by a board.

In 1804 a provisional committee was established, consisting of three stockholders, to which were granted all the prerogatives of the general meeting in confidential matters requiring decisions of a political character. Of the three seats on the committee, one was to be filled not by selection but by appointment, in accordance with a proposal by the Ministry of the Interior. In the words of the Minister of the Interior, "If the Company should choose by ballot two of the honorable members and His Imperial Highness should designate the third member as His agent in all matters pertaining to His Majesty, then the government would have the influence it has the right to reserve for itself, and in this way both the Company and the government would be mutually satisfied."[2]

The creation of the provisional committee, which was the first step in the transformation of the Company from a commercial organization into a direct agency of the Crown, met with no opposition, though, on the part of the Governing Board which was composed of merchants.

Only problems of a political nature were to come within the jurisdiction of the provisional committee. The Governing Board, being as it was in the hands of the merchants, preserved its full powers in commercial matters. At the same time the decisions of the Governing Board gained in importance upon the creation of the provisional committee, for they actually had the sanction of officials of the government, even before the government itself put its official stamp of approval on them.

The following were selected as members of the committee: Minister of the Navy Admiral N.S. Mordvinov, Assistant-Minister of the Interior Count P.A. Stroganov, and Privy Councilor I.A. Weidemeyer who was one of the most important officials of the Ministry of Foreign Affairs. A few years later the provisional committee, now called "Special Council

of the Russian-American Company," became a permanent
instrument of government control and of government direction of the political side of the Company's activities. Officially the initiative in creating the permanent council came
from the Governing Board. In its representation to the Tsar
in 1812 the Governing Board noted that as a result of the advance made by the Company in California, the American
penetration into Columbia which borders on the Russian colonies, the trade with China, and of other circumstances "one
often encounters matters which involve secrecy for commercial or political reasons, considerations which often neces-
sitate action on a level higher than that of the directors who
are in charge of the production of the Company."[3]

Taking this as its point of departure, the Governing
Board posed the question of creating not a provisional council but a permanent one, that would be qualified to make
decisions in political matters. This council, like the earlier one, was to consist of three stockholders and have the
same prerogatives with respect to making decisions for the
general meeting. "All important questions, or those that
require secrecy for political reasons, as well as those that
are inseparable from the development of trade, navigation,
and other undertakings of the Company, and the solution of
which may sometimes prove perplexing to the directors or
be outside their power, will be committed to the special
attention and solicitude of the Council together with the
Governing Board."[4]

The readiness of the commercial Governing Board to
submit to the State Council, which was now to become permanent, is explained by the very same reasons which, several years before, had compelled it to agree so willingly to
the formation of the provisional committee. By placing the
responsibility for the political line of the Company upon the
members of the Council, the Governing Board, as before,
was not formally deprived of its importance. It still hoped
to be able to exercise its influence in the solution of political
problems; for, in view of the joint sessions of the Council
and the Directors, the decisions were valid only when they
were adopted unanimously. The Governing Board proposed
to retain in full the direction of the commercial activity of
the Company. In the words of the statute referring to the
Council, "the directors are to maintain their former responsibility in those branches of the Company's activity which
have already been defined by the Company."

On October 16, 1813, the decision to form a permanent council of the Russian-American Company was confirmed by the Committee of Ministers. Although, by the provisions of the statute relating to the Council, one of the three posts on the Council was to be newly filled every year, some of the members remained in office for decades. This contributed even more to presenting the Council as a body consisting almost entirely of representatives from the various departments, appointed by the government. Thus, for example, Ya. Druzhinin, the Director of the Chancery of the Ministry of Finance and subsequently Head of the Department of Manufacture and Domestic Commerce, that is, the department to which the Company was directly subordinated, was a member of the Council for thirty-four years without interruption, from the first elections in 1814 to the day of his death in 1848.

The Council, as it was first constituted, included, in addition to Ya. Druzhinin, Senator I.A. Weidemeyer, a member of the Committee on Foreign Affairs, who had also been on the provisional committee, and Senator P.S. Molchanov. Later on Senator V.G. Politkovsky and Count N.S. Mordvinov, who was a member of the State Council, were added. Among the members of the Council we find the highest officials of the Ministry of the Navy, Admiral G.A. Sarychev, V.M. Golovnin, and F.P. Wrangell, all of whom had either participated in, or had headed a number of expeditions.

The "Commerical" Governing Board was mistaken, however, when it expected to be able to preserve its complete independence in commercial matters. It was not long before the government departments began to intervene in the conduct of the commercial activities of the Company. As a matter of form the Company was subject to government control with respect to its commercial operations from the very day of its founding. But the financial reports presented to the Tsar and then submitted to the Ministry of Commerce, were not examined by anyone, so that the commercial activity of the Governing Board remained practically without supervision.

The foundation for genuine financial supervision was laid the moment the Company was transferred to the jurisdiction of the Ministry of the Interior. The question of putting the Russian-American Company under the Department of Manufacture and Domestic Commerce which, in turn, was under the jurisdiction of the Ministry of the Interior, had been

raised in September, 1811, by the Minister of the Interior,
O.P. Kozodavlev. Starting with the idea that government
control of the Company should be the more direct since "any
abuse of the Company may lead to very harmful and perniciou
consequences to society and to the Empire itself,"[5] Kozodavle
urged that the government be kept fully informed both as to
the commercial activities of the Company and the degree to
which all the measures planned by the Company are co-
ordinated.

After examining the Company's representations to the
Tsar for the past years, Kozodavlev arrived at the conclusion
that these contained nothing except various solicitations and
incomplete financial accounts, the correctness of which "however, could be vouched for only by the Managing Directors."
In his memorandum to the Tsar, Kozodavlev dwelt on the
necessity "of designating the Ministry of the Interior as in-
termediary between the person of the Emperor and the
Company, to which the Company would be obliged to submit
complete accounts for presentation to Your Majesty, and
under whose direct supervision it would be placed."[6]

On December 15, 1811, Kozodavlev's proposals were accepted and the Company came under the supervision of the
Ministry of the Interior. This arrangement was not, however
of long duration. In 1819, as a result of the transfer of the
Department of Manufacture and Domestic Commerce to the
Ministry of Finance, the Company came under the jurisdiction of the latter Ministry. If, at first, the Governing
Board felt no particular constraint on its activities, it was
from this moment on to come under strict, systematic control.

At the same time the extension of government control over
the administration of the colonies was proceeding apace. This
extension of control was manifested, first of all, in the appointment to colonial positions of officers of the Navy Department. The filling of individual posts in the colonial administration by military personnel began, quite naturally, with the
Company fleet; the problem of creating a Company fleet was
equally important to the government and to the Company itself.

The grandiose plans of tsarist expansion required ships of
considerable tonnage to be manned by qualified seamen. From
its predecessors the Russian-American Company inherited
four galleys, built at different times in Okhotsk, and one

frigate, constructed in one of the Russian shipyards of the American colonies. This fleet was not, of course, the answer to the new problems which the Russian tsaris régime posed to the Company. The latter was compelled to raise virtually a new fleet. During the first two decades of its existence the Company owned altogether, including the five aforementioned ships, thirty-two ships of various sizes and types. During the same period the Russian-American Company spent 3,300,000 rubles on the fleet, but, even if one takes into consideration the rapid amortization of wooden vessels, it must be admitted that the amount spent was of little effect. At the beginning of the 1820's the Company had at its disposal only thirteen ships, ranging in tonnage from 50 to 300 tons.

Of the nineteen ships which, according to the overall registers of the fleet, were decommissioned during the same two decades, only two were destroyed "because of old age" and one was sold. The remaining sixteen ships, in the words of the management itself, "were shipwrecked" during that period, "as a result of accidents, and especially because of carelessness and lack of skill on the part of the Okhotsk pilots."[7]

Here we come up against a factor which played a very significant part in the activity of the Company--the lack of qualified crews, which was the result of the predominance of the institution of serfdom in the mother country. In the field of navigation the effect of serfdom was evidenced by the lack of qualified seamen, except in the Navy.

Even at the beginning of the Company's activity the government attempted to come to its assistance by militarizing the Company fleet. In 1802 an Imperial rescript enjoined the release from the Navy for service with the Company of an unlimited number of sailors, naval officers, and pilots, with half the salary being paid by the government, and with the men preserving all the rights and privileges appertaining to those on active duty.

Henceforth all round-the-world expeditions were manned by navy men, from among whom were to come not a few celebrated navigators.

As for the boats that were plying their trade along the coast, these continued to carry their complement of illiterate pilots who had signed up in Okhotsk. The naval officers considered it below their dignity to serve on coastwise vessels and to submit to orders of the governor of the colonies who was himself of the merchant class. A most striking instance though not the only one, was that taking place in 1845: A Lieu tenant Lazarev, not wanting to submit to the orders of Governor Baranov, instead of proceeding to seize the Hawaiian Islands, weighed anchor and wilfully went on to Kronstadt.

In this particular case Governor Baranov, tried, though unsuffcess-fully, to shell the departing Company vessel from the guns of the fortress, but in other cases he was forced to reconcile himself to the insubordination of these new employees of the Company. In fact, in the very first years after the naval officers had entered the service of the Company, Rezanov wrote to the management from Novoarkhangelsk about the abnormality of the arrangements under which former officers refused to submit to the orders of the Company authorities:

"To my distress, I must add to my conclusions regarding the naval side of the undertaking that it is incomparably more useful for the Company to recruit men from among foreign seamen, or from those who retired, if only they have not been in the service of the Crown, --otherwise, there is trouble. His Majesty's kindness is boundless, but, whether because of the training our officers have received, or the remoteness of the region in which they are serving and in which everything seems to be permissible , the Company, at any rate, stands to suffer great losses and the Fatherland--to lose its American domains. Unsuitable and spurious rules can be eradicated by exhortations only with great difficulty.... The contempt for the trading profession, which has struck deep roots among the nobility, has made them all masters here, and as you know too many cooks spoil the broth. Although there is a governor holding a high rank which he has won as a result of truly meritorious service, the fact that he was formerly a merchant means, unhappily for the Fatherland, in the eyes of most of our fraternity, the same as to have been a good-for-nothing. And so--to take orders from a man like that seems to them sheer mendacity; consider the benefits redounding to the Fatherland they cannot, for to do that they themselves must first realize the importance of those benefits."[8]

In the same letter N.P. Rezanov tells in detail of the acts

of violence and drunkenness and of the rows provoked by the officers in the American colonies. There was not a minute's rest: "now there is a disturbance of the Kolosh, now the nobles, having imbibed too freely, deign to raise the cry of Help. Murder." The officers appropriated everything that was being received for the other employees of the Company, mainly using the lash to obtain satisfaction from the employees belonging to the merchant class. "From the time that the officers made their appearance," writes Rezanov, "the poor and defenseless merchant class has been unable to buy anything for its money and has stopped ordering things from Russia, but is trying, at thrice the cost, to import things through skippers from Boston. What a flattering situation."[9]

Rezanov, in spite of his position as "correspondent," who was fully devoted to the interests of the merchant element in the Company, thought that the only way to avoid trouble between the officers on the staff of the Company fleet and the "commercial" administration was through the selection of suitable personnel who would be qualified to take the place of the aristocrats in the colonies. Hence arose the attempt to recruit crews of qualified seamen from among the native population.

However, the government was pursuing a different policy in this matter. In its aim to dominate completely the activities of the Russian-American Company, the government concentrated the whole colonial administration in the hands of the military command. In 1818 A.A. Baranov, Collegiate Councillor from "The Kargopol merchants," was removed, and Lieutenant-Captain L.A. Hagemeister was appointed in his place. Henceforth naval officers were invariably appointed as governors of the Russian colonies in America. This was provided for in an appropriate article in the charter of the Russian-American Company.

Only the Governing Board with its prerogatives sharply curtailed remained in the hands of the merchants, since even the conduct of the general meeting of the stockholders passed almost completely into the hands of the officeholders.

The minutes of two of the stockholders' meetings for 1819 and 1821, signed by persons "having the right to vote," have been preserved. We are not inclined to suppose that the number of people owning more than ten shares and hence having the right to vote was actually exhausted with the eighteen stockholders, whose signatures appear on the minutes for

1819 and the seventeen stockholders, who signed the minutes for 1821. Considering, however, that the general meeting was within its rights, we must arrive at the conclusion that the number cited in each case constituted a majority of the qualified stockholders, and that the bulk of the shares was in the hands of a very limited number of people.

It is noteworthy that in the two sets of minutes the number of signatures differs but slightly.

Of the eighteen people listed in the minutes for 1819, ten belong to the upper stratum of officeholders. Among them there are the Senators Count Marco Ivelich and Weidemeyer, the Director of the State Loan Bank Privy Councillor A. Khvostov, the Director of the Ministry of Finance Druzhinin, Prince Dondukov-Korsakov, Count Peter Ivelich, and others of the same class. Of the stockholders listed only eight are members of the merchant class.

The decline in the importance of the merchant class in the affairs of the Company, the actual removal of the merchants, first from the direction of the general political activities of the Company and then from that of the colonial administration, and finally the introduction of complete government control over the commercial activities of the Company--all this coincided, in point of time, with the actual suspension of further colonial expansion by the tsarist government on the American continent. The fear of provoking England into becoming more active on the European continent compelled Russia to make concessions on the American continent.

This fear was also reflected in the Anglo-Russian agreement concluded on February 16, 1825. For the same reason, and also because of its desire to uphold legitimism in Spain, the tsarist government did not feel free actively to encroach upon California, which then belonged to Spain and to which, furthermore, England also laid claim. Finally, France's penetration into Haiti raised new obstacles to any active policy by the tsarist government. Thus, barring the road to Russian expansion in the Pacific and to any extensive development of activity by the Russian-American Company was the desire of Alexander I to preserve the Holy Alliance, which forced him to focus his whole attention on affairs in Europe. This meant the collapse of all those grandiose plans which the government itself had at one time put forward and supported and to which the commercial circles associated with the Company clung so tenaciously. In these circles the policy of the tsarist government was, naturally, to arouse a good deal of opposition, which was most clearly formulated by the Manager of the Company Ryleyev.

Informing the Decembrist Steingel of the selection of the famous navigator V.M. Golovnin as a member of the Council of the Company, Ryleyev notes that he is very much satisfied with the choice. "I know that he is stubborn, that he loves to display his intelligence; but then he is firm in his attitude towards the government, and in the situation in which the Company finds itself today, that is a necessary asset."[10]

It is interesting to note that the obstacles which hampered the realization of the Company's plans acted in some instances to induce certain individual members of the Council of the Company to make common cause with the directors, these members being both representatives of the upper stratum of officialdom and stockholders as well. This was the stand taken by Mordvinov and other members of the Council who were making efforts to obtain permission for the Company to expand actively into California, Haiti, and so forth.

As for the merchants who were members of the Governing Board, they had further reasons for being somewhat dissatisfied with the policy of the government.

During the second half of the reign of Alexander I, Russia's foreign trade was experiencing a serious slump. In part this slump was a consequence of the Russo-Prussian convention of 1818. By the provisions of this convention not only were foreign goods allowed to penetrate into the Russian home market, but they were also granted free transit to Asiatic markets. The abrogation of this convention in 1823 and the new tariff of 1822 which imposed high customs duties on a number of foreign items did not, however, in view of the general slump, compensate in full the losses incurred by Russian colonial trade.

The dissatisfaction of the commercial groups as a result of the distressing trade situation is attested by the most diverse sources. We even read reports about it from secret agents. In a dispatch to the Ministry of the Interior in 1821 it is reported that "loud grumbling is heard from the stock-exchange and the stalls. Everybody engaged in commerce, with the exception of a few profiteers who have the proper protection, is indignant about the customs regulations and even more so about the way they are being carried out.... Never have there been such difficulties in trade."[11]

The Decembrists spoke repeatedly of this situation in their
depositions and letters. In a letter to Nicholas I, A. Bestuzh
wrote as follows:

> "The merchant class, hard-pressed by the guilds and
> hampered by the delay in the delivery of the goods, has
> suffered tremendous losses. Many a vast fortune was
> destroyed in 1812; others were dissipated. Their dealings
> with the Treasury brought ruin on a great number of mer-
> chants and contractors, and along with them on their client
> and creditors, by delays in payment, false accounting, and
> unjust exactions when the goods were finally delivered. Ex
> tortion penetrated everywhere.... Fraudulent bankruptcies
> multiplied and confidence declined. The weakness of the
> tariff reduced many manufacturers to a state of poverty
> and frightened others, and destroyed the faith which our
> own merchants as well as foreign traders had in the gov-
> ernment. As a result of this, there came a further drop
> in our rate of exchange (i.e. our foreign credit) in conse-
> quence of excessive government indebtedness, and there
> arose a universal lament that there was no cash. The
> prohibitory system, while enriching the smugglers, did
> not raise the prices of our wares and, following the
> latest fashion, everybody paid three times the actual value
> for the so-called confiscated merchandise."[12]

At the beginning of 1827, in one of the opinions expressed
in the Committee of Ministers, Count N.S. Mordvinov, basing
his conclusions on the totals for 1825, wrote as follows:

> "Almost all of our foreign trade is being carried on not
> with Russian capital but with foreign.... On the Petersburg
> stock-exchange, the most important one in Russia, native
> Russian merchants, who are engaged in foreign trade, will
> take goods sold on credit only to the extent of 1/40 and in
> the case of imported merchandise only to the extent of 1/60

The same section of the merchant class suffered, naturally
as a result of the general confusion which reigned also in domestic commerce. In the opinion quoted above, N.S. Mordvinov noted:

> "We are already experiencing the full weight of our de-

plorable situation, for throughout Russia domestic commerce has gone into a decline, and the reduction in the income of all classes has become painfully apparent."[14]

As we have seen, the merchant class was yielding its positions very reluctantly under pressure from the government.
In certain instances the merchants even attempted to give
battle, threatening to resign from the Governing Board of the
Company. This actually happened in 1817, in the wake of
complaints on the part of the local administration in Siberia
against a series of wilful acts of the Company. The Directors
of the Company Buldakov, Kramer, and Severin said in a
letter to the Minister of the Interior Kozodavlev:

> "We, tired of having to subject ourselves to the contin-
> uous task--one that in incompatible with our position--of
> excusing, and disputing the authenticity of, the shameful
> scenes presented for the consideration of the government,
> scenes which constitute a wearisome and improper burden
> for us because of our ignorance of the art of law and its
> procedures as observed and proposed by private authorities,
> shall finally be compelled to relinquish the duties with which
> the merchant class has charged us. This will be the begin-
> ning of its downfall. Others, elected in our place, once
> they have learned the cause of our withdrawal will not be
> willing to have their peace of mind disturbed by the neces-
> sity of combatting secret enemies such as envy and hate."[15]

But such demonstrations frightened no one.
Occasionally the Directors would undertake other measures
with a view of strengthening their position in the Company,
counting on bribing Arakcheyev. About these attempts, which
took place in Moscow and were made by the manager of the
Moscow office Prokofyev, we have very scanty information.
"In accordance with your request," wrote Prokofyev from
Moscow to the Director of the Company Buldakov on February 21, 1818, "I had the pleasure this past Monday, that is
the 18th, of entertaining at my house five of His Majesty's full
generals and nine adjutant-generals, whom I invited at the instance of Count Aleksey Andreyevich Arakcheyev."[16]
The conversation between the host and Arakcheyev revolved
around the condition of the Company, the reasons for its failure to pay dividends to the stockholders in previous years and,

finally, "the plans that were being contemplated for the future." According to certain sources, Prokofyev entered into some very secret negotiations with Arakcheyev during dinner, since Prokofyev would not even venture to inform Buldakov about them by mail. In the next letter to Buldakov, who, apparently, had asked for the details of the conversation with Arakcheyev, Prokofyev wrote: "With regard to the conversation I had with Count Arakcheyev concerning the Company, I cannot give you any detailed information at the present time."[17]

From the above letter of Prokofyev we learn that, at the dinner for the generals "who had been designated by Arakcheyev himself," there were present the military Governor-General of St. Petersburg, Count Miloradovich, Adjutant-General Chernyshev, General Uvarov, and others.

Almost in every letter of that period we find mention of persons close to the Court who visited the hospitable host. The reason for such close relationship between some of the dignitaries, particularly Arakcheyev, and Prokofyev, is revealed in a report by the latter to Buldakov saying that henceforth he will "always have 100,000 rubles on hand."

The above phrase follows immediately the information concerning Arakcheyev, who had accepted to dine again at Prokofyev's, upon his return to Moscow, wherefore Prokofyev "will not fail to come to him more often."[18] This "fund" was evidently created for Arakcheyev's benefit.

But it had already become quite evident in the beginning of the 1820's, during the time that Prokofyev moved to St. Petersburg and became one of the Directors of the Company, that it was not a question of enlisting the protection of individual courtiers, and that it was the general policy of the government that went contrary to the immediate interests of the commercial Governing Board of the Company. And it was at that very moment, when a rebellious attitude towards the government was quite natural on the part of the Company Directors, that they clashed with some prominent members of the Northern Society of Decembrists.

We know something about I.V. Prokofyev's connections with the Decembrists. "With I.V. Prokofyev," writes O.M. Somov to Ryleyev, "we are very friendly. Alexander [Bestuzhev.--Au.] and I dine at his home rather frequently, and there we meet Bulgarin, Grech, Batenkov and others, generally very many of our acquaintances."[19]

At these dinners new acquaintances were struck up and new members were drawn into the Society. "I had occasion often and almost on definite days," reports G.S. Batenkov, "to visit the building in which the American Company was housed, because I knew the Directors, especially Prokofyev.... It dated back to my life in Siberia and to the part that my uncle played in the occupation of the islands. Here, however, I made my first contacts with the secret society...."[20]

N.I. Grech, who attended these dinners, tells of the noisy, gay, and pleasant conversations that accompanied these get-togethers, and how "the generous host would walk around the table, pour the wine acquired from the sale of the skins of sea-otters and fur-seals, not having the slightest notion as to whom he was regaling."[21]

There is reason to believe that another of the Directors of Company, Nikolay Ivanovich Kusov, was also connected with some of the Decembrists. Elected as one of the Directors of the Russian-American Company in the middle of 1824, N.I. Kusov was mayor of St. Petersburg and co-owner of the old Petersburg commercial house of "Sankt-Peterburgskie pervostateinye kuptsy Ivana Kusiva synovia" (Ivan Kusov's Sons, First-class merchants of St. Petersburg), which conducted a large-scale grocery business. In addition, the Kusovs owned a sugar-refinery, a potash-plant, a distillery, and a tannery.

N.I. Kusov, very progressive for his day, had, it seems, long established contacts with groups of the opposition. He was a Mason, was treasurer of the "Izbrannyi Mikhail" (Michael the Elect) Lodge, and took an active part in the creation of the Lancaster schools.

According to Zavalishin, Kusov frequented the famous dinners at Prokofyev's which were attended by the Decembrists, and took part in the discussion of the events that were in the process of preparation. Some of the Decembrists, as, for instance, Ryleyev, associated themselves with the Company when they were already members of the secret society; others like Batenkov made friends with the Decembrists for the first time at Prokofyev's.

It should be noted that some of the Decembrists who had no formal connection with the Company, showed a deep interest in the Russian colonies in America in general. One of them was the Decembrist N.A. Bestuzhev, who was not formally connected with the Company. This we learn from the Decembrist V.P. Romanov, who visited America. Bestuzhev corrected his notes about the Russian colonies, urged him to have them published separately, and promised to assume the editing of them. Thanks to Bestuzhev, Romanov's articles about the Russian colonies were placed in a number periodicals. It was also at his initiative that the drafting division of the Navy Department drew a map of the Russian colonies in California.[22]

The Russian colonies in America served, apparently, on more than one occasion as a topic of conversation at the gatherings of the Northern Society. In his account to the Commission of Inquiry of his acquaintance with Küchelbecker Trubetskoy, who was in no way connected with the Company either, wrote that he had met him at Ryleyev's. Küchelbecker told them "how they shoot sea-otters and fur-seals, and all about our colony in America, called Ross."[23]

A number of factors tended to influence the Decembrists to seek a rapprochement with the leaders of the Russian-American Company. There was, first of all, the desire on their part to broaden their contacts because a portion of the merchant class was inclined to be in opposition to the government. "When M. Muravyov left here," Ryleyev says in his testimony, "I told him precisely that I would try to take in as members some of the local merchants. I wanted to do it with the approval of the Northern Duma so as to have members in that class, too."[24]

In addition to K.F. Ryleyev, the most pronounced tendency for a rapprochement with the merchant circles may be observed in the case of another Decembrist, who was very closely associated with the Company, namely, G.S. Batenkov. "More often than anywhere else," he informed the Commission of Inquiry, "I used to go to the merchants' houses, and inasmuch as that class is generally dissatisfied with the restrictive regulations on commerce, associating with them acted as an incitement to the desire for a change."[25]

A few of the Decembrists occupied definite positions with the Company, others were making ready to enter the Company's service.

Of the members of the Society the most important post with the Company was held by K.F. Ryleyev. He had been in the service of the Russian-American Company since the beginning of 1824 as office manager. He became one of the stockholders, receiving ten shares from the Company, each with a nominal value of 500 rubles in banknotes.[26]

Ryleyev was appointed to his position with the aid of Mordvinov. "I came to know Mr. Modvinov at his own desire,"
Ryleyev wrote subsequently in his deposition, "and went to
see him with F.N. Glinka. The occasion of the visit was an
ode I had written in which I mentioned him. Some time after,
he offered me a place with the American Company as office
manager, which I received at the beginning of last year."[27]

It is a rather widely accepted opinion in the literature of
the subject that Ryleyev, at first conscientious about his new
official duties, later neglected his work at the Company completely and lost all interest in the Company's fate. The testimony of Grech and Zavalishin, who never missed an opportunity to calumniate their former friends, serves as a basis
for such conclusions.

"From what the Director of the Company, Ivan Vasilyevich
Prokofyev told me," writes Grech "he [Ryleyev.--Au.] worked
zealously and with great benefit to the Company at the beginning of his term of service, but later on, befuddled by liberal
visions, he lost interest in his position and went about his
duties very listlessly."[28]

Bourgeois writers, seeing in Ryleyev primarily the poet
and ignoring him completely as a political figure, have usually
regarded his work with the Company as due wholly to his
straitened circumstances, and have pointed to the utter lack
of interest he ostensibly manifested in the activities of the
Company.

"There was very little of the spiritual in this new position,"
writes N. Kotlyarevský concerning Ryleyev's work with the
Russian-American Company. "The Company managed the
trade of the Russian colonies in America, and Ryleyev was
charged with the tedious secretarial duties. He performed
his secretarial functions very accurately and with a good
deal of zeal, so that he was presented with a very valuable
raccoon coat; but, of course, the whole business had little
attraction for him, and he probably accepted the position
because, after the death of his mother, his financial situation
became even more precarious, and the service with the Company was sufficiently profitable."[29]

But even the scanty data we have at our disposal on this
question bear testimony to a deep interest on Ryleyev's part
in the progress of the Company and to his enthusiasm for the
work to which he devoted a great deal of his time.

In one of his letters to V.I. Steingel, Ryleyev speaks

frankly of his relation to the Company. "They say that he,"
writes Ryleyev with reference to the newly elected member
of the Council of the Company, V.M. Golovnin, "does not
like me for some reason; but that doesn't concern me too
much.... I'll be allright without the Company, too, if only the
Company should flourish."[30]

The above letter belongs to March 1825, that is precisely
to the last period of Ryleyev's activity. It is possible to adduce many examples illustrating the deep interest that Ryleyev
showed in the affairs of the Company even at that time; in his
correspondence these affairs figure on a par with his literary
interests.

"Much work has accumulated in the Company, Furthermore
we have begun the printing of the 'Polyarnaya Zvezda' (Polar
Star)," writes K.F. Ryleyev to his wife on February 10, 1825
"and all this has kept me busy and has helped to dispel the
boredom and to fill the spiritual vacuum."[31]

A few days later, K.F. Ryleyev again informs his wife
that he is "terribly occupied with the affairs of the Company,"
and that at the very time when in the words of N.I. Grech, "he
went about his duties very listlessly."

People closest to K.F. Ryleyev, who were directly associated with him, also testify to the success of his work with
the Company. "His public activity in his capacity as manager
of the American Company," writes the Decembrist Ye.P.
Obolensky, "would deserve special consideration, in view of
the good he has done to the Company both by his activity and,
undoubtedly even more, by his substantial services because,
even before two years had elapsed from the time he assumed
his duties, the management of the Company expressed its
gratitude to him by presenting him with an expensive raccoon
coat, valued at that time at 700 rubles."[33]

We also read of the part played by K.F. Ryleyev in the
direction of the affairs of the Company in one of the letters of
O.M. Somov, a Decembrist who was in the service of the
Company. On November 25, 1824, O.M. Somov wrote to
Ryleyev that it was important to the Company in more ways
than one that he come at that ime; in the first place, "because
the time is approaching when dispatches and fur-hunters have
to be sent to America.... Both our directors, and Kusov, too,
when he comes here, always ask about you and are awaiting
your return with impatience." [34]

Indeed, the directors of the Company valued Ryleyev highly.

Following Prokofyev's advice, Ryleyev's wife, after his arrest, returned to the Company the beaver collar from the gift fur-coat and the shares she had in her possession. The Company paid Buldakov the 3,500 rubles which Ryleyev owed him. Ryleyev's debt to the Company to the amount of 3,000 rubles was remitted. "I am much obliged to them," wrote Ryleyev's wife to him on May 8, 1826 while he was in prison; "they haven't bothered me all this time about the apartment, I am still living in it, the same as when you were here with me, my dear."[35]

Through Mordvinov, D.I. Zavalishin also came in contact with the Company. Upon his return to St. Petersburg from California in 1824, he approached Mordvinov with a whole series of plans for bringing about improvements in the operation of the Company. Armed with Mordvinov's letters of recommendation, Zavalishin went to the Manager of the Company, Ryleyev, "who according to Zavalishin, was regarded as very well versed in the affairs of the Company."[36]

Zavalishin's plans were very enthusiastically received in Company circles, and he was immediately offered a permanent position with the Company as manager of the colony of Ross in California. The Tsar's permission was required, however, and this, in spite of lengthy negotiations, the Company was unable to obtain.

Like D.I. Zavalishin, another Decembrist, Lieutenant V.P. Romanov, also became associated with the Company. Returning at the end of 1822 from a trip to America where he had sailed on a Company ship, V.P. Romanov presented two plans in 1823 to the Chief of the Navy Staff. The first was a plan for the exploration of the territory from the Mednaya River to Hudson Bay and north to the Arctic; the second, for the exploration of the Cape of the Arctic to the east, with a view of having the Russian expedition link up with the proposed English expedition under Franklin. This plan was referred to the Russian-American Company, since it related to territory in its possession.

"If the Cape of Good Hope and New Holland attracted the attention of England," noted V.P. Romanov in his plan, "then the northwestern part of America deserves similar attention from our government."[37]

From then on V.P. Romanov started to frequent the directors of the Company, especially I.V. Prokofyev. In 1824 Romanov's plan aroused the interest of K.F. Ryleyev, who

declared that its achievement would bring not only glory to
the Company, because the Russians would be the first to
explore that region where no European has set foot, but it
would also prove profitable by establishing contact with the
Hudson Bay Company, and perhaps will also help to open up
a new branch of the business."[38] At the same time, K.F.
Ryleyev "offered to try to induce the Directors to agree"
that V.P. Romanov should be appointed leader of the expedition.

Steingel and Batenkov also established close contacts with
the Company as a result of their sojourn in Siberia.

A former naval officer, Baron Steingel had at one time
maintained close contacts with the correspondent of the
Russian-American Company, Rezanov, and later with the
Director of the Company, Prokofyev, whom he knew from
Moscow. There he had served as adjutant to the Governor-
General, and even intended at one time to enter the service
of the Company.[39]

Batenkov was also preparing to serve with the Company,
and the question of his service was almost settled in the affir-
mative. He was to assume the governorship of all the colonie
since the Governor of the colonies, Muravyov, had long sent
in his resignation. "The arrangements had almost been
made," Batenkov relates, "I pledged myself to serve for five
years, at 40,000 a year, intending to spend one half of the
salary and to deposit the other half in a foreign bank, so that
I could later settle permanently somewhere in Southern
Europe."[40]

In the process of realizing all these plans, a number of
responsible positions in the Company's administration might
well have fallen to members of the secret society. Ryleyev
would have remained as office manager actually in charge of
all current business; Batenkov would have been governor of
the colonies, and Zavalishin, manager of the colony of Ross.

Thus, 72 Moika Street, near the Blue Bridge, occupied
by the administration of the Russian-American Company, became, with the beginning of 1824, a sort of conspirators'
club. In this large building with the two-headed eagle on its
front, which the Company had purchased from A. Vorontsov's
heirs, was located the staff of the Decembrist insurrection.
Here some of the leaders of the Northern Society lived, here
the large meetings of the Decembrists took place, here rang
out openly the call to murder the Tsar, and here the decisions

on the preparation of the insurrection were made. Not accidentally, then, was the frequenting of the building of the
Russian-American Company identified with actual participation in the conspiracy.

"On the fifteenth [of December, 1825.--Au.]," the Decembrist Batenkov relates, "Speransky called me over and, no-
ticing that I was rather confused, asked me whether I had not
had a part [in the plot], since I had known Bestuzhev for such
a short time and had frequented the quarters of the American
Company."[42]

The notion that the Russian-American Company was a hot-
bed of sedition is most clearly reflected in the letters of the
famous fabulist and journalist A. Ye. Izmailov, who noted
down painstakingly all the rumors floating about St. Petersburg. Informing his son of the release from prison of the
head clerk of the Company, Orest Somov, who was implicated
in the Decembrist insurrection, Izmailov cites the following
characteristic anecdote:

"His Majesty asked Somov, 'Where are you employed?'
Somov replied, 'In the Russian-American Company.' His
Majesty exclaimed, 'You've collected some fine company
there."[43]

From the time that the directors of the Company began to
associate with some of the members of the Northern Society,
the refractory spirit of the Governing Board became more
intense. It may be surmised, on the basis of certain indirect
evidence, that there was suspicion even in government circles,
that someone was pulling the strings behind the directors'
back. D.I. Zavalishin relates that Ryleyev was reprimanded
by Imperial order for a memorandum supposedly written by
Zavalishin on the occasion of the Anglo-Russian and Russo-
American conventions. According to Zavalishin, Alexander I
"was infuriated at the idea of the merchants' trying to teach
the diplomats, and ordered that the manager be reprimanded,
saying that the merchants did not understand anything and
could not, of course, have written the memorandum."[44]

We do not have at our disposal the source material that
would confirm the information provided by Zavalishin. However, in the private archives of the Minister of Finance,
Ye.F. Kankrin, there has been preserved a very curious
document dealing with a similar incident, a reprimand to the
Directors of the Company for a representation apparently
composed by Ryleyev.

On February 17, 1825, the Governing Board of the Company
sent to the Minister of Finance, Ye. F. Kankrin, a memorandum over the signature of the two Directors I.V. Prokofyev
and A.I. Severin, and of the office manager K.F. Ryleyev.
The memorandum dealt with the Company order to build fortresses along the Mednaya River from the seashore deep inland.

This undertaking was intended to delimit, to a certain extent, the territorial concessions which the government proposed to make at the expense of the Russian colonies in Amer-
ca upon signing the Anglo-Russian Convention, the negotiations for which were already drawing to a close.

The establishment of armed outposts in the disputed territory along the Mednaya as far as the Rocky Mountains themselves [in the document at hand they are called "Kamennyaya"
(i.e., Stony).--Au.] was invoked to underline the fact that the
territory belonged to Russia. Such activity would, of course,
have been a direct provocation to England, which demanded
a reduction of the Russian-held areas on the American continent and their precise delimitation.

"It is well known," wrote the Board, "that the English have
already expanded their domains to the very range of the Stony
(i.e., Rocky) Mountains and will probably want to carry them
forward over to this side of the mountains.... Although the
Company is desirous, on its part, to expand its own colonies
as far as the aforementioned range of the Rockies, which is
indispensable for its stable existence, and towards which a
beginning has already been made, and which it will no doubt
achieve, unless it meets with dangerous competition; but
since the Company does not have such ample resources and
is not in a position to oppose the English government which
is cooperating in this matter, therefore, in order to prevent
the English government from coming into possession of the
territory lying on this side of the mountains, the Governing
Board of the Company is taking the liberty of noting that the
Stony (Rocky) mountains can and should be the boundary between the two powers in that region. Mutual benefits, justice, and nature itself demand it."[45]

In forwarding this memorandum to Nesselrode on February 27, Kankrin remarked that "he finds this representation
worthy of consideration." On March 4, however, Kankrin
was compelled to make a note on his copy of the memorandum
that he had been too hasty in finding "this representation

worthy of consideration." Word has been received from His
Majesty Himself," wrote Kankrin, "that the Company be ordered to discontinue immediately the construction of the little
fortresses, and when the order has been executed, it should
inform His Majesty by courier to that effect. Furthermore,
it should be pointed out to the Company that its very demand
does not suit either the circumstances of that region or the
rights granted to the Company. In addition, having called
the directors together, Kankrin should reprimand them most
severely for the impropriety both of the proposal itself and
of the expressions used, so that they should henceforth submit unquestioningly to the orders and views of the government, without overstepping the bounds of the merchant
class."[46]

Kankrin underscored a number of phrases, including the
one that "the Rocky Mountains can and should be the boundary
between the two powers," which were among the "improper"
expressions noted by Alexander, and wrote over them that
"a reprimand was made in February."

But immediately after the events of the 14th of December,
the merchants' "rebelliousness" cooled down. The directors
of the Company hastened to destroy everything that might in
some way have disclosed their connection with the Decembrists.

According to Zavalishin, "Prokofyev, who was Company
Director in 1825, in a state of fear after December 14, burned
all the papers where my name was even mentioned, and not
only those which emanated from me personally."[47]

For a while the "merchant class" continued to hold on to
the Company but, after the new charter had been confirmed
in 1844, the further participation of the merchants in the
direction of the Company became absolutely impossible
Henceforward the commercial activities as well as the questions of "higher policy" were to be the concern of major-
generals and vice-admirals. The provisions of the new charter
abolished the Company Council which comprised primarily
the higher officials who maintained government control over
the political activities without meddling with current commercial affairs. The direction of the Company was wholly
concentrated in the hands of the Governing Board. The
Board's composition underwent a change at the same time;
the members of the Council became Directors, and the
"merchant class" was practically forced out of the top offices
of the Company.

In accordance with the draft for a new charter, presented
in 1841 for examination by the Council of State, the Governing
Board was to consist not of four but of five members. Special
emphasis was placed on the condition that "there should be
admitted as members not only people who are experts in commerce, as stipulated in the old charter, but such noblemen
as are well known for their knowledge of commerce and
colonial affairs, and government officials with the consent of
their superiors, et al."[48]

In the definitive text of the charter "et al." was, so to
speak, decoded. There it was indicated that in addition to
"such noblemen as are well known for their knowledge of
commerce and colonial affairs, and government officials,"
"eminent citizens" and merchants of the upper two categories
could be elected to the Governing Board. But this was essentially a subterfuge, since now there was nothing for the merchants to do in the Company.

The Company had become an organization established not
"for trading on the mainland of northwest America and on the
islands," as its charter read, but for administering Russian
colonies in America, formulated in the draft for the new charter worked out in 1861.

Only one member of the old Governing Board, the merchant
Kusov, remained on the new Board. The remaining four places,
including the position of Executive Director in charge of current work, were filled by representatives of the higher officialdom, most of them members of the old Council. Vice-Admiral
Baron F.P. Wrangell was elected Chairman of the Board, and
the following were elected as members: Major General F.G.
Politkovsky, later to be Chairman of the Board almost to the
very liquidation of the Company, Lieutenant-General V.F.
Klüpfel, Rear-Admiral A.K. Etolin, Ret., and the merchant
N.I. Kusov. But though Kusov held on to his post for a rather
long period, he played no part in the management of the Company. Beginning with 1857, not one of the men at the head of
the Russian-American Company belonged to the "merchant
class."

In this way the Russian-American Company went through
the same process of development as the East India Company.
"The East India Company eliminated the plain people from
trading with India...."[49] The very same thing happened in the
case of the Russian-American Company with respect to trading
with America. Very soon, however, the English government

eliminated the stockholders of the East India Company from doing business with India, and turned the Company into a simple agency of the Crown, using for this purpose the so-called Board of Control.

As Marx points out, "the Pitt Act of 1784, which arranged a compromise with the Company and placed it under the jurisdiction of a Board of Control that was at the same time transformed into an appendage to the Ministry, confirmed and gave a permanent status to this system of dual administration--a system of accidental origin--and sanctioned it formally and actually. The act of 1833 strengthened the Board of Control, turned the owners of the East India Company into plain creditors whose debt was secured by the income of the Company, enjoined the Company to sell out its property, put an end to its commercial existence, and transformed it, as a political organization, into a simple agency of the Crown--in short, the Act dealt with the East India Company exactly as the Company itself had been wont to deal with the Indian princes: depriving them of their powers, it continued for a time to govern in their name."[50]

We have seen that the tsarist government treated the Russian-American Company in exactly the same manner: the functions of the English Board of Control were, in this case, carried out first by the Temporary Committee then by the Company Council.

But the complete transformation of the trading company into a weapon of government policy demanded the complete elimination from the management of the representatives of the commercial classes. The commercial directorate was, therefore, compelled first to renounce its special functions in the management of the Company and then to relinquish its duties altogether.

"Thus, beginning with 1833, the East India Company," as Marx points out, "existed in name only and, as it were, on sufferance."[51] Beginning with the 1840's the Russian-American Company suffered the very same fate.

Chapter VI

THE COLONY OF ROSS IN CALIFORNIA

EVEN AS EARLY as the 1790's California was regarded, in
the broad plans for expansion as outlined by the Rylsk merchant Grigory Shelikhov, as the natural boundary "of the
territory of Russian possession" in the western part of the
American continent. And even then, the Russian merchants,
by order of the government, hastened, in an attempt to provide for any contingency, to manufacture an excuse of some
kind for gaining possession of California in the future. Thus
Shelikhov wrote in February, 1790:

> "All along the American mainland from the island of
> Kitak [i.e., Kodia.-Au.] to California and far beyond the
> Cape of St. Elias, in many places, through the efforts and
> at the expense of the Company and according to my instruc
> tions, there have been distributed and left imperial marke
> namely coats-of-arms and plates with the inscription 'Lan
> belonging to Russia.' "[1]

The tsarist government never lost hope, either, that a
propitious moment would arrive, in the course of time, for
asserting its claims to the whole west coast of America and
that the markers which had been secretly buried would yet
serve their purpose. The activity of Shelikhov's company
"allows one...to hope" wrote Governor-General Pil of Irkutsk to Catherine in 1790, "that a continuation of its operations will in time reach California," and the presence in the
ground of the buried markers "may actually serve in the
future, when it will not be difficult for Your Majesty to increase Your forces in that area, as incontrovertible evidence
of the ownership of those places that should be subject to
Your throne."[2]
The coastal waters of California abounded in sea-otters;
this fact serves to explain, in part, the interest manifested
in that region by the Russian merchants. But, though the
quantity of sea-otters was decreasing from year to year, the

Russians' yearning for California was steadily on the increase.
This was quite natural, since the problem of organizing the
systematic exploitation of the American coast was contingent
upon the creation of a local supply-base for the benefit of the
Russian colonies. The northeastern Russian colonies of
Kamchatka and Chukutka were supplied primarily with grain
brought in from the mother country, partly by land. Any
further transportation of the grain from Kamchatka to the
American colonies was impossible, not only because of the
extremely high additional cost but also because the imported
grain did not even suffice for the northeast regions of Asia,
which also needed a local source of food supply. Furthermore the delivery of grain and other necessary provisions
by sea from St. Petersburg was not very reliable. The
slightest diplomatic complication exposed the Russian colonies to the threat of hunger, since in that event, round-the-
world expeditions would become impossible. It was necessary to keep this factor constantly in mind, in view of the
strained state of foreign relations at the end of the eighteenth
century and during the first half of the nineteenth.

All attempts to introduce farming into the region of Alaska
and the islands met with failure, not only because of the lack
of a native labor force qualified to work in the fields, but
chiefly because of the unfavorable climatic conditions. Of
the whole of the west coast of North America only California
was very well favored with respect to climate. A beneficial
climate, rich vegetation, a large quantity of cattle provided
all the elements necessary for the creation of a "granary"
for the Russian colonies in America. To be sure, in addition
to California, provisions could also be brought in from China
and Japan. But the frequent interruptions in trade relations
and the long distance separating China from the Russian colonies, tended to focus everyone's attention on California.

Towards the end of 1805 the Correspondent of the Company,
Rezanov, who was also appointed, at the same time, Envoy-
Extraordinary to Japan, visited the Russian colonies in
America. He found them in very difficult straits. "There
is no bread," he reported to St. Petersburg, "since, as I
hear, there is no one on Kodiak to prepare the fodder, and
people are dying of hunger on Sitka because the Kolosh, who
are armed with splendid rifles and falconets, are waging per-
petual warfare, and you have to catch your fish there under
gunfire."[3]

Rezanov's attempt to obtain provisions in Japan ended in failure, and at the beginning of 1806 he went to California to check up on the chances of purchasing supplies from the Spaniards who were then in possession of that territory. "I'll tell you frankly," said Rezanov to the governor of California, "that we need grain. We can get it from Canton, but since California is nearer to us and has a surplus which it is unable to dispose of, I have come to talk to you as to the ruler of these parts, with the assurance that we can agree on certain preliminary measures which we can submit to the decision and confirmation of our Courts."[4]

Trade with the Spanish colonies was rendered very difficult, however, by the fact that they were categorically forbidden to enter into commercial relations with any one except their mother country. This prohibition aroused bitter dissatisfaction in the colonies, inasmuch as the mother country did not supply them with anything. Still, as long as the Spanish rule had not been shaken, the colonies were afraid openly to violate the ban.

Not having been able to obtain in his negotiations with the local administration any assurance of normal trade relations, Rezanov, after his visit to San Francisco, began to develop the bold idea of wresting California from the Spaniards. He pointed out in a letter, dated June 17, 1806, to the Minister of Commerce that "if the government had given earlier thought to this part of the world...if it had continued to follow the perspicacious views of Peter the Great who, in spite of the limited means at his disposal, had planned the Bering expedition with something definite in mind, then one could positively maintain that New California would never have become a Spanish possession, since the Spaniards turned their attention to California only in 1760 and it is only through the spirit of enterprise of the missionaries that they have forever secured for themselves this tract of the finest land. Today there is only one unoccupied stretch, so useful to us and quite necessary, and if we should allow it to slip out of our grasp, what will posterity say?"[5]

But while Rezanov, in his letter to the Minister of Commerce merely said that the Spaniards "have forever secured for themselves this tract of the finest land," in a letter to the Directors of the Company he unfolded a practical plan for gaining possession of this "scrap" of land. To effectuate the complete conquest of California he considered it necessary

to wait for a propitious moment, but he also believed that it
was necessary right then to occupy the whole region extending
from the Russian colonies as far as California, which had
not yet formally come into the possession of any of the powers.
    Pointing to the necessity of establishing a Russian colony
north of California, in Columbia, Rezanov emphasized that
precisely from there "we shall be able little by little to expand
farther south to the port of San Francisco which marks the
boundary of California.... If only the means are provided
for the early beginnings of this plan, I can boldly say that we
shall attract people to Columbia from various places, and
shall have so consolidated our position at the end of ten years
as ever to have in mind the coast of California and, at the
slightest concurrence of favorable political circumstances
in Europe, include it among the Russian possessions....
The Spanish are quite weak in that area, and if in 1798, when
war was declared on the Spanish court, our company had had
the power corresponding to its activities, it would have been
an easy matter to utilize the part of California from the 34th
parallel of north latitude as far as the mission of Santa Bar-
bara and keep that piece of land forever, since, because of
a condition of nature itself, it would have been impossible for
the Spanish to receive any assistance from Mexico by land."[6]
    The preparations of the Russian-American Company to
establish itself in California began as early as 1808. The
well-tested method was put into operation: copper markers
were buried in the ground, bearing the inscription "Land of
Russian Possession." According to reports submitted by the
Company to the Minister of Finance and later transmitted to
the Ministry of Foreign Affairs, those little plates were
buried "considerably to the south of the designated line of
the 51st parallel of north latitude, namely at the 41st and
38th.[7] In 1808 the peasant Sysoy Slobodchikov placed iron
marker no. 1 in Trinidad Bay, at latitude 41°N.... In 1809
Commercial Councillor Kuskov placed narker no. 14 in
Little Bodega Bay.... In 1810 he also placed marker no. 18
on a little island near Dundas Island opposite the Charlotte
Islands. In 1811 an unnumbered marker was placed on the
promontory of Little Bodega in the northern arm of San
Francisco Bay, where the fortress and the Spanish mission
were located."[8]
    In the fall of 1808 two of the Company's vessels under the
command of Assistant-Manager of the Colony, Kuskov, set

out for California. While he was ostensibly engaged in hunting for sea-otters, Kuskov was secretly trying to find appropriate sites for a settlement. However, the attempt to effect
a landing in Little Bodega Bay, which Kuskov had marked for
a landing, miscarried that year. One of the vessels of the expedition was wrecked and nearly the whole crew perished. As
to the second vessel, the crew, according to Tikhmenev, who
had at his disposal certain of the Company's archival material
which was subsequently lost, was so unreliable that Kuskov
could not persuade himself to leave it in California. "The
lack of building materials and, above all, the attempt made
by many of the Russians and Aleuts, who were with him, to
excape compelled him to postpone the execution of his design
to a more propitious time," reports Tikhmenev. [9]

Kuskov's later attempt, in 1810, to win a base in California ended just as unsuccessfully. Near the Charlotte Islands
the natives fell upon Kuskov's hunting party and forced the
expedition to return to Novoarkhangelsk. Only in 1811 was
Kuskov successful in locating a site for the first Russian
settlement in California. It was decided to establish it on a
small bay named after Rumyantsev, fifteen Italian miles
from Bodega Bay, at latitude 38°N. and longitude 123°E.
The following March, in 1811, everything necessary for the
establishment of the settlement was put ashore at the designated spot.

Subsequently the management of the Company expressed
its opinion once and again that the site for the Russian colony in California had not been well chosen. Its proximity to
San Francisco, the seat of the Spanish authorities, the considerable distance separating it from Rumyantsev Bay which
had a splendid harbor while there was none in the occupied
section, and a number of other disadvantages provoked continual reproaches on the part of the Company. Tikhmenev,
however, justly observes that all these disadvantages became
manifest only when the Russians were compelled to limit
their settlement to the section they had occupied in the very
beginning. Indeed, if one takes into consideration the as-
sumptions of Baranov and Kuskov, who believed that the
given settlement was only the first step in the conquest of all
of California, one must admit that the choice of the site presented a number of advantages both as a springboard for
further offensive action and for defense.

The site taken for the settlement was a flat elevation, more

than a square mile in area. On the side of the sea it was protected by a precipice no less than seventy feet high; on the
side of the land it was not very open to attack, either. The
fortress built on that spot, between twelve to fifteen feet high,
with turrets mounting twenty guns, was a reliable defense.
"The presense of these guns" notes the American historian
Bancroft, "with the natural strength of the site and the strict
system of sentinels and drill never relaxed, gave to 'Ross'[10]
the appearance of a military fortress rather than a fur-hunting
and trading post. The fortress was impregnable to the abo-
rigines and even to any force the Spanish Californians could
have brought against it."

The harbor was built in Bodega Bay. Half-way down to
the port were the quarters of some of the Company's employees. In addition, the Russians occupied a small island
in the Farallones group fifteen miles from Cape Drake, where
some seal-rookeries were located.

Both the decision to discard Rezanov's plan, which was a
long-range plan and presupposed an offensive on the Californian coast only after Columbia had been made a Russian possession, and the change to direct action after a foothold in
California had been consolidated, were conditioned by changes
in the international situation.

The revolution in Spain was the signal for the Spanish colonies in America to intensify their fight for independence and
liberation from the unrestrained exploitation by their mother
country. At that very period, the end of the first decade of
the nineteenth century, as a result of England's struggle
against the continental blockade, there was a slackening in
the interest that the British government was taking in events
occurring on the American continent. The United States of
America took advantage of this circumstance to intensify its
expansionist activities in the Pacific area.

While the first two factors, the civil war in the Spanish
colonies and the slackening of England's interest, tended to
create a situation favorable to territorial conquests, the intensified activity of the United States in the regions adjoining
the Spanish colonies, hastened perforce Russia's attempts
to secure the possession of California.

The opposition of the United States played a decisive role
in the renunciation by tsarist Russia of the conquest of
Columbia and in diverting Russian expansionist efforts towards
California. When in 1810 the Company made an attempt to

consolidate its holdings in Columbia, "the United States of No
America sent, at the same time, its own expeditions both by l
and by sea to the aforementioned Columbia River, with the fir
intention of settling along the river and farther on, on the coa
New Albion." This circumstance, according to the Company,
the reason why the governor of our colonies, Collegiate Counc
and Knight Baranov decided also to send an expedition to make
survey of the coast below Columbia, between the Gulf of Trini
and San Francisco Bay, and thus steal a march on the North
Americans."[12]

While preparing to seize the Spanish colonies in America,
management of the Russian-American Company presented a pe
in 1809 to the Ministry of Foreign Affairs for government assi
in establishing some colonies in California. The Minister of I
eign Affairs reported, in turn, to Alexander I that "the Goverr
Board solicits Your Majesty's protection in connection with th
projected colony of New Albion, in the event that the Americar
states should attempt something out of envy." In view of the fa
that the Company did not have sufficient means to hold the terr
once it had gained possession of it, the Governing Board regar
it necessary "to request those means from the Treasury." Ale
however, "refusing in this instance, to create a colony on Albi
the expense of the Treasury," granted to the Governing Board
right "to establish it freely in its own name, with the encourag
ment, at any rate, of His Majesty's Imperial protection."[13]

Alexander's refusal to lend direct government assistance to
Company and his simultaneous promise of "Imperial" protecti
the establishment of Russian colonies on the territory of Cal
fornia are explained by the policy which tsarist Russia was
suing at that time with relation to Spain. That policy was very
clearly formulated in the draft of the instructions handed, in tl
name of the Tsar, to Count Pahlen who was sent that year, 18(
as envoy to the United States. Bound to France by the Peace o
Tilsit, Alexander was compelled to support the candidacy to th
Spanish throne of Joseph, the brother of Napoleon, as a counte
balance to the candidacy of Ferdinand VII, who had England's s
port. Alexander did not believe, however, that his recognitior
Napoleon's brother as king of Spain necessarily entailed his su
of the reestablishment of the former colonial might of Spain. (
the contrary, the desire to overthrow the power of Spain and th
hope of new colonial acquisitions as a result of the partition of
Spain's colonial heritage, are manifested in every line of the
Tsar's instructions to Count Pahlen. "Remember," says the t

of the instructions, "that in order to restore the peace of
Europe I have recognized as king Joseph, who is indeed the
only king that may be found in Spain, but do not on that account see some special predilection in my political relations
with Spain. I am always guided only by the interests of my
country, and I have not yet arrived at a decision as to whether
or not it will be good for my country if South America should
share the fate of the throne of Madrid."[14]

In another part of the instructions there is indeed talk of
wresting from Spain not only her South American colonies
but all of her colonies in America. "I expect that if the war
in Spain should continue, the vast and wealthy territories she
has under her control in America...will form one or more
independent states. It is difficult precisely to take into account all the changes which such an event would produce in
the political and commercial relations of Europe, but it is
to be hoped that it will lead to considerable changes. You
will render me a service by finding out all about the intentions
of the inhabitants of these various states."[15]

Thus, the necessity, made obligatory by the provisions of
the alliance with France, for recognizing Joseph as king of
Spain, and at the same time, the hope for the collapse of
Spain's colonial empire prompted Alexander to pursue a dual
policy with respect to the seizure of California. On the one
hand, it was suggested that the Russian-American Company
should initiate operations on its own responsibility, and on
the other hand "Imperial" protection had definitely been
promised to the Company. This was a continuation of the
policy of camouflaged expansionism which the government
had been pursuing consistently from the very beginning of
the Russian-American Company. In the event the Spanish
Empire should come out stronger, the tsarist government
would be in a position to avoid foreign complications by as-
cribing the occupation of California to the Company's private
initiative; in the event, however, that the colonies should be
separated from Spain, the tsarist government would obtain a
base for further expansion on the American continent.

Some time elapsed and the "friendship" with France was
replaced by "friendship" with England. At once Alexander
recognized as legitimate king of Spain Ferdinand VII, whom
he had but recently ignored, and promised him every support.

If tsarist policy was directed towards undermining the colonial might of Spain even when Joseph, the Russian-recog-

nized pretender to the Spanish throne, was backed by the
armed might of Napoleon, so now, after recognition had
been extended to the essentially impotent Ferdinand, the
Russian government considered it possible actually to set abo
the wresting of the Spanish colonies.

On July 8 (20), 1812, at Veliky Luky the representatives
of Russia and Spain solemnly signed an agreement according
to which "not only friendship, but also genuine agreement and
an alliance"[16] were to be established between Alexander and
Ferdinand. But, no later than August 30 (Old Style) of the sa
year there took place, on Spanish territory in California, and
just as solemnly, the founding of a Russian colony, named
"Ross."

Inasmuch as the central Spanish government, preoccupied
as it was with events in the homeland, had not had an opportunity actively to react to the events taking place in the colonies, the Russian-American Company did not consider it
necessary to pose the question of the legal formulation of the
conquest. In the diplomatic exchange between Russia and
Spain there was no mention as yet of any "Californian question." Officially Russia had not seized anything, and Spain
had not lost any of her overseas possessions. As for the
protests of the local Spanish administration, the Company
tried to satisfy them as best it could.

In October, 1812, there began a lengthy exchange between
the governor of the colony of Ross and the local administratio
on the one side and the Mexican viceroy, the highest represen
tative of the Spanish administration in North America, on the
other side. The viceroy demanded the immediate liquidation
of the Russian settlement. The governor of the colony aiming
at drawing out the negotiations, pleaded ignorance of the
Spanish language which purportedly made it difficult for him
to understand the substance of the viceroy's demands. In a
few of the cases that arose, the governor of Ross suggested
that the viceroy address himself, for the purpose of negotiatir
to St. Petersburg. He justified his stand by maintaining that
he was not cognizant of the aims of the higher authorities by
whose orders the settlement had been established, and that
his own responsibility "consisted in maintaining [Ross] and
in defending himself in the event of attack."[17]

The relations with the local administration were even more
aggravated when the "Suvorov" brought to California the so-
called proclamation of the Governing Board of the Russian-

American Company. This was the second appeal of the Company and, like the first one, was addressed not to the local administration but directly to"the noble and most honorable Spaniards living in California."[18]

The Company called upon the local Spanish population of California to trade with the Russians, notwithstanding the drastic ban on such trade by the central Spanish government. The Governing Board frankly hinted that, considering the helplessness of the Spanish authorities, there was nothing to fear from any countermeasures on their part. "We had the honor to write to you on March 15, 1810," read this proclamation in reference to the first one, "and in the hope that in view of conditions then prevailing in Europe and in Spain itself, you will no longer encounter any difficulties in maintaining trade relations with the Russians, the more so as such relations are mutually beneficial."[19]

The relations with the local Spanish administration became more and more unfriendly. In 1815 the Company's commissioners were detained in San Francisco. Aleuts, who were engaged in the hunting of fur-bearing animals in the proximity of Spanish territory, were taken captive. The trade relations which were just getting into working order were definitively broken off. The Company continued, though, to send equipment to the colonies. The year 1814 saw the completion of a tannery, a mill, workshops, store-rooms, a cattle-shed, dwellings, and so forth.

Finally, in 1817, the Spanish government entered its first protest. In a note of April 27 (May 5), 1817, the Spanish Foreign Minister, de Cea Bermúdez, demanded in the name of the King that the Russian settlement in California be liquidated.

Inasmuch as the question of the seizure of California by Russia had not been raised by the Spanish government until then, but came up only as a result of the relations with the representatives of other powers, particularly with England, the Company pleaded that the territory it had occupied was not colonized. Alluding to the common practice of the English themselves, the Board wrote that "the Company was availing itself of the same national law which all European nations have been utilizing in colonizing their own people in the two Indies."[20]

When time came to send a reply to the Spanish government, the Company at first tried to represent the case in such a way

as to imply that everything stated in the Spanish note was not i
accord with the facts, and that there were in reality no Russia
fortifications in California. The Company assured the Spanish
government that "the settlement which the Spaniards call 'a fo:
tress'" was fenced in with a wooden paling only "for protectior
against unexpected attacks by the Indians, without which it
would have been impossible to sleep in peace.... Similarly
the cannon mounted there were set up to keep the respect of
the natives."[21]

Sensing, however, how unconvincing such pretexts were,
the Russian-American Company tried to maintain that the territory occupied by Ross had not belonged to anyone except the
Indians. The latter ceded it to the Russians of their own free
will, fearing that it might be seized by other Indian tribes who
were hostile to the local population, or by the hateful Spaniard

As for the juridical formulation of the "cession" of the Ross
territory by the Indians, the Company, foreseeing that it would
inevitably need legal sanction, took the necessary steps to secure it even before it had received the protest of the Spanish
government. In 1817, Hagemeister drew up a paper which was
signed by the Indian chiefs Chu-gu-an, Amat-tin, Hem-le-le,
and others, stating that "they are very much pleased with the
occupation of the place by the Russians, that they can now live
in security from the other Indians who used to attack them, tha
this state of security came only with the establishment of the
settlement." In the same paper it was, as though accidentally
asserted again that the territory in question had belonged to the
aforementioned Indians and was voluntarily ceded by them to
the Russians. "Lieutenant-Captain Hagemeister," the document read, "presented them [i.e., the Indian chiefs.-Au.] with
an expression of gratitude in the name of the Russian-America
Company for the cession of land to the Company for a fortress
buildings, and institutions on sites belonging to Chu-gu-an."[22]

The "agreement" concluded with the Indians was the only
document which established the Company's rights to the Ross
territory, but there was no special reason to depend much on
this "agreement." The rights of the Russian-American Company to the exclusive possession of the Ross territory were,
as the Russian envoy to the United States, Poletika, correctly
indicated in a letter to the Minister of Foreign Affairs, "far
from being evident.... It is enough to look at the map to see
that the colony in question was wedged into the Spanish posses-
ions in California and the neighboring territory. One rather

old Spanish colony is situated thirty miles south of Ross. The
city of Monterey, the principal town in New California, is only
a distance of 1° latitude from Ross."[23]

In Poletika's opinion, the Company, in basing its rights to
the territory on the absence of Spanish settlements in the given
region itself, lost sight of the fact that "it is providing the
English and the Americans with arms against itself; for they
might, on their part, call its attention to the fact that
along the full extent of the northeast coast of America, beginning with the 57th parallel, to which the Company is laying
exclusive claim, it has only one single colony, Novoarkhangelsk.[24] And, according to Poletika, the Americans had
already had recourse to this argument in the negotiations about
the affairs of the Company.

For just at that time the United States began to activize its
colonial policy and also came out with claims to the Spanish
possessions. Florida had actually become a part of the United
States. Furthermore, the pact signed in February 1819, between Spain and the United States recognized the 42nd parallel
of north latitude as the boundary of the Spanish possessions.
Thus the Russian colonies in California came to be threatened
from the north by the United States.

In these conditions, the legal formulation of the California
colony became a serious problem for the tsarist government.
It was a question, in substance, of placing a foundation under
all further expansion on the American continent.

After it had received, in 1817, Spain's note of protest
against the seizure of her colonies, the Russian Ministry of
Foreign Affairs decided to examine the conditions on which it
would be possible to reach an agreement with the Spanish government. The examination was made cautiously and without
undue haste. At the beginning of 1820 a plan was even advanced
for the liquidation of the Russian colony in California. While
it raised no objections to the plan, the Russian-American
Company demanded suitable compensation. The Spanish government was supposed to grant the Company the right of free
trade with California. "Under this arrangement," wrote the
Governing Board to the Minister of Foreign Affairs Nesselrode, "the Russian-American Company would be glad to liquidate that colony, which has given rise to envy or fear on the
part of the Spaniards, and would never again contemplate
searching for another place on the Albion shores, if it could
make good the loss of that colony by permanent trade with

New California, into which the entry of foreigners is forbidden
by colonial law and, especially, in order not to reveal the
amazing carelessness and weakness of the administration."[25]

This was a cleverly calculated move on the part of the
Company. By announcing its assent to the liquidation of
Ross, the management intended to place the responsibility for
retaining the colony squarely upon the government, so as to
be able, in case of necessity, to demand its active assistance
and support. The Company was very well aware that the plan
propounded by the Ministry of Foreign Affairs was nothing but
a diplomatic subterfuge. The tsarist government did not even
think of divesting itself of its colonies in California, for the
Russian Emperor Alexander was still all-powerful in the Holy
Alliance and his assistance and cooperation were eagerly
sought after by the Court at Madrid. Indeed, it was with the
aid of the ships purchased from Russia that Ferdinand was
planning "again to bestow those benefits upon Europe of which
it has long been deprived because of the disturbances in the
New World," that is, to suppress the revolution in the American colonies. To be sure, the "powerful" squadron purchase
from Russia, consisting of five ships of the line armed with
74 cannon each and three frigates armed with 44 cannon each,
and intended to revive the glory of Spain of the time of the invincible Armada, proved to be only junk. Still, Russia was
the only power holding out any hope to Spain in her struggle
with the rebelling American colonies that were, furthermore,
being supported by England.

Not without reason did the tsarist government prolong the
negotiations about California. At last the long-awaited momer
had arrived when there could no longer be any question of not
complying with the demands of the government. Tatishchev,
the Russian Ambassador in Madrid, having learned of the Com
pany's desire to relinquish its colony in California in exchange
for the right of free trade with the Spanish colonies, hastened
to assure Nesselrode that one thing did not necessarily preclude the other. On February 4 (16), 1820, he wrote to the
Minister as follows:

"It will be more expedient to begin by considering the
question of establishing trade relations, in order to render
secure, by that very means, the acquisition of territory
which is here taking place. The right of possession will
in this way be given legal sanction."[26]

While he began his negotiations by asking that the Russian-American Company be allowed to trade with the California colonies, Tatishchev proposed later to obtain sanction for retaining Ross, if only in the form of a trading-post or a storage-place.

Spanish assent to the cession of colonies in California to Russia was, indeed, at that time, only of formal significance, since the American colonies no longer recognized the rule of their mother country. However, armed even with such a sanction, it would subsequently be possible for Russia to argue her right to that territory. At any rate, the assent of the King of Spain, who was about to lose his possessions, was still quoted at a higher figure in international legal usage than the cession of the same territory by two Indian chiefs who had never owned it.

Poletika, the Russian Ambassador to the United States, pointed out very sensibly to Nesselrode that same year that "Spain, which is holding Mexico only by moral bonds that are apt to snap, if they have not already irrevocably done so, will not wait to be entreated before yielding to us the site occupied by the colony of Ross. Having thus secured the assent of the government, it will be possible for us to attempt to secure the same from the actual government existing in Mexico, as soon as the Imperial government has arrived at a final decision in this matter."[27]

It was impossible, however, to bring the negotiations with the Spanish government to a successful conclusion; in the same year of 1820 a revolution flared up again in Spain.

After the Restoration, the hopes of the Russian-American Company revived once again. A part of the members of the Council were no longer satisfied with the mere consolidation for Russia of the territory under actual occupation in California. They insisted on the necessity for obtaining the sanction of the Spanish government to expand the Russian territory so as to include also the port of San Francisco. Another, more cautious part of the Council, while not denying the necessity for possessing San Francisco, considered it perilous, though, and premature to attempt to obtain any kind of sanctions from Spain. Such a policy, in the opinion of these members of the Council, could only arouse the animosity of the Mexican government which was the actual master in California.

The first group was led by the famous navigator I. F. Krusenstern, the second, by the no less famous navigator

V.M. Golovnin. In a memorandum presented to the Ministry of Foreign Affairs, Krusenstern maintained that Spain "in the condition in which she finds herself" would cede to Russia both the territory of Ross and the port of San Francisco. "Keeping the port of Ross in the possession of the Russian-American Company does not involve any considerable difficulties, and is possible beyond a doubt; but the place the possession of which would be incomparably more beneficial to Russia is the port of San Francisco itself, which today unquestionably still belongs to Spain. There, right now and before conditions have changed, the Spanish government has the full right to cede that port to Russia."[28]

As a reason for such a cession Krusenstern regarded the circumstance that the Spanish government was under obligation to pay a considerable amount of money for the naval squadron it had purchased from Russia. Krusenstern did not deny the possibility of a protest on the part of the government of Mexico. But, in his opinion, it was properly to be expected that the moment the question arose of the recognition of Mexico's independence by the European powers, that country would agree to sanction the cession of territory in California.

Golovnin, on the other hand, believed that "it may be said with certainty that the cession made by the King of Spain will not be recognized by the republicans, and even though we, should gain possession of the land, it would still be perilous to invest any capital in the improvement of Ross, for the republicans, having learned of the cession, will no doubt desire to assert their rights for reasons of their own. They will then break off all relations with us, will insist on the destruction of our establishments, and will perhaps even employ force." Golovnin suggested that contacts be established in advance with local California authorities and "that their attitude both towards our colony of Ross and the future cession of San Francisco Bay be thoroughly scrutinized."[29]

Alexander I himself understood, however, that Ferdinand's cession of colonies in California to Russia would have practically the same effect as his cession of any other territory not belonging to him. In October, 1824, the Minister of Finance, Kankrin, at the instance of the Governing Board of the Russian-American Company, made a proposal to the Minister of Foreign Affairs, Nesselrode, that the negotiations with the Spanish government on the subject of Ross be resumed. Nesselrode replied that after the "old order" had been reestab-

lished in Spain, he reported about the matter to the Tsar,
and that "His Majesty saw fit to regard as nothing but useless
the resumption of the discussions with the Spanish government, inasmuch as it is not within its power in the present
confused situation in its American colonies, to extend its
authority over those colonies." As for the revolutionary
government of Mexico, wrote Nesselrode, "we shall not enter into any relations with it and we cannot, consequently,
approach it on matters relating to our rights over the colony
of Ross and the land it occupies."[30]

In the meantime the situation of the Russian colony in California became more and more difficult. The claims of the
United States to Spain's "colonial heritage" grew stronger
from year to year. American trader-pioneers were rushing
to California in ever-increasing numbers. The activities of
the American traders tended to break even the slender commercial ties between the local Spanish people and the Russian
colony which had been supplying them with many of the things
they needed. Moreover, the American traders, who, not
infrequently, were the agents of their government, stirred
up the local population against the Russians in every way
possible. They made skillful use of the fact that the tsarist
government, on the other continent, was supporting Spanish
absolutism which was so hateful to the people of California.

Yet, in spite of the ever-intensified claims of the United
States to the Spanish colonies, Monroe's message to Congress
which was subsequently to exert such tremendous influence
on the whole process of European colonization on the American
continent, and which even in 1824 compelled Russia to make
a number of concessions in concluding the Russo-American
convention, was as yet of no effect in the colonies. Since
the conditions set forth in Monroe's message to Congress
were not supported in the colonies by bayonets, they were
regarded as nothing but a doctrine; the real danger to the
Russians in California lay with the opposition on the part of
the Mexican government.

As early as 1822, when Iturbide was proclaimed Emperor
of Mexico, there appeared in his name in the colony of Ross
Don Agustin Fernández de Vincent and demanded of the governor of the colony documents proving the right of the Russians
to the territory occupied by them in California. Not obtaining
the required proof, for of course there was none, the Mexican
envoy declared that the territory in question belonged to Mexico

and that the Russians should evacuate it. At a conference
with Khlebnikov, the agent of the Russian-American Company
in Monterey, Fernandez de Vincent declared again that "the
government of the Empire of Mexico demands most insistently
that the colony of Ross be removed within six months, otherwise Mexico will take forceful measures."[31]

The continuous threats of the Mexican government, together with the steady and persistent American penetration into
California, posed even more sharply the question of the clari-
fication of the juridical status of the Russian colony. In 1824,
therefore, the local colonial authorities, having lost all hope
of seeing the question settled through Petersburg, determined
to take some decisive steps themselves, which they believed
would lead to the consolidation of Russian rule in California.
The initiator of the new plan for consolidation and further expansion of the Russian colonies in California was the Decembrist D.I. Zavalishin, who arrived in the colony of Ross at
that time.

Although the literary heritage left by Zavalishin is quantita
tively much more extensive than that left by the other Decembrists, investigators have largely ignored everything coming
from his pen. The result of his well-deserved fame as a
petty intriguer and liar, whose writings are full of incessant
boasting, has been that up to the present time no one has
made a study of the valuable material comprised in his manu-
scripts. The papers preserved in the archives of the Commission of Inquiry, which reveal the role he played in the
activities of the Russian-American Company, are of the
greatest interest.

At the beginning of 1824 Zavalishin arrived in the colony
of Ross on the frigate "Kreiser" which was making a round-
the-world trip. Here he was able to see for himself the tremendous possibilities that were inherent in the exploitation
of the region, as well as the insignificant results obtained
until then by the Russian-American Company.

The colony of Ross represented at that time a small wooden
fortress, that mounted seventeen small-caliber guns. In
addition to the Aleuts, who were engaged in the hunting of
fur-animals, there were some fifty Russians in the settlement. This supposed granary of the Russian colonies, for
it had been intended to supply with grain not only the Russian
colonies in America but Kamchatka as well, sowed a total of
only 200 poods of wheat and 40 poods of barley. It was im-

possible for the colony to conduct any trade of considerable
dimensions with the local population, because of the drastic
ban on such trade by the California authorities. Hunting also
fared badly. By the 1820's the animals yielding the high-
priced furs had all but been exterminated in the region of the
colony. To be sure, sea-otters could still be had in San Francisco Bay, but the Russians were unable to hunt there because
of the opposition of the Spaniards. The colony brought nothing
but losses to the Company. In addition, Ross was in constant
danger of being wiped out either by the Spaniards or by the
native population. It became apparent that to retain the colony of Ross under such conditions was very difficult, and it
was only the hope that the Revolution in Spain and the agitation
enveloping Mexico would turn Ross into an outpost for further
Russian expansion in California, that kept the Company from
liquidating it.

Immediately after the Spanish colonies had proclaimed
their independence in 1818, the Russian-American Company
made an attempt to extend its possessions in California. This
attempt, however, met with such violent opposition on the
part of the local authorities, that any further progress became
absolutely unthinkable. In order to preclude the possibility
of further territorial seizures by the Russians, the local authorities decided to surround Ross with a chain of Spanish
settlements. In 1819 was founded the rancho of San Pablo,
in 1822 were established the ranchos of Solano, Sonoma and
others. The Spaniards, however, had neither the means nor
the men to encircle the Russian settlements completely. This,
in the 1820's, was, in general terms the unenviable situation
of the colony of Ross, whose strength rested only on the weakness of the Spanish authorities.

Zavalishin writes that soon after his arrival to that colony
he became cognizant of: "1) the unsuitability of the place, 2)
the weakness of the colony, and 3) our indecision which encouraged the claims of the Spaniards and stimulated such
actions on the part of the California authorities as they would
otherwise not even dare consider." Summing up, he arrives
at the conclusion that "the possibility of developing the colony of 'Ross' depended mainly upon taking possession of a
more suitable place than the one seized originally."[32]

Zavalishin realized full well the extremely important strategic situation of California. Later on, while giving an account
of his activities in California, he expressed this thought in a
letter to Nicholas I, dated January 24, 1826:

"California, if ceded to Russia and colonized by Russia
would forever remain under Russian rule. The acquisition
of its harbors and the low cost of maintenance would allow
us to keep there an observation fleet which would give to
Russia mastery over the Pacific and control over the trade
with China, consolidate our possession of the other colonie
and serve to restrain the influence of the United States and
England."[33]

What Zavalishin had in mind was the further expansion of
the territory of the Russian colony in California. In the north
ern direction the colony was to be extended as far as the bound
ary of the United States, in the eastern to the Sacramento Rive
or the Sierra Nevada, and in the southern to San Francisco
Bay. These boundaries had been projected even before Zavalishin; they were the very same frontiers to which the Company was aspiring all along. The novelty of the Zavalishin
plan consisted in that the action it proposed was to be carried
out by other methods.

Before we examine this plan, let us dwell awhile on the political situation that had developed in California. The Mexican
Empire, created in 1822, was torn by civil war. General
Iturbide (Don Agustin I) was overthrown. California was no
longer subject to Mexico, but had not proclaimed its independence officially. Two parties were fighting it out in California
the Mexican and the Spanish, called also the Royalist party.
The dominating position in the Mexican party was held by the
top-ranking military and civil officials, in the Spanish party
by the missionaries. The backbone of the Mexican party was
the urban population, of the Spanish party the missions.

The Mexican party was somewhat stronger than the Spanish
since, after all, it drew its support from the armed forces,
small as they were, that were to be found in California, while
the missionaries derived their sole strength from the baptized
Indians on whom one could not seriously depend. We might
add, that the term "armed forces" as applied to the Mexican
party is to be understood very relatively, since the soldiers
had not been paid for a long time and had neither rifles nor
gunpowder. The condition of the military supplies in California may be illustrated by the incident that took place during the
arrival in California of the Russian frigate "Kreiser." On
entering San Francisco Harbor the "Kreiser" fired a seven-

gun salute. The customary reply failed to materialize. An
officer was sent ashore to find out the reason for such a show
of disrespect to the Russian flag. He was informed by the
commander of the port that he would gladly have ordered a
return salute, if the "Kreiser" had sent him seven charges,
since he had none himself.

It was during that period, in 1824, that Zavalishin came
to California with the ambitious design of annexing it to the
Russian empire. "The true situation in which I found the
province," he subsequently reported to the Commission of
Inquiry, "would , of course, have been favorable, if the
annexation was to be accomplished by the force of arms. But
since the policy of the powers, especially that of England,
would not have allowed us to go to that extent, the only method
to which no one could have raised an objection and, at the
same time, the most trustworthy, would have been the voluntary submission of California to Russian rule. All my efforts
were indeed bent in that direction."[34]

"California would have had to declare herself independent
of Mexico," continues Zavalishin, "under the pretext that no
government had as yet been established there and--in order
to mollify the Mexican party--that this independence would
last only until such time as a government had been established. Then would come the freedom for foreigners to
settle in California, whereby it was intended to bring in the
Russians, since it is much easier for them to come there,
and so forth."[35]

Zavalishin's attempts to establish contacts with the Mexican party did not lead anywhere. He then began to orient himself on the Spanish party. He made the acquaintance of the
missionaries, establishing contacts, first of all, with José
Altimira, head of the Mission of St. Francis, an intelligent
man and, what was even more important, an ambitious man.
Zavalishin used all means at his disposal to win the monks
over to the Russian side--"some through fanaticism, others
through cupidity, others still through hate for the republican
government, and the rest by inspiring them with misgivings
with regard to England."[36]

It was at this point that Zavalishin's secret desire to create the "Order of Restoration"--a desire that had occurred to
him before--was to be realized. It would be the function of
the Order to promote the annexation of California to the
Russian Empire.

Adjutant-General Levashev in his summary of the Zavalishin case notes that "California, being in the situation in which it finds itself, [he is referring to the state of anarchy reigning there.-Au.] could easily have become the scene of operations for a man endowed with intelligence and the spirit of enterprise. Zavalishin had both. In the very <u>Order of Restoration he saw the way to accomplishing this end.</u>"[37]

In Zavalishin's note-book there has been preserved an entry which he entitled "Sketch on the colonizing, organizing, and consolidating of the land appurtenant to the Military Order of Restoration" that gives a clear exposition of the purposes of the organization.

He considered it necessary "to fortify the north bank of the sound in the port of San Francisco, keeping in mind the possibility of a landing there. Enclose the woods by a wall with concealed batteries. Find rocks in the sound and build lighthouses on both shores, construct a harbor for rowing vessels; establish telegraph and mail service, dam up the canals with water, and build mills and test the soil from the bottom of the sea for possible use; erect walls around the low places, dig canals, and build locks for the loading of ships. Raise a fortress in Bodega and set up a shipyard there. Inspect the port of Trinidad and intrench ourselves there."[38]

In his negotiations with the Spanish party, Zavalishin represented the Order, whose object was "the throne and a crusade of extermination against the Masons" (the monks applied the term "Masons" to all revolutionaries) as already organized, under the Russian Emperor himself, whose stand at the Congress of Verona was well known to the monks. Zavalishin expected that these supporters of the restoration of the Spanish monarchy would be duly impressed by his portrayal of the Order.

In his very first conversation, then, with Altimira, Zavalishin strove to give a picture of the activity of the mythical order that would be in perfect consonance with the inclinations and purposes of the Spanish missionaries in California. " Combining political reasons with religious considerations," he says in his deposition, "I began to tell him of the Order I founded, of the similarity between its aims and the purposes for which they had been coming to California, of the future power of the Order when it had obtained the protection of the sovereigns, and, finally, of the assistance which the Order

itself would render them in their affairs. He listened atten-
tively to everything and at almost every word I said he exclaimed 'Oxala fuese así (would it were so.)'"[39]

Experienced politician that he was, Altimira realized from
Zavalishin's very first words just what benefit he might derive from trying to win adherents to Russia's cause on the
basis of mere rumors of a supporting secret international organization. Knowing full well that the "Order of the Restoration" existed only in Zavalishin's imagination, Altmira
hastened to "recognize" it. "Altimira knew everything concerning the Order," writes Zavalishin, "that is, he knew
that it was still in the process of being established."[40]

After his conversation with Altimira, Zavalishin felt that
he was on solid ground. From then on he began to call himself Grand Master of the "Order of the Restoration."

Zavalishin endeavored to win over to his side the president
of California, who was, naturally, expected to play a decisive
part in the adoption of the constitution proclaiming the separation of California from Mexico. All his attempts, however,
to influence President Don Arguello, a former adherent of the
Mexican party, came to naught. Then he decided to utilize
the next session of the consultative junta to replace the president. Don Noriega, an adherent of the Spanish party, was
nominated for the office. Zavalishin succeeded, with the aid
of Altimira, to win over to his side three of the four members
of the junta. The selection of Noriega and the proclamation
of the independence of California seemed to be a matter of the
very near future.

Zavalishin's sudden recall to Russia, however, by order of
Alexander I deprived him of the opportunity to continue his work
for the fulfillment of the above plan. But even after his departure, Zavalishin, in letters addressed to the junta and to
Altimira himself, endeavored, by arguments about the might
of the Order, to induce the Spanish party to take decisive
action. In the letter of "Grand Master" Zavalishin to "Grand
Restorer" Altimira, the vague phrases about the Order are
accompanied by some very practical proposals: "The designated vessel will bring gunpowder for your own use and for
sale, cannon, rifles and other ammunition."[41] Very soon,
however, it became apparent that the Spanish party, if it
should adhere to its pro-Russian orientation, would have to
fight not only the Mexican party but also England and the
United States. Neither England nor the United States could,

of course, allow Russia to intrench herself in a region which would secure for its possessor the hegemony over the whole of the northern Pacific. The subtly conceived plan of Zavalishin was a total failure.

More than twenty years had passed since the ceremonious founding of the Ross colony, and the Russian-American Company had not even succeeded in obtaining formal recognition of its rights to the territory occupied by the Russian settlement. The colony was visited by foreign vessels; it carried on trade operations, with the Company footing the considerable bill for maintaining it, but de jure the colony had no existence. Nor did Ross become a base for further advances into the interior. The future of the Russian colony in California did not presage any favorable developments. On the contrary, year by year as the power of the United States grew stronger and as the influence of Russia on the American continent grew weaker, the situation of Ross became more and more difficult.

The results were deplorable in every respect. Ross had not become the "granary" of the American colonies, since neither the size of the territory belonging to Russia nor its geographic situation was such as to admit of a broadly developed agriculture. In the best of years, according to the testimony of the manager of the colony, Khlebnikov, "a stretch of land totaling 88 dessiatines or 211,600 square sagenes"[42] was sown in the colony of Ross.[43]

The proximity of the colony to the sea had a negative influence on the sowing-seed. The gramineous plants, according to the reports of the administration of the colony, were covered with blight, as a result of the excessive dampness of the climate, and this also had a bad effect on the crop.[44]

Let us utilize the detailed report of the governor of the Russian colonies in America, Baron Wrangell, who visited the colony of Ross in the middle of 1833, to obtain a picture of the economic conditions of the colony twenty years after its founding, during the period when the Company made a last effort to pull the colony out of the impasse in which it found itself.

The fortress itself still consisted of a quadrangle, surrounded on all sides by a wooden paling. Each corner of the fortress had a wooden turret which mounted a cannon. This fortress, according to the governor of the colonies, still "appears quite strong, and perhaps even invincible in the

eyes of the Indians and the local Spaniards."[45] The governor adds, though, that "almost all the buildings and the paling
itself with the sentry-boxes are so old and decrepit" that they
should be either repaired or replaced by new ones.

The adult population of Ross numbered 199, including 128
males. There were 41 Russians, 42 Aleuts, the rest consisting of Creoles and Indians. By the 1830's agriculture had
shown considerable progress over the middle 1820's. Still
there was just enough produce to feed only the population of
Ross. Between 1826 and 1833 inclusive, that is during an
eight-year period, a total of about 6,000 poods of wheat and
barley was sent from Sitka to Ross, averaging no more than
750 poods annually. Besides the dearth of fertile soil, another
factor contributed to aggravating the situation--the unusually
extensive methods of cultivation. The land was not fertilized,
and since there was not enough land suitable for sowing, none
of it was allowed to lie fallow. As a result, the most fertile
sections were very rapidly exhausted. For lack of manpower,
threshing was done with horses that were let out into a so-
called "circus" with the floor covered with sheaves. Forty
horses with eight drivers threshed out about 900 sheaves in
twenty-four hours, but the loss of grain by this method was
very considerable.

Another branch of farming, cattle-breeding, which, according to the original plan was to supply all the Russian colonies in America with salt meat and dairy products, failed to
achieve the expected results. Under a rational system of
economy, no less than fifteen hundred head of horned
cattle were required to supply Sitka with the necessary a-
mount of salt meat (400 pounds annually). In Ross, however,
there were only 700 head. It was impossible to increase this
number because of the absence of pasture land. Between
July and November, when the grass burned up, the Russian
colonists found it necessary to let out their cattle beyond the
confines of the colonies.

The hunting of fur-bearing animals had, by this time, almost come to a complete standstill in California. In the
areas occupied by the Russians the animals had been exterminated, and in the Spanish areas, hunting was forbidden by
the local authorities. In 1826 the Aleuts had processed 287
sea-otters and 455 fur-seals in California, while seven years
later, in 1832, they processed only one single sea-otter and
188 fur-seals.

At first the colonies derived a certain income from the orders of the California Spaniards for wheels, barges, and dishes. These orders were good for an annual income of some 6,000 rubles. But, along towards the 1830's there was hardly any income from that source. The governor of the colonies wrote as follows:

"Such transactions are now rare and unimportant, because the foreigners, who have captured the California trade, have brought in all kinds of things that the people need and have been supplying them at such low prices that we simply cannot compete with them."[46]

During the whole existence of the colony in California no way was ever found of solving the most important problem of manpower. The required workers were recruited either from among the laborers who were brought under contract from the mainland, or from among the local population of Indians. The Russian laborers, bound by contract to a state of servitude and having lost all hope of ever returning to their native country, utilized the proximity of foreign territory to desert systematically from Ross. As early as 1817, Lieutenant-Captain Hagemeister, in the course of the round-the-world voyage of the frigates "Kutuzov" and "Suvorov," carried on a lengthy exchange with the Spanish authorities about the handing over to him of a number of deserters from Ross, among whom were also some Creoles. The Spanish authorities agreed to extradite only those fugitives who were found in San Francisco. The governor gave a variety of excuses for his refusal to hand over all the other deserters. He adduced, for example, his inability to deliver them to San Francisco in the nearest future, and even the necessity of utilizing these deserters in consolidating the friendship with the Russians, since, with their knowledge both of Spanish and Russian, they could serve as interpreters.

In this connection Hagemeister wrote to the governor:

"It seems to me perfectly impossible that you should not return all of them without exception, taking into consideration both the friendship between our two sovereigns and the fact that Russia is perhaps the only empire that, unlike other nations, is lending no assistance to the American insurgents."[47]

The Spanish authorities blocked the return of the fugitives to Ross mainly because the Spanish colonies were in great need of manpower themselves. Under these conditions there was no sense in concentrating a considerable number of Russian laborers in Ross.

The other source of manpower, that of the Indians, was also unreliable. Since the Company paid the Indians very low wages for their labor, they were quick to stop hiring themselves out for work in Ross. At the same time, even with the small crops, no fewer than 150 people were needed to gather in the harvest. Thus, according to information of the year 1833, during the summer season 210 people in all were employed at different tasks. Of these 49 were Russian or Creole (the Aleuts were engaged in the hunting of fur-bearing animals) and 161 were Indian. The Russians nd Creoles were mainly employed as sentries and mechanics, while the Indians were directly employed as workers on the land.

In what manner, then, did the Company manage to gather such a number of Indians? Baron Wrangell, Governor of the Colonies, reports on this as follows:

"When the crop is being harvested and the Indians gather in the colonies from the nearest tundras, either because they are properly paid or because they need the work, and when there are few volunteers, then as many Indians as can be assembled--sometimes as many as 150--are driven together by force and are put to hard work in the fields for a period of about a month and a half." The Indians were handed out "only flour for thin gruel." As a result of this scanty food and the hard labor, notes the Governor of the colony, "the Indians reach in the end a state of complete exhaustion."[48]

The local administration was perfectly aware of the results to which such methods of exploitation of the Indians might lead. The Governor of the colony pointed out to the Governing Board "that not only humanity but good sense itself demands that the Indians be treated more kindly. As a result of the bad food and the poor pay, the Indians have stopped coming to the colony to work of their own accord, wherefore the office found itself compelled to search them out in the tundras, fall upon them unexpectedly, tie their hands and drive them like cattle into the colony to work. Such a group of 75 men, women, and children, was brought in to one of the colonies in my presence about 65 versts[49] from here. There they were told to leave their things, with-

out anyone watching them, for about two months. We need
not dwell on what the long-range consequences of such conduct toward the Indians are bound to be; we are certainly
not making any friends among them."[50]

There were solid grounds for the apprehension expressed
by Governor Wrangell. There were repeated Indian uprising
in the vicinity of Ross, in which fugitive Russian fur-hunters
also participated. The administration preferred not to pub-
licize such incidents, or activities of any kind that were
directed against the Company as a result of its unrestrained
exploitation; it did not even report them to the government.
However, some information may be gleaned from the papers
of the Company. For instance, in the abstract made of the
colonial dispatches for 1825 by Manager Ryleyev we find the
following report:

> "During the past year the Indians rose in the vicinity
> of Ross, in several of the Spanish missions. The Mission
> of St. Inez was laid level with the ground. According to
> the governor of California, the rebelling Indians were led
> by the fur-hunter Prokhor Yegorov who had fled from Ross
> But the rebellion was brought to an end through the efforts
> of the government and the clergy. On this occasion the
> authorities of our colonies had an opportunity to render
> an important service to the government of California by
> supplying it with a considerable quantity of powder and
> rifles. This sensible step taken by M. Muravyov[51] con-
> tributed to strengthen our bonds of friendship with Cali-
> fornia, and the hostile actions of Prokhor Yegorov (finally
> killed by the Indians themselves) compelled the local au-
> thorities to stop protecting our fugitives, but to hand them
> over to us--which they have already begun to do."[52]

On the whole, the colony of Ross during the 1830's meant
an annual loss to the Company of some 10,000 rubles. In
the year 1832, the most fruitful of the past few years, the
loss was 7,599 rubles. "It may positively be stated," wrote
Governor Baron Wrangell, "that the Company will always incur losses, even in the most bountiful of years, in trying to
maintain the Russian sector, if the colony stays on the site
it now occupies, a site that does not admit of any considerable
improvements in the field of agriculture."[53]

Wrangell sharply posed the question of occupying the plains

of the Slavyanka River, between Rumyantsev Bay and the colony of Ross, so as to liquidate the existing settlement and
transfer it in toto to a new site. The main obstacle to such
a change of location was, as it had been earlier when similar
plans came up, the fear that "such an undertaking would a-
rouse the envy of the foreigners living in California who would
shrewdly set the government of Mexico against us; it might
also expose us to our own government's displeasure with the
wilful occupation on our part of places that are so distant
from the established boundaries of the Russian possessions
in America."[54]

If the core of Zavalishin's plans was to attain the independence of California by separating it from Mexico--which
would, naturally, place weak California in a position of
total dependence on Russia--then Wrangell's plan was based
on an agreement between Russia and Mexico, which would involve keeping California dependent on Mexico. The Mexican
government was, at that time, interested in obtaining de jure
recognition by Russia. Such recognition would, in the first
place, have strengthened the government's internal position
and, in the second place, would have given some assurance
against the possibility of intervention by England and the
United States. It was on this possibility that Wrangell was
counting when he included in his plan the recognition of the
Mexican government, in return for territorial concessions
to Russia in California.

"They will understand full well," he wrote to the management of the Company, "that the proximity of a handful of
Russian peasants, torn away, so to speak, from their own
country, can never be a danger to the integrity of the Mexican possessions, but, on the other hand, a Russian settlement there might block, or, at least, render difficult the
encroachments of the English and the United States, which
would be far more dangerous to Mexico."[55]

In order not to goad the other powers into presenting
claims of their own, the subject could be broached not as a
question of transferring the new territory to Russia's possessions but merely as one of leasing it to the Company for
a definite period. Such a form of ownership would, in fact,
be even more acceptable. A fifty-year lease on Bodega Bay
and the plain along the Slavyanka would establish the Company
on a firm foundation. The Mexican government itself, eager
to obtain Russia's recognition, was also greatly interested in

arriving at an understanding with that country. On April 11, 1833, Brigadier-General Figeroa, who had newly been appointed by the Mexican government Head of Military and Civilian Affairs in California, dispatched a letter to Governor Wrangell. In it he apprised the Russian official of the desire of the Mexican government to enter through him "into friendl relations with the Imperial cabinet in St. Petersburg and to inform it that in asserting its independence the Mexican natio is acting in accordance with the tenets of reasonable policy, and fully intends to maintain with all other nations the union and concord that are an absolute requirement of good relatior and of mutual advantage among neighboring powers."[56]

Wrangell understood that if the moment should be allowed to slip by and other powers given a chance to steal a march on Russia by granting recognition to the Mexican government the last hope for the firm establishment of the Russians in California would vanish.

"We must rush the start of the negotiations with the government of Mexico on the aforementioned subject," Wrangell urged the management of the Company. "Procrastination may jeopardize our success, allow the English or citizens of the United States not only to hamper our efforts but even to occupy those places themselves and thus deprive the Russian-American Company of one of the finest acquisitions in this region."[57]

The Company failed, however, in its attempt to induce the tsarist government to grant immediate recognition to Mexico, and Wrangell was not given any official powers to negotiate about it. The Director of the Ministry of Foreign Affairs informed the management of the Company through the Minister of Finance that "having examined the question of recognizing the new order of things introduced into the former Spanish possessions, in connection with a number of current problem of great political importance, His Majesty has not yet wished to recognize as possible a decision to extend such recognition at this time."[58]

Wrangell was permitted to visit Mexico only in the capacit of representative of the Russian-American Company, "charge in addition, with the duty of ascertaining on the spot the exten to which the recognition of the independence of the republic by the Russian government might influence the Mexican government to agree to the formal cession of the territories actually occupied by the Russians in California." In the unofficial instructions to Wrangell, the Minister of Foreign Affairs wrote that "the question of recognizing the new order of things introduced into the former Spanish colonies is rather delicate and very closely bound up with too many very important political considerations for our cabinet to be able at this time to proceed to a definitive solution."[59]

The attention of the "international policeman," Nicholas I, was wholly focused at that time on events taking place in France and in Poland. At the same time, tsarist policy on the Eastern question contained a real threat of a collision with England. To come out at that moment with the recognition of Mexico was not without danger to the tsarist government. Such a step was prone to exacerbate even further the relations with England, which had already been distrubed by Russian penetration into Asia and by the rising threat to England's Indian possessions. The most essential consideration in the position of the Russian government, however, was the fact that the recognition of Mexico went counter to the policy, pursued by Nicholas, of unconditional support of legitimism in Spain. In contradistinction to Alexander, Nicholas did not lose the hope that Spain would in the very near future be able to cope with the situation in her colonies, and that Russia would then obtain all she needed in California.

This thought permeates the aforementioned instructions sent Wrangell by the Ministry of Foreign Affairs. Thus we read: "It is possible, however, that in the near future the opportunity will present itself to Russia for a final decision with regard to Mexico, without swerving from the principle by which she has been guided until now in all things relating to the Spanish colonies in general."[60]

Not having received any official diplomatic powers, Wrangell found himself in a very difficult position in Mexico. Time had been allowed to slip. England had already recognized Mexico, and the Mexican government was not satisfied with Russia's proposal to conclude a trade agreement without formal recognition. Furthermore, in the words of Wrangell, "the ministers of England and France were using their influence against letting the ministers or the vice-president of Mexico enter into any negotiations with me."[61]

In the long run Wrangell did succeed in having the Mexican envoy in London authorized to enter into negotiations with the Russian representative for the conclusion of a trade agreement without recognizing Mexico de jure.

The Company endeavored to utilize at least this opportuni
to maintain contact with Mexico and, at the proper time, to
take advantage of the complications which were bound to aris
in the relations between the Mexican government and the
United States. "The attitude of Mexico towards the United
States of North America contributes a great deal to a rapprochement with Russia," wrote Wrangell upon his return
from Mexico, "especially when the province of Texas has
bècome a part of the northern confederacy." Butler, the
American Ambassador to Mexico, said frankly in a conversation with Wrangell about the interests of the United States
in San Francisco Bay:

> "We are not neglecting that part of California. We
> have people there who report to us and supply us with
> every kind of information, and the time is not far off
> when northern California will join our northern con-
> federacy."[62]

But in vain did the Company strive, in every possible way
to prove to the tsarist government that the threat from the
United States was forcing Mexico to make concessions to
Russia and, this being the case, even the conclusion of only
a trade agreement would serve a certain purpose. Nicholas I
"did not consider it appropriate to expedite the matter in any
way," and flatly refused to enter into any agreement with the
Mexican government. Soon there was no longer any necessit
for negotiating with Mexico on matters pertaining to Californi
in October 1836 California proclaimed her independence and
expelled all Mexican officials.

While in the early 1820's, when the Russian-American Co
pany was endeavoring to bring about the separation of Califor
nia from Mexico, the proclamation of California's independence would have meant her becoming completely dependent
on Russia, the situation was very different now. A new powe
had grown to maturity, the United States, that was biding the
opportunity first to subjugate California and then to incorpora
it in its own territory. "The Americans are using all means
at their disposal to inflame the Californians against the Mexicans and, it seems to me," reported the Governor of the colony of Ross, "they hope that California, having seceded from
Mexico, will, if not actually become subject to the United
States, then at least come under her protection."[63] The

Company strove in every way possible, during that period, to make sure that California would remain under Mexican rule, for that was the only thing that might have rendered difficult the penetration of the United States into California.

The results of the overturn were soon to become apparent. Some thirty versts (twenty miles) from the colony of Ross the American Cooper established a rancho. Another rancho was planned on Cape Drake. It was evident that Ross would very soon be encircled by American settlements on all sides. The Company, without even soliciting government approval, made a decisive attempt to secure the possession of the contiguous areas. The governor of Ross was enjoined "to plow up at least the places near the bay itself...in order, by furnishing all possible means for the successful pursuit of agriculture, to secure possession of Bodega Bay itself; under the present circumstances," wrote the Governor of the colonies, "we should avoid all excessive modesty in our dealings."[64]

But this attempt to profit by the civil war in California produced no tangible results, either. The ring of American settlements around Ross was tightened even more.

The colony of Ross always brought nothing but losses to the Company. It was being retained only in the hope of propitious circumstances in the future. Now this last hope was also gone. In the summary memorandum composed by the Governing Board of the Russian-American Company at that time due note is taken of the fact that the influence of the United States, having become stronger in California from year to year, has led to the establishment of populous settlements of American citizens in Monterey, San Francisco, and in the adjacent areas. "As the trading activity of these new-comers, who are experts in speculation, has found new ways of making profits," we read in the concluding part of the memorandum, "the small, barren colony of Ross was to lose its profits and even the hope for a future amelioration of the conditions which have so radically changed."[65]

For a time after the news of the events in California had reached St. Petersburg, and when the part played by the United States had not yet become quite clear, the Directors of the Company and some government circles even had a gleam of hope that it would be possible to take advantage of the civil war to round out the territory of the Russian colony. However, when the management of the Company received the detailed reports on the situation in California, it petitioned

the Ministry of Finance on March 31, 1839, for permission
to liquidate the colony of Ross.

The management, observing that the Company had never
given up the hope of expanding its territory in California for
the purpose of establishing farming and cattle-breeding on a
large scale, declared that "under present circumstances that
hope has come to naught," and that, therefore, "it sees no
reason for, ano no valid purpose in, the further occupation
of the colony of Ross."66 Politically, clinging to the colony
offered nothing but unpleasantness, since its possession had
remained unsanctioned by international law. Finally, the
Company opined, that strategically, too, the loss of Ross was
immaterial to the Russian colonies in America, since "the
English have their own harbors in close proximity to our
borders anyway; the Mexicans or Californians are in possession of splendid San Francisco Bay not far from Ross, the
citizens of the United States are colonizing the shores of the
Bay in droves and do not need the inaccessible rock of Ross."

To these very weighty arguments the management of the
Company added some purely commercial considerations. Even
in former days, the management pointed out, the maintenance
of the colony of Ross amounted to 45,000 rubles annually; by
1839 it had reached 72,000 rubles. There was a time when the
hunting of fur-bearing animals in California brought in an
annual income of 29,000 rubles, now in 1837, such hunting did
not bring in anything. There was only the income from farmi
which amounted to between 8,000 and 9,000 rubles, and from
small crafts, such as brickmaking, tanning, and so forth
which, in the last years, had hardly produced any income at
all.

When the reports of the proposed liquidation of the colony
reached Bodisko, the Russian Ambassador in Washington, he
lost no time in informing the Ministry of Foreign Affairs as
to the possible effect of such a step on the diplomatic world.
"I make so bold as to observe," wrote Bodisko on August 10
(22), 1839, "that our retirement from Bodega and Ross would
make an unfavorable impression in the minds."68 And immediately after Ross had been liquidated, the Company began
to lose its holdings on the North American coast bit by bit in
the guise of leases.

The colonies in California were now lost to the tsarist government. True, several years later, at the beginning of 1848
when California was already occupied by American troops but

had not yet been officially admitted to the Union, the same
Bodisko intimated to Secretary of State Buchanan that Russia
might still return to California, if it were so desired. This
statement, made in a semi-jocular vein, was the result of
the failure of the Company to collect a single penny from
Mr. Sutter, a citizen of the United States, who had purchased
the property of Ross. Prior to the appearance of American
troops in California the Company had obtained the promise
of the Mexican authorities to become surety for Sutter's payment of the debt. This pledge was even duly recorded in a
special agreement. After the occupation of California, it
became necessary to enlist the cooperation of the American
authorities, or to attempt to resell the property of the colony
to them.

"In the course of my conversation with Mr. Buchanan,"
wrote Bodisko to the Minister of Foreign Affairs, Nesselrode,
on February 12, 1848 "I made casual mention of the extremity to which the Russian-American Company might be
driven in order to save its investment, namely, to return to
Ross and resume its farming and commercial operations....
I added laughingly, 'At one time you were a little envious of
that little colony, so here is your chance to pay $30,000 for
the privilege of depriving the Company of any excuse for
staging a comeback.'" Buchanan, by the way, had as little
faith in such a possibility as did Bodisko himself. "Of
course, Mr. Buchanan" writes Bodisko, "answered me in
the same vein, 'let us begin, though, with an explanation and
then we'll be able to agree on the conditions on which we can
negotiate.'"[69]

The discovery of gold in California brought regret to the
tsarist government that it had relinquished its colonies in that
region. Nicholas I even saw fit in 1849 to inform the Russian-
American Company that it would be to its benefit to preoccupy
itself with the extraction of gold in California, following the
example of other private individuals."[70]

The Company, however, alleged that there were no reliable
people available, and even made no attempt to carry out the
imperial order. According to the report of the management,
"under the existing practice of allowing the gold to become
the property of every one who extracts it, it is very difficult
to keep the employees of the Company from running away."
In reality, however, from the time of the discovery of gold in
California the Company incurred nothing but losses. It was

able to participate only to a limited degree in the trade that
was developing on a broad scale in California, thanks to the
influx of masses of immigrants. At the same time the rise
in the price of grain in California deprived the Company of
the opportunity of purchasing products there for the other
colonies. As the governor-general of Eastern Siberia observed in his report, "the Company is in a difficult situation
...because, on account of the excessively high prices in
California, the colonies have been deprived of the means of
procuring their food at reasonable prices, and they have to
procure it in the region of the Baltic Sea."[71]

Chapter VII

THE COLONIES ON THE HAWAIIAN ISLANDS AND THE
PLANS FOR SETTLEMENT ON THE ISLAND OF HAITI

THE ATTEMPT made at the beginning of the nineteenth century to gain a foothold on the Hawaiian or Sandwich Islands
was not the personal accomplishment of a swindler, as it
later came to be treated in official sources, but an integral
part of a carefully thought-out plan for expansion in the Pacific, a plan perfected and approved by the tsarist government
itself.

If the establishment in California was intended to assure
Russian domination in the western part of the north Pacific,
the colonies on the Hawaiian Islands were expected to secure
Russia's predominant position in the eastern part of the
ocean. Domination of the Hawaiian Islands would have given
Russia effective control of the most important sea-lanes of
Pacific commerce. The Hawaiian Islands were an inter-
mediate point where ships were bound to call on their way
from American to Asia and, particularly, to China, which
had become a principal fur-market. Not without reason,
then, did the Russian merchants say that "the highway to
Canton leads through the Hawaiian Islands."

This favorable situation of the islands spurred on the Company, first of all, to make an effort to gain possession of
them. "In order to maintain the balance of power in Asia,
Russia needs the Sandwich Islands. Having taken possession
of them, she will be in a position to offer her friendship to
China, Japan, the American colonies that have been freed
from under the Spanish yoke, and her protection to the
Philippine Islands and others," wrote Dr. Scheffer, Commissioner of the Company, to Alexander I.

The Company was also tempted by the vast natural resources of the Hawaiian Islands. Even though the Company
had only a vague notion of the wealth of the islands, it knew
enough to be fascinated by the prospect of a partial freeing
of Russian industry from the necessity of importing raw
materials, and of the establishment of a base for supplying

the Russian market with the products of the colonies. It was
proposed to establish such hugh cotton plantations on the islands, that "a considerable portion of the Russian people wil
be dressed in cotton goods." It was planned to cultivate the
mulberry tree, and, with the assistance of invited Chinese
specialists, to go in for the manufacture of silk. The Company's plan also provided for the breeding of merino sheep
and the manufacture of coarse woolen cloth and blankets, th
cultivation of sugar can, spices of all kinds, and finally, the
exporting of sandal-wood, peltry, and other products.

The Russian-American Company had done some recon-
naisance on the Hawaiian Islands in 1806, when the Company
vessel "Neva" under Lisyansky's command called at the island of Atuwaii (Tuau-Kauai). Tomari, the native ruler of
Kauai, who was preparing just then to make war on Tomi-om
the ruler of the island of Owaihi (Hawaii), made an attempt t
enlist the aid of the Russians. He asked particularly that the
supply him with gunpowder and arms. The officers of the
Company, however, would not risk intervening in a conflict
between Hawaii's petty kings. In 1809 the same "Neva," under the command of Lieutenant-Captain Hagemeister, again
put in at the island of Kauai. According to the officers, King
Tomari again turned to them for assistance, asking them to
leave some Russian colonists on the island as a measure for
defense against Tomi-omi.

All this was only in the nature of preliminary reconnais-
sance. The attention of the Russian-American Company was
focused at that time on gaining possession of the coastal stri
of California. The Company vessels were busy transporting
equipment for the colony of Ross, and the voyage of the
"Bering" to the Hawaiian Islands in 1814 ended in a fiasco.
The ship was wrecked not far from the shores of Kauai, and
the whole cargo fell into the hands of King Tomari. It was
this cargo, by the way, which was subsequently to be used
as a convenient excuse for sending Russian expeditions to
that island ostensibly to retrieve the merchandise. Thus,
only in 1815 did the Company have the opportunity seriously
to set about the realization of its plan for penetrating into
the Hawaiian Islands.

However, the political situation, which had been favorable
to Russia at the beginning of the second decade of the nineteenth century, now took a sharp turn for the worse. The
direct seizure of the Hawaiian Islands had become out of the

question. Napoleon was crushed, the war between England and the United States had come to an end. This allowed both the English and the Americans to turn their attention to the northern basin of the Pacific. The three powers, England, the United States, and Russia were keeping a sharp eye on one another for any move to seize the islands. Cloaking their predatory designs, they were now attempting to solidify the independence of the islands. This circumstance strengthened the native rulers, since each of the three powers endeavored, by bribing these kinglets, to secure for itself, the domination over the islands.

With the aid of British agents the native ruler Tomi-omi of the southern part of the island of Hawaii, disposed of the other petty rulers and became actual ruler of almost all of the Hawaiian Islands, with the exception of Kauai and Onihau (Nihau) which came under the control of Tomari, the son of Dojio, the murdered ruler of Oahu, Kauai, and of other small islands.

Tomi-omi, who later assumed the name of Kamehameha I, supplied his troops with fire-arms with the aid of the English and managed to procure some artillery and even a few ships of European design. Surrounded by foreigners as he was (even the governor of the island of Hawaii was a runaway English sailor, named John Young), he could do nothing but favor that power which, at the given moment, disposed of larger forces on the islands and also paid higher prices for the goods it purchased.

In 1794, when Captain Vancouver sailed up to the island of Hawaii, Tomi-omi announced his desire to become an English subject--which did not prevent him, after Hancouver had left, to grant exclusive privileges to American traders, including an export monopoly on all merchandise. The cabinet of St. James, which had long kept silent, was finally compelled in 1812, when the relations between England and the United States had become exacerbated and when a mere suspicion of England's designs on the Hawaiian Islands might have given the United States excuse for seizing them, to reject Tomi-omi's petition for British citizenship.

His rival Tomari oriented himself on the Americans. With their help he fitted out an army, acquired a few guns, and even fancied raising a fleet to give battle to Tomi-omi.

Such was the situation on the Hawaiian Islands in 1815, when the Russian-American Company began to take definite

steps to consolidate its foothold there. Baranov, the governor of the Russian colonies in America, intended at first to
entrust this operation to Lieutenant Lazarev who was then
on Sitka. But a misunderstanding between the two resulted
in Lazarev's sailing away to Kronstadt on the "Suvorov."
Then Baranov entrusted the job of taking possession of the
Hawaiian Islands to the commissioner of the Company, Dr.
Scheffer, the only one of the crew of the "Suvorov" to remain
in the colonies.

Scheffer, a Doctor of Medicine, was a typical adventurer
of the kind that was very common in those days in the colonia
possessions of all the powers. Arriving in Russia in 1808, h
was appointed the following year police physician in Moscow,
in which position he served until 1812. In 1813 he entered
the service of the Russian-American Company and was sent
on the "Suvorov" as ship doctor and commissioner on a roun
the-world expedition. Having fallen out with most of the
officers in the course of the voyage, Scheffer, upon arriving
in Sitka, was released from the "Suvarov" "as an intolerable
person on board ship." To Baranov he appeared as a perfectly suitable candidate for the position of leader of an expedition to the Hawaiian Islands, since, as a physician, he
enjoyed a number of advantages that would help him in ef-
fecting a rapprochement with the native little king.

For greater secrecy it was decided to send him on the
American boat "Isabella" which, in October, 1815, landed hi
on the island of Oahu (Ahu) that belonged to Tomi-omi. Following him, two well-armed Russian vessels, the "Kodiak"
and the "Otkrytiye" (Discovery) arrived at the Hawaiian Islands in March of 1816, with the ostensible purpose of bartering with the natives.

Scheffer, whose official mission it was to recover the
property of the wrecked Russian boat "Bering," decided at
first to act through Tomi-omi who ruled most of the Hawaiian
Islands. However, as we read in his travel journal, "...be-
fore Scheffer was able to come ashore, some of the captains,
or skippers, who had been in our colonies before coming her
with their vessels--the oldest being Ebets Gunt, Adams and
old John Young (who had long been living on that island as
governor and exercised a tremendous influence on the king)
--managed to convince Tomi-omi and many of the best islanders that Scheffer's coming and the expected arrival in
the near future of some Company vessels from Arkhangelsk,

were unmistakable indications of the hostile intentions of the Russians. Wherefore the letter with the medal sent to Tomi-omi in advance was returned unopened."[2]

Nevertheless, Scheffer did succeed in going ashore. He managed to become physician to King Tomi-omi and in "grati-tude," as it were, for the medical assistance he had rendered, he was given some plantations on the island of Oahu, where the American Winship brothers had already established theirs.

In the six months between Scheffer's arrival and that of the Company vessels he built a few houses on the plantations assigned to him and started to raise tobacco and various other plants. He strove to expand the territory he had re-ceived as a "gift" by buying up land from the natives. It was not long before his activities aroused the American traders against him, for, aside from everything else, it seems that he was claiming the exclusive rights to the export trade in sandalwood. For this reason the Americans tried in every way to make mischief between Tomi-omi and Scheffer and, according to witnesses, "they so upset King Tomi-omi that they almost had him consent to have Scheffer killed."

He was saved by the timely arrival of the Company's ships. He then decided to change his course completely and to orient himself on King Tomari of the islands of Onihau and Kauai, who was Tomi-omi's enemy.

To escape persecution Scheffer ran away from the island of Oahu, leaving a few of the employees of the Company to keep guard over the Russian trading-post. On the Company ship "Otkrytiye" he roughed it to the island of Niihau and thence to Kauai which was under Tomari's control. As Scheffer observes in his journal, King Tomari received him "in friendly fashion, to be sure, but evinced a certain con-fusion which, it was revealed later, arose from the same sort of hostile insinuations on the part of the North American skippers as they had been making to Tomi-omi."

It was not long, however, before Tomari came to feel that the assistance of the Russians would be of substantial value to him in his conflict with Tomi-omi. For that reason he suddenly conceived uncommon respect for Russia and asked Scheffer to obtain for him the protection of the Russian emperor.

On May 21, 1816, Tomari officially "accepted Russian . citizenship." According to one of the officials who accom-panied Scheffer, the ceremony was performed with great solemnity. "The king himself brought the Russian flag from the ship to the shore and there raised it to the top of the flag staff..." Having received the approval "of the gods and the priests," for his actions, Tomari, in token of gratitude, "built a new Morai or sanctuary to his statues, and made the offerings of various fruits, cattle, and, if we are not mistake of two humans as well."[3] To mark the occasion "the king handed over to the Company as a gift in perpetuity a whole area containing some 400 Indian families, for plantations, factories, and so forth."

In the name of the Russian-American Company Scheffer concluded four agreements with Tomari. By the provisions of the first agreement Tomari granted to the Company the ex clusive rights to the export of sandalwood from the island of Kauai, allowed it to set up trading-posts everywhere and establish plantations "with the aid of the islanders." The secor agreement dealt with the cession "in perpetuity, in favor of the Company, of one half of the island of Oahu together with the inhabitants and all that may be found in the soil thereof." But since that islands was still in possession of Tomi-omi, t. Company was "to come to the aid of the king, under the direc tion of the same Dr. Scheffer as commander of his troops, with a force of 500 men to be utilized in winning back the is lands of Oahu, Lanai, Maui, Molokai and the other islands that had been wrested from him. These islands, too, the king yields to the high protection of His Majesty the Emperor

By terms of the third agreement the Company was obliged to buy, at its own expense, one armed vessel from the Bostor skipper Whittemore for an expedition against King Tomi-omi with Tomari reimbursing the Company with sandalwood. Scheffer actually bought the ship and sent the bill to the Governor of the Colonies, Baranov. And, finally, by the provisions of the fourth agreement, Tomari "gave" to Baranov three harbors on the same island of Oahu, "without levying any taxes on them for himself."[4]

The decisive steps that Scheffer took received the open approval of the management of the Company. On August 20, 1817, the Company sent to Scheffer the following instruction: "On defending King Tomari against the other island rulers, only when they do not hold power as a result of the influence of some European nation, or have that power given to them not by that nation itself.... On respecting that king to the exten required by his savage mode of life." A report was presente

to Alexander on August 25, 1817, dealing with Scheffer's adventures and Tomari's negotiations for Russian citizenship.
The report met with no objections on the Emperor's part.

In the meantime Scheffer continued his activities aimed at
taking possession of the Hawaiian Islands. By order of Tomari
"the elders of the province in which the port of Hanalei is situated , handed it over with due solemnity to Scheffer, together
with population comprising thirty families. He inspected the
port, looked over the Waimea River, the lake and the whole
lay-out, then built fortresses on the three heights, calling
one Fort Alexander, the other Fort Elizabeth, and the third
Fort Barclay. The Hanalei valley he named, at the king's
desire, after himself: Scheffer Valley. In like manner he
renamed the other little places, rivers; lakes and people
with Russian names. The king gave of his own men to build
those fortresses."[5]

In a short article in "The Hawaiian Spectator," based on
eye-witness accounts (the author of the article landed on the
island in 1820), dealing with the attempts of the Russians to
establish themselves on Kauai, there is information to the
effect that the forts built by Scheffer (he is called Schoof in
the article) were "so far finished that a number of guns were
mounted on one side, the magazine built and a flag staff
erected, on which the Russian colors were seen flying on
public occasions."[6]

Similar information was given by one of the men in the
Company's service who returned from the Hawaiian Islands
on the "Otkrytiye." He had seen the trading-post and the
storehouses which the natives built for Scheffer. The latter
sent word to Baranov that he "would soon take over a whole
province, which the king had given to the Company on the island of Oahu. Whence, as the Company reports, it must be
concluded that he, Scheffer, would set out for that island
with Tomari's troops on a ship purchased especially for him,
or on some other Company vessel.

At the same time the Company made aggressive attempts
to win possession of Tomi-omi's territory from the other
side. As early as November, 1816, when Tomi-omi expelled
Scheffer, Captain Kotzebue brought over on the brig "Riurik"
a new assistant to Scheffer, an employee of the Company,
named Eliot, of Portuguese extraction. John Eliot de Castro
resembled Scheffer in more ways than one. He, too, possessed a certain knowledge of medicine--he even served at one
time as physician in the hospitals of Rio de Janeiro.

Following in Scheffer's footsteps, de Castro soon became chief adviser to Tomi-omi, who was left without the necessar medical assistance upon Scheffer's departure. According to Kotzebue, Tomi-omi also gave to his new confidant, Eliot, "a large tract of land."[8]

Thus the Russians were already in possession of two areas in Tomi-omi's territory. As for the further expansion of the Russian possessions on that region, particularly on the island of Oahu, which had been "given" to Russia by Tomari who, let us note, had no rights whatsoever to it, Scheffer imagined that he could carry out his expansionist plans by main force. He intended to do away with Tomi-omi's troops with the help of the schooner "Lady" which he had bought.

The Council of the Company reported all this to the head of the Ministry of Foreign Affairs on January 19, 1818. However, the international situation had undergone a change durin the brief interval. The stand that Russia took in the Holy Alliance on the question of the Spanish Colonies in America compelled the government to refrain from giving its approval to the seizure of the Hawaiian Islands. The tsarist government, afraid that England might seize the Spanish colonies that were ablaze with revolution, came forward verbally as a defender of Spain and her colonies, basing its position on the "principles of international law"--which did not prevent it from laying claim to a portion of the Spanish colonies in California. Still, any open seizure of quasi-independent islands in the Pacific, the priority to which had belonged to the Spaniards by right of discovery and in the eighteenth century to the English, was now out of the question.

Nesselrode, the head of the Ministry of Foreign Affairs, informed the Minister of the Interior, Kozodavlev, on February 24, 1818, that "His Majesty the Emperor has pleased to believe that the acquisition of those islands and their voluntary entry under His protection would not only bring no substantial benefit to Russia but would, on the contrary, present some very great difficulties in many respects. And, therefore, it has pleased His Majesty that while King Tomari is shown all possible friendliness and a desire to maintain amicable relations with him, the aforementioned act should not be accepted from him."[9]

It was suggested to the Russian-American Company that it adhere in its relations with the Hawaiian Islands to the rules generally accepted by other governments. At the same

time, Nesselrode pointed out that "the reports received...
from Dr. Scheffer indicate that his rash conduct has already
led to some unfortunate results."[10]

In view of the position taken by the Ministry of Foreign
Affairs, the Council of the Russian-American Company hit
on a very clever way out. Baranov, according to the Council, was ostensibly ordered to take all the necessary steps
to recall Scheffer and send him to St. Petersburg. "But
since he is a foreigner," we read in the Council's report,
"and might, after his separation from the Company, wish to
go back to the Sandwich Islands on his own and take possession of the land given to him by the other King Tomi-omi, in
which we cannot be hindered without clear violation of his
rights to freedom of action, especially when he has found out
that King Tomari has not been taken under Russia's protection
--so, should he really undertake to go back to those islands
for the time being on a foreign vessel and possibly even with
some plausible excuse, it will be incumbent upon Mr. Baranov
to make him a friend of the Company to which, otherwise,
he might be in a position to do great harm."[11]

In other words, the Company was planning to make use of
Scheffer's foreign citizenship to be able to represent all his
activities on the Hawaiian Islands as his personal actions,
for which Russia was not to be held responsible but from
which she was, at the same time, to benefit. However, the
government itself, while not in a position at the moment to
give its approval to the seizure of the Hawaiian Islands, did
not purpose to lose sight of them. The problem was one of
waiting for a more propitious moment.

As early as August 5, 1818, according to a memorandum
of the Russian-American Company, Alexander I "pleased to
recognize as necessary, in order to encourage those relations,
to bestow upon the local ruler by the name of Tomari a gold
medal on a St. Anna ribbon to be worn around the neck with
the inscription 'To the ruler of the Sandwich Islands Tomari
as a token of his friendship for the Russians.' And in addition, to present to the King as a gift a cutlass in the proper
setting and a crimson cloak with gold tassels and trimmings."
On August 8, 1818, the management was informed that
Alexander had ordered the original act of Tomari's acceptance
of Russian citizenship not to be sent back, "in the belief that
it might humiliate its owner."[12]

But only five days later, the management of the Russian-

American Company reported to the Minister of the Interior
that it had received a letter from Scheffer from Macao, dated
September 20, 1817, saying that "for political reasons the
Russians have been compelled to abandon the island of Atuwa
and that he was on the way to St. Petersburg. According to
information presented by Lieutenant Kotzebue, "Scheffer and
his contingent were driven off the island of Atuwaii by the
owner himself, Tomari, who would not even let him have the
looted Company property that was left from Bering's wrecked
vessel."[13] Advising the government of the situation, the Com
pany asked that the preparation of the gold medal and the other
gifts for Tomari be suspended.

The collapse of Scheffer's plans was brought about by the
determined opposition which the Company encountered on the
part of American merchants who had very substantial commercial interests on the Hawaiian Islands. These islands
were not only an indispensable naval base on the commercial
route to China, but also the only export center for sandalwood, which the American merchants sold in Canton at a
considerable profit.

In the beginning, the struggle with the Russian-American
Company was being waged by economic means. In addition
to the existing trading-post of the Winship Brothers on the
island of Oahu, which was under the rule of Tomi-omi, the
Americans set up a trading-post also in Tomari's territory.
In their constant endeavor to induce Tomari to establish
commercial relations with them, the Americans repurchased
from him at a high price the same merchandise which he had
already sold to the Russians. "On the island of Atuwaii
[Kauaiz]," reported the Company employees to the Governing
Board, "they [viz. the Americans.-Au.] established a trading-station in 1816, in the name of the local King Tomari
and his chiefs to counteract the Russians and the Russian-
American Company. For this purpose they bought from the
king land, plantations, and all the sandalwood that could be
found on that island, and whatever the king asked of them
they paid. In addition, they bought up provisions to last
them a whole year, such as dry tare,[14] salt, coconuts, and
so forth, which the king was really under contract to deliver
to the Russians, in return for 12,000 dollars' worth of such
merchandise as he might need."[15]

Still, the Company's aggressive policy, which found expression in the purchase of a man-of-war and in the prepa-

rations for offensive action against Tomi-omi's territory, forced the Americans to decide on a more drastic course of action.

When the armed schooner "Lady" that Scheffer had bought from its American skipper arrived at the island of Oahu in Tomi-omi's territory, where there was a Russian trading-post with a few Company men, the trading-post was found to be completely destroyed. The havoc was wrought under the direction of the "minister" himself of Tomi-omi, John Young, who had been bribed by the American merchants.

"Thus our trading-post on Ahu [Oahu] came to an end, and the lands given or sold by Tomi-omi's family reverted to their original owners," laments Scheffer in his journal.[16]

The employees of the Company were forcibly put on board the schooner and sent to Kauai. But on that island,too, the Russians enjoyed only a brief stay. In May of 1817, five boatloads of natives, with a letter, came over from Oahu, and soon after, in Scheffer's words, "a revolution broke out against the Russians."

The Americans who were in the service of the Company, including Captain Vozdvit (Wadsworth) of the Company vessel "Ilmen" that was in dock at Kauai, abandoned their ships. Together with the natives they seized Scheffer and his companions, forced them into a boat, and took them to the Company vessel "Kodiak" which was anchored in the harbor. Under the threat of having the ship shot up from under him with cannon, Scheffer was given twenty-four hours to leave the island.

But the "Kodiak" had a hole in its side and was, moreover, without provisions and water. With difficulty it made its way to the island of Oahu and there, within three miles of the harbor of Hannorua (Honolulu), it came to a stop and gave the distress signal.

The Company's employees surrendered all their guns, rifles, and even swords and spears under the threat of not being allowed into port. But even after all the arms had been surrendered, the "Kodiak" was still kept for another week outside the port limits. The captain of the American vessel "Voiles" was then in command of the port.

Scheffer managed to transfer to one of the foreign ships that called at Honolulu by accident. He made his way to Canton, and from there to St. Petersburg, where he hoped "to win new support for his rights to those islands."[17]

In the memorandum on the Sandwich Islands which "Collegi-

iate Assessor" Scheffer submitted to Alexander I upon his
arrival in Russia, we find a description of the islands "with
respect to their physical advantages...their commercial
advantages" and, finally, "with respect to their political advantages." Scheffer's arguments were subjected to scathing
criticism in the Department of Commerce and Manufacture.
His memorandum was being examined at a time when the
tsarist government really had no hope whatever of gaining a
foothold on the Hawaiian Islands.

Scheffer brought forth a plan for the establishment of vast
cotton plantations on the Hawaiian Islands. Starting with the
calculation that he had picked 3-1/2 poods of "pure paper"
from 10 sagenes of land, he figured that it was possible to
raise in the Hawaiian Islands, and then sell in China and
Japan, 4 million piasters' worth of cotton annually. In this
connection the examiner from the Department observed ironi-
cally: "Even if it is really true that cotton grows so abundantl
there, the question still remains as to who would process it
profitably and as to where it could be sold without trading
directly with China and Japan."

Scheffer's assertions that "the climate of the Sandwich Islands favors the introduction of clothmaking," that "the cotton to be grown there will supply half of Russia with goods,
and the benefit therefrom will be quite considerable," that it
is possible to breed merino sheep, grow mulberry-trees, and
cultivate silk-worms and subsequently to establish silk factories and sugar-refineries--all these met with the same skep
tical reaction. "It will be difficult for the government to establish factories on islands situated in the other hemisphere,"
was the objection raised to Scheffer's plans by an official in
the Department of Manufacture and Domestic Commerce.

However, it was not Scheffer's economic plans that met
with the most serious objections, but his political schemes
for seizing the Sandwich Islands. Taking as its point of departure Scheffer's own report that the barter trade with the
natives was wholly in the hands of the Americans, who supplied the islanders with everything, including fire-arms,
cannon, and cannon-balls, the Department of Manufacture
pointed out quite logically that the Americans, "being their
neighbors and being strong on the sea, will be most reluctant
to allow any other power that does not have a fleet in those
waters to establish such relations" with the islanders. The
Department found confirmation of this opinion in the refusal

of the English government in 1812 to bestow British citizenship upon King Tomi-omi of the island of Oahu. Scheffer's
report on the negotiations between Tomi-omi and the English
brought forth this laconic remark: "Certainly there were a
sufficent number of political reasons for the English cabinet
not to admit under its jurisdiction the ruler of the Oahu Islands."

Having been completely sidetracked, Scheffer, Doctor of
Medicine, went to Brazil in quest of new adventures. He gained
the confidence of the Emperor of Brazil, attained a high position, and even received the title of Count of Frankendahl.
He was commissioned by the Emperor to go to Europe to recruit soldiers for the Brazilian guard.

In spite of the failure of Scheffer's Hawaiian expedition,
the Russian-American Company was unwilling to abandon its
plans for expansion. Apart from Scheffer and his memoranda,
which he submitted to Alexander in person, the Directors and
the members of the Company besieged the government departments and, by means of "Opinions of the Management" which
they distributed among a number of influential officials, tried
to prove that the Hawaiian Islands should belong to the Russians.
Neither the Spaniards, nor the English, nor the Americans,
asserted the management, had any right to the islands. The
Spaniards, although they were the first to discover the Hawaiian
Islands at the beginning of the eighteenth century, could not
and would not block their seizure, for even previously they did
not claim the ownership of these islands. As for the English,
although Cook and Vancouver did put in at these islands at an
early date, and though the islands were named the "Sandwich
Islands" after Lord Sandwich, they still could lay no claim to
them, since the English government itself had refused to receive Tomi-omi into British citizenship. And, finally, the
Americans, for whom the islands constitute a convenient
transfer-point on the route to China, had no right to them in
the opinion of the Company, inasmuch as they had not officially
announced their claims. Hence the Company drew the conclusion that Russia alone had the right to the Hawaiian Islands.

While agreeing that Scheffer's proposal to send a new expedition to the Hawaiian Islands for the purpose of seizing
them by force of arms was not feasible, the management
brought forth another plan. It called for the sending of two
ships, one a warship as an escort vessel and the other loaded
with Russian fur-hunters who would settle in the Hawaiian

Islands. The cooperation of the same King Tomari was count
upon. The management maintained that the regular yearly dis
patch of one warship would be entirely suffcent to prevent any
one from laying claim to the Russian possessions in the Hawa
Islands.

But the political situation would not allow the government t
accept this plan for entrenchment on the Hawaiian Islands. Wh
it raised no objection to any attempt on the part of the Compan
to consolidate its position on the islands, the government absolutely refused to come to the aid of the Company with armec
force. The Minister of Foreign Affairs, Nesselrode, in a let
ter to the Minister of the Interior, Kozodavlev, apprised him
of the following opinion of Alexander I in this matter:

> "As for the Company's intention to attempt the establish
> ment of friendly relations with those islands, His Majesty,
> while approving such an intention and wishing the Company
> the best of success, is convinced that under a prudent ar-
> rangement and a careful selection by the management of
> agents who are discreet and cautious in their activities,
> the Company will secure by these means, and with greater
> dependability, the very same benefits and advantages that
> are anticipated from the precarious seizures of those is-
> lands."[18]

The Russian-American Company failed, however, to obtain
any degree of success by following this plan. Although it continued to send its boats to the Hawaiian Islands (in 1819 it dispatched there the newly purchased brig "Brutus," the captain
of which was supposed to meet with Tomari), it failed to obtain any substantial results. The management could only regret Scheffer's excessive enthusiasm which had led to the
loss of the Hawaiian colonies. "If that agent of Baranov's,"
writes the Director of the Company Khlebnikov, "had not gone
about it with such fervor, but had been more circumspect and
cautious, then by applying moderation and a knowledge of conditions, he would, at the start, have remained in possession
of some small plantations on Oahu and Atuwaii [Kauai], and
later might have been able, consistent with the forces at his
disposal and with prevailing conditions, to strengthen his holdings, if not actually to expand them."[19]

The seizure of the Hawaiian Islands was to be, as we have
noted, merely the first step in the consolidation of Russia's

position in the northern Pacific. The failure of this attempt, however, did not put a stop to the efforts of the Russian-American Company to realize similar plans in the northwest Atlantic.

The attempt made in the early 1820's to win possession of the island of Haiti--one of the group of the large Antilles--is intimately associated with the name of the Decembrists who were close to the Russian-American Company.

The island of Haiti, as an object of future Russian expansion, served as a topic of conversation among the Decembrists. Even in the letters that he addressed from prison to Nicholas I, the Decembrist Steingel did not fail to mention Haiti. He said: "I had the good fortune to submit to the late Emperor a plan for reviving the fleet and stimulating honest people to engage in navigation--something to which Haiti and America are beckoning us."[20]

The seizure of Haiti was to have been accomplished by the Decembrist Zavalishin, with the aid of the French General Jacques Boyer who had served in San Domingo for a long time. A participant in the march on Moscow, taken prisoner on the Berezina, Boyer made his permanent home in Russia. It is known that in 1822 General Boyer, with the permission of Alexander I, travelled to San Domingo, ostensibly in the interests of the French government. But, to judge by the testimony that Zavalishin gave before the Commission of Inquiry on October 4, 1826,[21] Boyer's trip to Haiti was of an entirely different character. According to Zavalishin, Boyer submitted to Alexander I a plan for initiating commercial intercourse with Haiti. This plan was approved, but it was pointed out that it was necessary first of all to obtain French recognition of the independence of Haiti. Only then would it be possible, without aggravating the relations with France, to attempt to secure an economic foothold on Haiti. Boyer's trip to Haiti in 1822, at the very moment that France recognized the independence of the island, was not at all in "the interest of the French government," but in the interest of the Russian government.

French recognition of the independence of Haiti coincided with a worsening of the international situation as a result of the Greek rebellion and of events in Spain. It was natural, therefore, that Russia's interest in further expansion on the American continent should flag. On the other hand, Boyer's plans seemed quite attractive to the Russian-American Com-

pany, with which he soon established close contacts. For the
Company Boyer was doubly valuable, since, in addition to possessing an excellent knowledge of the situation and of the
nature of the trade with Haiti, he knew how to maintain friend
relations with the local authorities. According to some reports, General Boyer was related to the President of the Hait
negro republic, the mulatto Boyer. [22]

It was decided to send a ship with merchandise to Haiti under the command of Zavalishin, who had returned from California. In his own words this was the plan:

> "I shall lead the ship, General Boyer will come with me
> and I shall set forth the main reasons why the republic
> should establish friendly relations with Russia. This is the
> way it should be done, so that we may not appear unduly
> hasty by sending a special agent. And while the reasons
> that I have put forward are being studied, and the cargo
> sold, I shall preoccupy myself with scientific studies on
> the Sea of the Antilles, and visit various ports both on the
> islands and on the mainland, gathering information, at the
> same time, on the subject of direct trade between Russia
> and the places I shall have visited." [23]

The expedition to Haiti was to be launched in September,
1826 but the events of December 14, 1825, interfered. It
devolved upon Mordvinov to obtain the government's permission for the expedition to Haiti, when some of the authors of
the plan were already in prison or in exile.

The question of allowing the Russian-American Company
to trade with Haiti did not come up for consideration before
the Minister of Finance until October, 1826. The conditions
on which the Company proposed to initiate that trade were the
same as those noted before. An absolute prerequisite was the
provision that "the government will give [the Company] prefer
ence over others by raising the customs duties." [24]

In spite of the fact that the Committee of Ministers found it
possible to permit the Company to make two trips to the island
of Haiti without paying any duties, the question, in view of the
protest of the Minister of Finance, was submitted for examination to the State Council.

Both in the memorandum of the Russian-American Company
and in the separate opinion expressed in January, 1827 by
Admiral N.S. Mordvinov at a session of the Committee of

Ministers, a great deal is said about the aims which the Company had set for itself when it came out with the plan for establishing commercial relations with Haiti. The Company put especial emphasis on the fact that "the island of Haiti might serve as a most convenient place for storing merchandise shipped between the countries of North and South America, and for sending it on from there to the Russian-American colonies and to the east coast of Siberia."[25] The importance of storage-places in the development of colonial trade was also emphasized in Mordvinov's separate opinion. He said: "The foundation of England's foreign trade has been the chain of storage-places that she set up for the most convenient disposal of her manufactured products."[26]

And indeed, the establishment of storage-stations was usually the first step towards the economic and occasionally the political conquest of foreign territory. It was of particular significance with respect to Haiti. Just as the Hawaiian Islands served as an indispensable transit-point between America and Asia, so Haiti was intended to become a transit-point between the Russian colonies in North America and the islands of South America and, at the same time, to bind more closely the Russian colonies to the European mainland.

Speaking of the necessity for establishing trade relations with Haiti, Mordvinov maintained that "the attempt should be made even if it involves losses, for what should be kept in mind are the benefits that will accrue to Russian commerce and to the establishment, well in advance, of reserves of all the things needed by our north-west colonies and of the goods to be bartered with the savage tribes of that region, as soon as navigation is opened up through the isthmus of Panama, the shortest route to the Pacific."[27]

Farther on Mordvinov notes: "An additional advantage is the fact that the present trip, conjectural as to time and distance," may be divided "into the two shorter trips, one from the Baltic Sea to the island of Haiti and the other from Haiti to the colonies, with special ships to be used in these two crossings; wherefore there will be less need of taking on provisions for the ships' crews, and commercial cargo could be taken on instead. The Company will derive many other benefits and advantages from shorter trips."[28]

The plans for gaining a foothold on Haiti were not only calculated on possible direct commercial benefits to the Company, but also on the advantages to be derived from the importance

which this island had attained as a result of the change in
Russia's situation after the conclusion of the convention of
1824-1825. The colony of Ross had still not become the
granary of the American colonies, and, as we have pointed
out more than once, there was no basis for hoping, in view
of the obstacles interposed by England and the United States,
that the Company would be able to expand any further on the
North American continent. The Company was fully aware that
"under the conditions in which the European trading nations
now find themselves, that nation which fails to expand its com
merce, extend the boundaries of its business activities, or
discover new markets, will inevitably lose its old business
as well, for it may be pushed out of its positions everywhere
by the vast resources of the other nations and by the abundance and the low prices of their merchandise."[29] In the
opinion of the Company, securing a foothold on Haiti was also
intended to facilitate the penetration of the Russians into the
South American countries.

All these arguments, however, were ineffectual. The rumors that the Company intended to import from Haiti free of
duty coffee, indigo, and, especially, sugar, caused great
consternation among the St. Petersburg merchants and induced them to come before the Minister of Finance, Kankrin,
with a special petition. By a majority vote the State Council
rejected the Company's request for the right duty-free trade
with Haiti. As for establishing commercial relations with
Haiti on generally recognized principles that involve the payment of all requisite duties, the Russian-American Company,
brought up, as it was, on the enjoyment of government-grante
privileges, would not dare take that step. So this plan was
not realized.

Chapter VIII

LABOR CONDITIONS IN THE RUSSIAN
COLONIES IN AMERICA

THE RUSSIAN-AMERICAN COMPANY was constantly troubled by the shortage of labor. It was, moreover, very important for the Company to create in the colonies a permanent and settled Russian population, without which the firm possession of the region would be impossible. In trying to solve this question, however, the Company encountered insurmountable obstacles. The system of serfdom which then prevailed in Russia reduced to a minimum the number of free workers in the country and was a determining factor in the policy of the government. The latter actually hampered the settlement of Russians in America, in spite of what seemed to be its natural interest in colonizing the region.

The question of attracting a permanent Russian population to the colonies was raised almost at the very beginning of the life of the Company. "Since the real strength of those regions should rest upon the number of settlements and the density of the population," wrote Rezanov in his plan for reorganizing the colonies which he submitted to the management, "it is necessary to invite more Russians over there, who, setting an example of a settled life, would tend gradually to temper the savagery of the Americans and turn them into a desirable social group." Rezanov considered it necessary to concentrate in the colonies as many free Russians as possible, and to give the same rights to the Creoles, whose numbers had been increasing from year to year, since there were scarcely any Russian women in the colonies.

It was to be a population enjoying complete independence of the Company, something in the nature of the American farmers. According to Rezanov's idea, "they were all to be assigned land for cultivation and to receive assistance from the Company in erecting their buildings."[1]

In 1808 the State Council examined the request of the Company, which had been approved by the Minister of Commerce, for permission to settle in the Russian colonies "free men,

such as merchants, townspeople, so-called state and economic peasants, those paying tribute in furs, retired soldiers,
and so forth, and serfs with the consent of the landowners."

The Company pledged itself to assume all the taxes due
from those settling in the colonies. However, this plan
aroused sharp opposition in the State Council. Fears were
entertained by the big serf-owners that the opportunity to
leave for the American colonies might appear very alluring
to too large a number of Russian subjects. The plan was regarded as an encroachment on the interests of the nobility
and was unanimously rejected. The Minister of Commerce
alone persevered in his separate opinion. The State Council
gave as the formal reason for its rejection the fact that among
the men going to the colonies there might be some who had
district and city tax obligations, or were subject to military
service--that is, state-owned peasants, townspeople, and so
forth. The State Council considered it necessary to preserve
the old order, according to which the people sent to the colonies would conclude only temporary contracts with the Company and were not to be exempted from the payment of general
taxes and obligations.

The Governing Board of the Russian-American Company
was informed that "with regard to the Russians who have their
own little houses and their families with them on Kodiak and
who have requested to be allowed to remain in the colonies
for good, no such authorization has been granted to them pur-
suant to a report to His Majesty, and they are ordered to remain there on the same basis as before, according to the
provisions of their contracts, that is, to stay for seven years,
with their passports, to pay their taxes at their domicile, and
to leave America and return home only by order of the authorities."[2]

The Company, however, invariably violated these time-
limitations on the stay of the workers on the hunting-stations.
It adduced all possible pretexts for failing to send back home
the workers who were under contract and for keeping them in
the colonies for decades on long-expired passports. The local
administration, often antagonistic to the Company because of
its "impertinent reports to the government," constantly al-
luded to this in its accounts to St. Petersburg.

The Company defended its course of action on the ground
that "it does not possess the means, when the passports of
the workers have expired, to send them out of the colonies

immediately, because they live in various places which are
widely separated from each other and where seagoing vessels do not put in every year, and when they do put in, they
do not have any new people to replace those who have been
in the colonies for a long time, and it is impossible to leave
any post unoccupied. For this reason some of the workers
decide, of their own free will, to stay another term, in order
to pay up their debts and to make some money."[3]

In 1821, when its new charter was confirmed, the Russian-
American Company succeeded in obtaining the abrogation of
those provisions that called for the return of the worker to
his home upon the expiration of the seven-year term of his
passport. According to the new regulations, the term of
the passport could be prolonged another seven years on petition of the Company, without the worker's having to appear
in person.

When the new charter of the Company was approved in
1844 for the third twenty-year period, the Governing Board
obtained a juridical formulation of its right to keep the worker
in the colonies until he has repaid his debts, which meant
practically to the end of his days. Article 12 of the new charter reads as follows:

"If those serving in the colonies desire to remain in America after the term agreed upon has expired, or if they are in
debt to the Company on their accounts, the Company cannot be
forced to send them back to Russia but may request that new
passports be issued to them prior to their departure." The
only requirement for detaining the worker in the colonies was
a statement from the Company of his indebtedness.

But while the new charter settled the question of the workers' extended stay in the colonies, the problem of attracting
settlers on a broad scale remained unsolved. The natural
solution, under the conditions of serfdom, would have been
to grant to the Company the right to acquire serfs. And the
Company did, in fact, solicit that right at the very beginning
of its existence. However, the government found it impossible
to accommodate the Company in this matter. The acquisition
of serfs was the perogative of the nobility, and a régime
founded on autocracy could not possibly grant that right to
the Company, composed as it was of merchants.

Even before, in 1835, the Company had made an attempt
to form a free estate of so-called "colonial citizens" from
among the Russian fur-hunters. These "colonial citizens"

were not to be recruited from the young Russian fur-hunters who came to the colony, but from the very old workers who, because of advanced age or physical disability, were unable to return to Russia. It was they whom it was planned to leave in the colonies for good to form an estate of "colonial citizens

By imperial decree the Company was authorized "to colonize on the Kenai coast of America, or wherever the Company should deem it proper in the interior of the Russian possessions, all hired Russian townspeople and peasants who are to be found in the American colonies in the Company's hire, who have taken Creole or Aleutian wives, and who, because of ill health, old age, a very long stay in those parts, or because they have become accustomed to the climate and the way of life there, or because, during their long absence from Russia, they have been bereft of their nearest relatives in that country, will manifest their desire to the Company to settle there in perpetuity and submit petitions in writing to that effect."[4]

In establishing such colonies for the disabled the Russian-American Company intended to profit by the right granted to it of accepting into its service the children of the colonists. In other words, the Company was planning to organize its own cadres of manpower and to form new bases for the acquisition of new areas. Actually, however, this did not bring any results, since the total number of fur-hunters colonized, who were given the pompous appellation of "colonial citizens," did not exceed, by the time the Company was being liquidated, the ridiculously low figure of 94, of whom 54 were males and 40 females.[5]

Captain Golovin, who inspected the Russian colonies in America in 1860-1861, laid special stress in his report on the fact that "the colonial citizens, in the conditions in which they find themselves at the present time, constitute a class of people that is absolutely useless and a burden to the Company as long as its exists, and will be so to the government, if the government should decide to take over the administratio: of that region. If any hope had been entertained, when the estate of 'colonial citizen' was established of colonizing the region little by little, then that hope has come to naught. Indeed, how could anyone have expected superannuated, decrepit invalids to contribute to an increase in the population? It would have been a different matter if the young people had been allowed to marry, and had been assigned land by the

Company in perpetuity; and if several families of them had
been settled together, so as to be able to guard their property
against attack from the independent natives; if, in other words,
they had been converted into something in the nature of the
American squatters."[6]

Thus the problem of creating a sedentary population in
the Russian colonies in America remained unsolved.

Yet from whom, then, and in what way did the Company
form its basic workers' cadres?

Throughout the vast expanse from Irkutsk to Okhotsk there
were found, at the end of the eighteenth and at the beginning
of the nineteenth century, though not, to be sure in large numbers, many so-called "idle people." Runaway peasants,
small merchants and artisans who had lost everything--they
were all trying to reach the distant borderlands, drawn both
by the chance to find cover from the watchful eye of the authorities and by the rumors of easy gains. It was from
among these people that the workers for the Russian colonies
in North America were recruited, both during the period
when there were still in existence a great many bankrupt
associations that were antagonistic to each other, and also
later on, when the Russian-American Company alone held
complete sway in the colonies.

Every ship leaving Okhotsk for Novoarkhangelsk--a colonial center situated on the Island of Sitka--would carry away
under contract some tens of workers of various occupations.
On the way over they worked as sailors, upon arrival in the
colonies they would invariably become either workers at
hunting-stations or artisans, and during the frequent attacks
by Indian tribes they would become soldiers.

A few days before the ships sailed for America, all the
drinking establishments in Okhotsk would be crowded with
promyshlennosty, whom the Company entertained lavishly,
without sparing expense. Here in the saloons the recruiting
agents would slip the contracts into the hands of the promyshlennosty for their signature, contracts which would bind
them for many years to come and in which, in the guise of
advance pay, was included the cost to the last penny of the
entertainment at the time of enlistment.

When the promyshlennosty were brought to the ship they
would be in an impossible state, and when they recovered,
the ship would be far out at sea, on the way to America. If,
for some reason, the boat was not sent out to sea at once,

the clothes of the contract workers were taken away and they, wrapped up in sacks, would submissively await their departure, for it was not an easy matter to seek "redress" from the Company.

Whatever the merchants' associations perpetrated somewhat warily in their day, the Russian-American Company, being as it was under His Majesty's protection, was able to do rather openly. The commandant of Kamchatka, Koshelev, outraged, apparently, by what he regarded as the inadequacy of the amount paid him by the Company for failure to see or hear what it was his duty to see and hear, draws a very lifelike picture in his report to the Tsar for the year 1803 of the arbitrary rule of the Company administration:

"The people who manage the affairs and the trade of the Company in the Irkutsk region were scarcely known among the merchants before. Not only were they no better than the others in any way, but they were in fact regarded as the worst of them all. But the moment they entered the Company service, they forgot their condition and began to entertain exaggerated opinions of themselves. While going around proclaiming everywhere His Majesty's protection, they do not allow the weaker ones to open their mouths. Placing their hope on the direct intercession of a large number of persons of quality, they have declared themselves members of the Company, or more correctly, are trying to convince people that they are members, and boast about it. They have intimidated the Irkutsk authorities into looking at their activities with closed eyes. Where their method of intimidation is ineffective, they employ bribery with dazzling effect."[7]

During the period when the Company was engaged in recruiting new workers for the colonies, the Okhotsk authorities preferred to do nothing. The same Koshelev writes as follows:

"The workers, during the hiring out to the Company and the division of the stuff brought in from the islands were given to drink in a way that was an insult to the human race, and the police did not find itself in a position to put an end to the daily drinking and rowdyism."[8]

This, then, was the manner in which workers were being

recruited and sent to the colonies in America. And many
years later, these workers, almost wholly disabled, wearing
the same rags they had on their back when they went to America, would be returning to their homeland utterly disillusioned.
Every one of them had, through hard, back-breaking labor,
earned a considerable sum of money in the course of his
stay in the colonies. But the result of the deductions for the
merchandise purchased at high prices in the Company store,
"His Majesty's taxes," the debts paid off for them by the Company, and, finally, of open deceit and cheating, was that the
many years' labor invested by the workers at hunting-stations
were not always enough even to pay off the debts shown on
their accounts.

In the early stages of its activity the Russian-American
Company continued in full the system of settling the workers'
accounts that had prevailed during the period when a great
number of associations of various kinds were active in the
colonies. The greater part of the workers received their
pay not in money but in furs. All the peltry was divided into
a definite number of parts, depending upon the number of
workers, then each part was divided equally between the
workers and the Company. The worker received a so-called
"half-share." It was, in effect, a system based on a piece-
wage, with the pay not in money, but in kind. The right of
the workers, however, to one half of the furs procured in
the colonies was actually only a formal right; there were
many ways in which the Company was able to appropriate
all the furs secured by the workmen. These methods were
so effective that only a small minority of the workmen succeeded in returning from the colonies with a portion of the
"half-share" credited to their account. In the first place,
the Company tried to select for work in the colonies persons
who were burdened with debts. When such a worker entered
the service, the Company paid off all his debts, including the
money spent on the "farewell"drinking. Thus, even before
he ever arrived at the colony, he was already under considerable financial obligation to the Company.

The worker at the hunting-stations was under obligation
to liquidate this debt to the Company in kind, that is by leaving with it a portion of the"half-share" credited to him--at a
very low evaluation, by the way, which did not at all corres-
pond to the market-value of the furs. In this way a certain
portion of the "half-share" came into the hands of the Com-

pany. Another method of appropriating the "half-share" was by using the credit which the Company gave the workers in its shops.

According to the provisions of the agreement with the recruited workers, they were supposed "beginning with the managers of the Company during the time of their labor at the hunting-posts to receive their maintenance and subsistence wholly from the products of their own labor." Thus all the workers had to live in the colonies at their own expense. But since they could have only fish as "the products of their own labor" in the colonies, they were naturally compelled to turn to the Company shops and stores not only for clothing but also for foodstuffs. This was the more necessary since they were prohibited from making purchases from foreign merchants. A clause had prudently been inserted in the contract which empowered the Company to collect "twice the Okhotsk prices" on all merchandise sent into the colonies over and above the quantity needed for the organization of the post. Actually, however, as we shall show later, the prices in the Company stores were not twice but many times in excess of those prevailing in Okhotsk. The workers were being robbed, then, in two ways, since, along with the raised prices on the merchandise, the deductions for them in terms of furs were calculated according to a rate established by the Company--and that was considerably below the market-price.

A certain portion of the very much reduced "half-share" accrued to the Company in the form of fines. The contract read as follows:

"If anyone is disobedient, or arrogant, or refractory, or, having gotten drunk, commits impertinences and crimes not for the first time, the managers of the Company have the right to impose a fine upon such persons, after a detailed report, according to the law, on the guilt of the culprit."[9] According to the contract, one of the most serious crimes in the colonies was the purchase of spirits from foreign merchants and the home distillation of liquor. Article II of the contract reads as follows:

"Everyone in the service of the Company is forbidden, under any pretext whatsoever, to distill liquor from herbs, roots, berries, Company grain, and so forth; or to buy or barter liquor from visiting foreigners and trade in it on Company premises, to make loans or give money to each

other for drinking purposes, then drink the liquor or use it
in any way at all."[10] Those committing such crimes lost all
their earnings and were immediately exiled to Okhotsk. The
workers on the hunting-posts were expected to buy their liquor
only in Company stores.

At first the liquor trade in the colonies was the monopoly
of the small companies, then it came under the Russian-
American Company. The liquor would "pick up" the last bits
of the "half-share" which, through some lucky circumstance,
the worker had managed to put away. The Company was very
solicitous of this source of income. In one of his letters to
Shelikhov's widow, Baranov told with perfect candor about
the important role that liquor played during the time that the
income from the hunting-stations was being divided up among
the workers:

"Here there is no need of gold, silver, or precious
stones. Among the provisions there is only one which is
more expensive and more important, as you yourself
know who have lived here at the proper time. Next to
articles of clothing and footwear liquor is dearer to the
workers than anything else in the world. And if it is a
question of getting people into debt, just send over some
[liquor] and have it sold in moderation when necessary,
especially at times when the income is being divided up,
and you will see how much of the income will be passed
out and how many people will get into debt."[11]

Finally, in the case of those promyshlennosty who, after
all their fines and indebtedness to the Company for goods
bought at three times their price had been deducted, still
had something left of their "half-share," the administration
of the Company did not hesitate to employ strongarm methods.
One of these cases is recorded in the testimony of Verigin,
who had taken part in the uprising of the workers on Sitka in
1809--and this was not the only case. The Company owed
him 574 rubles, but shortly before his departure from the
colonies, he was called into the office where he was asked
to sign a paper that the Company owed him only 300 rubles.
At the same time he was informed that if he refused to sign,
he would be reported to the Governor of the Colonies, Baranov, who "will not fail to supply him with a ticket home, that
is to say, will punish him with a cat-o'-nine tails or gaskets,

fearing which he put his signature below the item in the book.

If, after they had stayed in the colonies for many years, some few lucky ones did succeed in returning home with the right to collect certain sums from the Company, their chance for collecting those amounts were practically nonexistent. The settlement of the accounts with the workers who had returned from the colonies dragged on for several years, and was rarely decided in favor of the worker. According to the provisions of the contract, the definitive settlement was to be worked out in Okhotsk, immediately upon the worker's arriva from the colonies. But when he came into the Okhotsk office, the new arrival would usually be asked to wait a little, since the data for the settlement had ostensibly not arrived from the colonies. While retaining the final account, the Okhotsk office would force the workers to perform certain tasks for the Company, and by supplying them with certain necessities, would again involve them in debts to the Company.

One of the reports to St. Petersburg of the Okhotsk administration in 1815 has this to say about the above machinations:

"The Company office is detaining the workers of the hunting-posts in Okhotsk absolutely against their wishes, under the pretext that it has to work out their statements of accounts. It is doing it in order to force them, by dragging out the final accounts with the workers who, in the meantime, are engaged in various tasks for the Company, to take on credit, against their will, more of the Company's merchandise and provisions, and then, when their indebtedness has been considerably increased, compel them to go on a sea voyage. As proof of this we may adduce the fact that some workers who returned from the islands in 1807 have since been waiting for their accounts from the office, but to date [i.e., 1815.-Au.] have not received them, and have been compelled all that time to take on credit provisions and other things from the office, and have hence been obliged to proceed, for the time being to America in order to work out their indebtedness."[13]

This cynical method of cheating and then enslaving the workers became so intrenched in the practice of the Russian-American Company that it even gave rise to a special association in Siberia which bought up the Company's obligations.

Voinov, Secretary to the Governor, and Golenitsky, a Tiumen merchant, would buy up the Company's obligations at half-price from the workers as they returned from America, and would then collect payment for them at their face value, for their own benefit, of course. But even these enterprising business-men failed in their attempt to wrest some money from the Company, although they lodged countless complaints against it in all possible instances.

Somewhat more fortunate was Tolstopyatov, a merchant of the First Order from Yenisei, who bought up the right to the "half-share" from the relatives of the workers who had died in the colonies. After his lawsuit had dragged through various courts, where he had to show that most of the "bor-rowings" were added to the workers' accounts after their death and that they, "being dead, could not borrow any more," the case was settled "by agreement, to the satisfaction of both parties." As a result, Tolstopyatov, according to his own testimony, received less than was due him by more than 52,000 rubles and about 11,000 fewer sealskins. Not only were the individual workers no match for the Company, but even the enterprising Siberian merchants and the expert legal pettifoggers came out second best in their legal en-counter with that organization.

It was a very different story, however, when the debtor happened to be one of the workers. When a worker owed the Company a certain amount, then, in the words of the local administration, "the office makes up his accounts (in spite of the fact that it has received no such accounts from Amer-ica) without the slightest delay and, presenting them to the authorities for collection, demands either that it be paid or that the debtor be sent on an ocean voyage, in spite of the fact that the worker, not considering himself in debt, does not wish to remain in the service of the Company for any amount."[14]

It is clear, then, that once a worker on the hunting-posts fell into the Company's paws, he was unable to free himself to the end of his days.

Not unintentionally did the Russian-American Company, even after the colonies passed into its hands, preserve for a time the "half-share" as the chief method for paying the workers. While thus stimulating them in their work, the Company also made the colonies more attractive to them. But it should be pointed out that the payment of the "half-

share" also had a number of very rral disadvantages for the
Company. Notwithstanding the system of "pumping out" of
the workers the furs that were rightfully theirs, a part of
the peltry, though a very insignificant one, did remain in
their possession, and finding its way to the Siberian market,
sold at a lower price than the Company furs. The desire of
the workers to sell the furs they had left after the division,
impelled them to return to the mother country as fast as
possible, since the furs soon lost their value because of the
primitive processing they had undergone.

At the same time the "half-share" system gave the worker
some right to meddle with the Company's affairs and even to
demand an accounting. That this factor was of some importance may be gathered from the "solemn" oration that Baranov delivered to the workers on Kodiak. He began by express
ing his gratitude for the fine order in which he found the colony, but finished quite unexpectedly with these words:

> "Not a month passes without some show of animosity
> and affrontery to your fellow-workers and to the authori-
> ties; some disparagement of the administrators appears
> at every step. This is in spite of the fact that more than one
> of you did nothing in his home village except feed the swine
> or frequent the saloon, yet here he has become a pene-
> trating intellect, a judge of everything, a high-minded
> minister."[15]

The Company took the first step towards the abolition of
the "half-share" in 1803. The payment of the "half-share"
was henceforth made not in furs but in money, by calculating
the value of the processed skins according to a set rate. This
innovation tended to aggravate even further the situation of
the workers, since the Company assessed the peltry many
times below the market value. The Company was now to
keep the full difference between the market value of the furs
and the assessed value, which, small though it was, used to
accrue to the worker--if he managed to take a few skins out
of the colony.

"The management of the Company," wrote Pestel, Governor-General of Siberia, to the Minister of the Interior,"when
it drew up the master-contract for all the workers in its
hunting-stations--a contract which was not endorsed by the
home government--stipulated, strictly on its own responsi-

bility, that not one worker, when on a hunting expedition, would be allowed to sell one animal falling to his share to strangers outside of the Company, but should deliver it to the Company at the price set by it, which is to say, at the lowest and most disadvantageous price to the hunter. But on the other hand, whenever the poor people take something they need for themselves, they are compelled to pay the amount that the head of the Company will arbitrarily set. Wherefore these hunters always find themselves between two extremes, and, running into debt from time to time, they accumulate so many obligations that they cannot pay them back in a lifetime."[16]

This abolition of the payment of the "half-share" in kind was only the first step towards the complete liquidation of that kind of payment. As early as 1805 Rezanov, during his stay in the colonies, brought up the question of putting the workers on a firm wage basis. In his letter of instructions to the Governor of the colony, Baranov, Rezanov noted that the "half-share" system was the main obstacle in the way of attracting Russian workers to the colonies. He wrote that "fewer than 400 people or shares constitute at the present time our whole strength in America. Upon this small number has devolved the duty of keeping whole tribes in submission, help with construction, and, at the same time, though in the form of a very weak cordon, guard as well as possible the whole stretch of the American coast. As a reward for their labor, they receive, out of the animals procured, half a share or portion, and the artisans receive a whole share. The number of people is extremely inadequate, in view of the vastness of the establishment and interferes with our success; and it will be inexpedient both for the Company and for themselves to increase their number on that basis; inasmuch as the profits from hunting will become so scanty as to make it burdensome for both classes.

In view of all this, workers on the hunting-stations themselves remain in a state of uncertainty until the very end of the four-year period, when the division takes place, because they do not know their lot and are apprehensive that, instead of the expected profits, they may easily have been toiling for nothing; for the Company, in expanding its operations, must look for profit in trade in which only the stockholders take part and not the hunting-station workers. Consequently, it becomes self-evident that the situation of these workers cannot long be allowed to continue on the present basis. I believe, Rezanov concludes his thought, "that the number of 'half-shar should gradually be reduced, and that in time all the profits from the portions should go to the Company, while the people should everywhere be employed on a salary basis."[17]

The Company, however, would not stand the hazard of adopting such a measure at once, for fear of losing even those inconsiderable cadres of workers that were to be found in the colonies. The payment of the "half-share" in money continue therefore, down to 1815.

A number of changes were introduced in the administration of the colonies in 1817, upon the arrival in Novoarkhangelsk o the fourth round-the-world expedition under the command of Lieutenant-Captain Hagemeister. He replaced as governor of the colony the senile Baranov, whose methods of administrati tended more and more to discredit the Governing Board. The activities of this Kargopol merchant had gained very wide note riety through the continual visits of foreign merchants to the colonies and the frequent calls of Russian men-of-war. At that very period, when the Company did not grow weary of priding itself on every occasion on the "prosperity" that the natives enjoyed in the Russian colonies, the administration decided to remove the one man who, for more than a score of years, instilled, with iron and blood, into the consciousness of the natives and the hunting-station workers the incontrover tible truth that they were born, that they lived and that they died for the profits accruing to the Russian-American Compar

Not receding one step from Baranov's basic principle--not to disdain anything that might bring profit--the Company now demanded that all this be clothed in a more "European" form. There began the expulsion of the remnants of the merchant class, and, along with that, the complete liquidation of the "half-share." By order of Hagemeister of February, 1818, the pay of the workers in the colonies, beginning with the last general account in 1815, was to be figured in terms of money. Every worker was to receive 300 rubles in paper-money annually. According to the Commissioner of the Company, Khlebnikov, the average earnings of a worker under the old system of pay reached 1,561 rubles for a four-year period. Now the same worker would receive 1,200 rubles for the sam period. It is evident, then, that the introduction of the system of payment in money brought about a reduction in the worker's wages of more than 20 per cent.

The new pay system gave rise to some agitation among
the workers on the hunting-posts. As Khlebnikov observes,
"the workers, and even many belonging to other classes, find
it more seductive to live on the hope of an unknown future than
to be satisfied with a definite, permanent arrangement."[18]
Hagemeister was compelled to make certain concessions,
such as giving every worker one pood of flour a month, in
addition to his regular wages.

Under the new pay system the hunting-station workers no
longer had any opportunity of leaving the colonies. The longer
a man worked, the more debts he accumulated. A very curious document has been presented from the pen of the governor
of the Russian colonies in America, which serves to illustrate
by figures the condition of slavery in which the workers of the
colonies were kept to all intents and purposes. In 1834 the
governor paid a visit to the colony of Ross in California. In
his report to the Governing Board he had something to say
about the condition of the workers. In California the condition
of the Company workers was a little better than in the other
colonies. Here the annual wage was 350 rubles and, in addition to the monthly pood of flour, every worker received a
pound of meat a day. In order to acquaint himself with the
condition of the hunting-station workers the governor calculated the credit that one of the workers received in the colony store in the course of one year. A certain Vasily Permitin,
on whom a wife and five children depended for subsistence,
during 1832 bought on credit in the colony store, on account
of his annual salary of 350 rubles, various articles to the
amount of 728.28 rubles, or more than twice his earnings.
"The list, enclosed as a sample, of the articles and provisions purchased by Permitin shows," wrote the governor
of the colonies to the Governing Board, "that he had purchased
nothing that he did not need. Consequently one cannot but
acknowledge that it is impossible for these people to maintain
themselves on a salary of only 350 rubles a year."[19]

The merchandise sold in the colony stores was not only
expensive but also of exceedingly poor quality. This, in turn,
had a bearing upon the increase in the quantity of goods that
the workers bought on credit. Kostlivtsov, who made a tour
of inspection of the Russian colonies in 1860-1861, reports
that "the poor quality of the ready-made clothes and shoes
for the common people is beyond belief; boots will last only
a few days and a cloth garment will wear out in about two

months. How much, then, does a worker have to spend on
clothes, who receives between 300 and 350 rubles in paper-
money a year, when the price of a cloth outer garment (sail-
or's pea-jacket and trousers) runs to from 20 to 30 rubles,
and boots cost 10 rubles? He will hardly have enough to dres
not counting shirts, underwear, gloves, caps, which he also
needs to buy."[20]

The Company stores ate up all of the worker's earnings.
It was impossible to do without these stores, since the wages
were paid out not in money but in Company stamps. The
foreign merchants would not, of course, accept these stamps
and the natives could not use them in the Company shops, because it would at once come out that they had come into possession of these stamps through some illicit traffic with one
of the employees of the Company, or one of the hunting-post
workers. The Company stamps that were received as a part
of the salary could be used only in the Company stores, and,
considering the permanent state of indebtedness of the worke
it is clear that it was quite possible to avoid exchanging the
stamps for government notes even when the account was fina.
settled with those departing from the colonies.

During the decade from 1816, when the issuance of the
stamps was first authorized, to 1826, the Russian-American
Company issued stamps to the value of 42,000 rubles, in
denominations from 10 kopecks to 10 rubles, In 1826 the
Company was authorized to issue more stamps to the value o:
30,000 rubles, in order to exchange those that had become to
worn. Finally, in 1834 the Company was again allowed to
print a supplementary issue of stamps to the amount of 30,00
rubles. Inasmuch as there was no government control over
the immobilization of the stamps that had become worthless
and over their replacement by new stamps, the was was open
to the administration of the Company to pay all its colonial
expenses in stamps that had no security whatsoever behind
them. The government regarded the issuance of the stamps
as a private affair of the Company, granting the administrati
complete freedom of action in this matter. When the questio:
of a new issue of stamps was brought up to a session of the
Committee of Ministers in 1826, "the Committee, taking into
consideration the fact that the use of stamps in our American
colonies in place of current money depends entirely upon the
confidence that the local inhabitants place in the Russian-
American Company, has proposed that the Minister of Financ

be asked to inform the administration of the Company that
the government is not opposed to the replacement of stamps
used there by new ones, but does not consider it necessary
to give its formal approval of the transaction and will not
stand surety for it in any way."[21]

The stamp system served as an additional source of income for the Company and as one more device for the unrestrained exploitation of the workers. Deceived even while
they were being recruited, systematically cheated when
their accounts were being settled, and having lost all hope
of ever breaking loose from their servitude to the Company,
the workers on the hunting-stations were living in the colonies under monstrous conditions that doomed them to ruin
and extinction.

The famous traveler Captain Krusenstern writes that the
workers "for scarcity of dwellings...are living for the greater
part in mud-huts, that is to say, in very unhealthy quarters
below the ground, and are suffering from the same lack of
wholesome food as one does at sea. Often they do not even
have salt, that indispensable condiment for our viands. Although they are given bread, it is only in very small quantities, due to the difficulties in transportation. The only item
of which there is no scarcity is vodka."[22]

This finds confirmation in memoirs of another member of
Krusenstern's expedition, the physician Langsdorf, who took
notice of the extremely high mortality among the workers on
the hunting-posts. He had an opportunity to look after one
group of such workers who arrived in the colony in late
autumn. "Of the one hundred and fifty young and healthy
people that had been selected in various places and sent over
to Sitka," writes Langsdorf, "eight had died by February and
more than sixty were laid up in bed, in their barracks. Those
buildings had no ovens, no fire-places, and the only source
of heat were the contaminated exhalations of a host of people,
who had no conception of cleanliness. On coming home in the
evening drenched to the skin, the workers lie down in their
wet clothes and sheepskin coats or hang them up for drying
in their sleeping-rooms. Those who have scurvy are forced
to stand guard and patrol the premises as long as they can
stand on their legs and do not collapse utterly with the cold,
the dampness, and general exhaustion."[23]

The workers on the hunting-stations were not given any
opportunity to complain of their miserable situation, to say

nothing of the fact that is was absolutely futile to lodge a com
plaint against the all-powerful Company. There were no gov
ernment officials in the colonies. A worker could leave the
colonies only when the Company itself wanted to take him out
of there; all the ships belonged to the Company. As for the
transmission of a complaint through a third person, that cam
under the head of a petition composed by common effort, and
the contract read that "whoever initiates a petition or a reque
or a denunciation by common effort or by conspiracy, that
person is to be put under arrest and handed over to the court
of law." True, as a rule it did not come to "handing the person over to the court of law." Wishing to avoid publicity, the
administration of the Company preferred to take care of the
complainants on the spot.

There were instances of unrest among workers. Their
indignation expressed itself not only in their refusal to take
orders from the administration and in presenting it with lists
of demands, but also in attempts to dispose of the colonial
authorities altogether. In some cases these uprisings were
preceded by a secret agreement among the workers and by
the election of leaders.

As early as 1795, prior to the formation of the Russian-
American Company, large-scale disturbances took place on
the concessions of the Shelikhov-Golikov Company. "The
hunting-station workers were highly agitated, and the winter
was a most turbulent one," wrote Baranov from the colonies
to Shelikhov about the winter of 1794-95. The workers refuse
to take orders from the administration of the Company. "As
for the uprising of the settlers," reported Baranov, "they
have shown their true colors here, too, at the very beginning
They have completely stopped obeying your Ivan Grigoryevich
have tried to carry out some insolent and high-handed act,
and to interfere with the exchange of furs with the foreigners
threatening Mr. Polomoshnov that they would break up the
store, and so forth, loudly blaming you for their ostensibly
having been cheated in their expectations of the usual handing
out of provisions, and asserting that none, or very little is
being handed out now, and that they have not become accustomed to the food provided while traveling."[25]

Soon after, in a letter to Count Zubov, Shelikhov's wife
reported that "the hunting-station workers have hatched a
conspiracy to the effect that when the guns are issued to them
for protection against the savages and while they are proceed

to the mainland by boat, they will take possession of the boat
and set out for the Kuriles, and they have chosen one among
them as navigator. They have managed to put away three
guns and supplies. But the Company manager, having discovered their conspiracy, punished the three leading mis-
creants with gaskets, in accordance with the instructions set
down in the orders of the local commander-in-chief, and then
sent them away to different artels, to join the hunting-station
workers. And thus he liquidated their undertaking."[26]

During the life of the Russian-American Company the most
serious disturbances among the workers took place on Sitka
in 1809. At the head of the administration of the colony at
that time was the same Baranov, who instituted a real prison
régime in the colonies. For the slightest infraction of the
rules the workers were punished with gaskets, cats-o'-nine-
tails, or were deported for a term of several years to some
thinly populated island where no provisions of any kind were
ever delivered. Baranov's cruelty in his relations with the
native population and with the Russian workers reached truly
monstrous dimensions. According to Captain Golovnin, who
visited the colonies in 1818, Baranov made himself famous,
as it were, "by his long sojourn among the savages, and
even more so by the fact that instead of making them more
enlightened he became wild himself and sank to a level below
that of the savage."[27]

To rid themselves of Baranov, to go away from the hateful
colonies somewhere to some unknown island and to start a
new life there, these were the bright perspectives which
lured a group of workers into preparing the uprising. In the
organization and the plan of the uprising may be detected the
influence of the famous uprising of 1771 on Kamchatka under
the leadership of Benyevsky, who seized the peninsula and,
with a group of workers belonging to the merchant Kholodilov,
started out on a government vessel in search of new lands.

In 1809 a secret organization in the manner of a Cossacks'
circle sprang up among the workers on Sitka. At its head,
temporarily, was a duly elected "cornet",[28] who was later
to be replaced by a hetman. The elections were held at a
meeting of a group of workers in the woods, a good distance
from the fortress. When the question arose as to "who would
be in command of them and direct the revolution," they decided
to wait with the election of a hetman for the return of the other
conspirators who were then busy on the posts, and elected a

"cornet" for the time being. The man chosen was "Ivan Pop‹
one of the original instigators, who, instead of the seamly
title of hetman, was given that of cornet--a title highly honor
among the Cossack troops of the Don."[29]

The rebellion of August Benyevsky served as a constant
topic of conversation among the workers. Almost all of thos‹
who were subsequently prosecuted in this case testified that,
in talks among themselves, "what was most frequently discussed and vehemently approved was the villainous and trai-
torous revolution that had been perpetrated in Kamchatka.
This would be accompanied by an exposition of how the commander, Captain Nilov, was the first to be killed, how the
treasury was robbed as well as many private estates, how
the rebels seized Kholodilov's ship and went off--that fellow
August with his accomplices, the clerk Chuloshnikov and
trappers belonging to the aforesaid company--on a trip to the
island, how they spent the winter there, and so forth, and
how, finally, they themselves intended to follow the same
course as the best open to them."[30]

It was planned to launch the revolt by killing Baranov and
the officials close to him. "They intended first of all to take
his--Baranov's--life," testified one of the hunting-station
workers by the name of Sidorov, "then to do the same to the
officers, or merely tie them up, and to kill, without exceptio
the most honored of the officials who were especially attache
to him, to Baranov, and who had been rewarded with medals
in recognition of their services." The burning hate for the
officials who had been rewarded with various tokens of distin‹
tion and who occupied minor positions of authority in the colonies was very well founded. For it was these petty officials
who constituted that top layer of the bureaucracy in which the
company found its main support in its exploitation and oppres
sion of the workers. It is noteworthy that the rebels intende‹
to mete out the same punishment to the higher circles of the
native population whom the Company had also bribed to do its
bidding. It was planned, with respect to the "honorable" natives, the "toyons," or the chieftains, "to kill those who wou
stand in the way, or to tie them up and put them away in a
convenient place."[31]

There was a good deal in these plans that smacked of the
naively fanciful. This was especially manifest during the
discussion over the destination of the vessel that was to be
seized. It was decided that "as soon as the business at hand

had been finished, the ship would be loaded and they would
set out for the Philipisian [i.e., Philippine.-Tr.] Islands,
discovered, as the story goes, by Naplavkov on the other
side of the equator, and beyond Turkey in the fourth part of
the world there are plenty of places and no people at all, and
there is a strait that is one hundred versts wide beyond which
live the negroes." This longing to go off to some place where
it would be possible to live "at one's own free will,"[32] was
shared by all the participants in the plot.

The treachery of one of the participants helped Baranov to
find out about the planned insurrection. The investigation
dragged on for eight years. At first it was conducted by Baranov himself, who subjected the prisoners to refined and varied
forms of torture. A few years later, when the accused were
brought to Okhotsk, the case passed into the hands of justice.
There and then it became clear to the Governing Board of
the Company that it was a serious blunder to bring over the
workers to stand trial in the mother country. At the judicial
examination there came to light the monstrous abuses of the
colonial administration, which, if they had been made public,
would have threatened the Company with a major scandal.
Khlebnikov, the Commissioner of the Company in Kamchatka,
wrote to the Directors when the prisoners arrived that if they
"should be tried in open court, they might reveal certain
facts that would be bound to bring harm and disgrace upon the
Company."[33] Khlebnikov suggested that it would be best "to
bury the whole affair in oblivion." But it was impossible to
stop the case, and the administration exerted all its energy
to prevent the discreditable material which had been collected
as a result of the investigation from being publicized; or, as
Captain Golovnin says in his "Remarks on Russian America,"
to see to it that the workers on the hunting-stations are prosecuted, while the Company's sins are being covered up."[34]

Reports of the disturbances on Sitka reached the Committee of Ministers which proposed to the Senate that it carry
out its own decision, not only in the matter of the imprisoned
workers but also "that it should make a decision with regard
to the cruel treatment of the Company workers at the hands
of the Governor of the American islands, Baranov."[35]

The case was heard in the Senate from April to May 1817,
or eight years after the plot had been discovered. Here, too,
the Company succeeded in turning the affair to its own advantage. While it sentenced those of the defendants who had re-

mained alive during the intervening years to various terms
of imprisonment, the Senate "did not find" in the documents
of the investigation any evidence against Baranov, inasmuch
as the accusations against him emanated from "criminals"
who had already been convicted as plotters and who were,
consequently, the sort of people "in whom the law does not
allow to place any credence."

By imperial decree a naval officer was yet to be sent to
the colonies to make an investigation. The affair dragged,
however, until the report came that the very old Baranov had
died. Then the Senate decided "that it is no longer possible,
because of Baranov's death, to carry out the investigation
of his activities as ordered by His Majesty."[36]

Chapter IX

THE NATIVE POPULATION IN THE RUSSIAN
COLONIES IN NORTH AMERICA

IN ITS REPORTS, the Company was wont to divide the native population of the North American colonies into three categories; "actually dependent," "semi-dependent," and "completely independent."

Among the "actually dependent" the administration of the Company included, first, the Aleuts who inhabited the Aleutians and whom the Company colonized throughout the territory of the numerous islands it occupied, and secondly, in all probability, the Eskimos who pass as Aleuts in the Company's documents. Among the "semi-independent" were comprised first the so-called Kenai people who inhabited the coast near the Kenai Peninsula, and who were a branch of the numerous groups of Atabasks, and secondly, other Atabask tribes living in the interior of Alaska. As to the Tlinket, they were regarded as "not completely independent."

In reality, the last two categories might well be considered "completely independent," and it was only the Aleuts and Eskimos who experienced to the fullest extent the whole weight of colonial oppression.

Simpson, the Director of the Hudson Bay Company, who visited the Russian colonies in America in 1842, noted in his memoirs that the number of Aleuts was barely one tenth of the number of natives who were there when the Russians captured the area. "There is nothing mysterious about it," wrote Simpson, "it happened in the wake of privation and oppression. Alone the natural wealth of the country served as an instrument for its impoverishment; its fur-seals and otters brought about its ruin, just as sandalwood was the ruin of the people of the Sandwich Islands and silver mines of the Indians of Spanish America."[1]

In the hunting of sea-otters, the most valuable variety of fur-bearing animals, no one could take the place of the Aleuts. Even many years later, almost on the eve of the liquidation of the Russian-American Company, the Governing Board observed that "neither the negro of Guinea nor the Chinese coolie nor the European worker can take the place of the Aleut in the art and practice of hunting."[2]

Decades of grievous exploitation and the most cruel chastisement of the rebellious were necessary to reduce a freedom-loving people to slavery. S.S. Shashkov explains precisely on these grounds the mass murders of the natives during the first period of the Russian conquest:

"What spurred on the fur-hunters to exterminate the 'strangers' was not the mere desire for loot and certainly not the zeal for the government's interests but more subtle considerations. The Aleuts know excellently well how to process sea-otters, something the Russians have not mastered to this day, and knew nothing about at all in thos days. It was necessary for the fur-hunters to enslave the Aleuts and make laborers out of them; but it was impossible to do this, in view of the large native population that would always rise up in mutiny and receive the Russians arms in hand. It was necessary to exterminate the greater part of these recalcitrants, so that the rest might inevitably become Russian serfs."[3]

This also fully applies to the Eskimos. As early as 1784, when Shelikhov was on Kodiak, he ordered all the captured "males to be beaten up and taken away to the tundra and kille with spears," which was indeed done.[4] No wonder that a few years later Baranov felt relatively safe on Kodiak. A naval officer who visited the Russian colonies in America describes the methods Baranov used in fighting the Aleuts and the Eskimos in the following manner:

"Woe to those who resisted him: he destroyed them without pity, deported them to desert islands, took away all their means of getting together, and mixed up their tribes, so they would be unable to plot any evil against the Russians. The savages dreaded him; they looked upon him as a terror from heaven and, being unable to oppose him, were forced to become his slaves and forget their former freedom which they had but recently enjoyed without any restraint."[5]

The erstwhile free natives became the slaves of the small

hunting companies, and a little later of the Russian-American
Company. "The Russians are coming to America and to our
Fox Islands and Andreanof Islands to hunt sea and land animals,"
wrote the Aleuts in 1799 in one of their letters of grievance to
Paul I against the Russian fur-hunters. "We receive them in
friendly fashion, but they act like barbarians with us. They
seize our wives and children as hostages, they send us early
in the spring, against our will, five hundred versts away to
hunt otters, and they keep us there until fall, and at home
they leave the lame, the sick, the blind, and these, too, they
force to process fish for the Company and to do other Company work without receiving any pay, and, since the fields
have not been sown, they are dying of hunger. The remaining
women are sent out on Company labor and are beaten to death.
They are removed by force to desert islands, and the children
are taken away from those who walk with crutches, and there
is no one to feed them."[6]

Exhaustive data on the way the hunting companies ruled the
Aleuts were brought back by I.I. Billings from his trip, and
by other navigators. All the information was published more
than once and came to the attention of the higher administration.
Now and again orders were issued calling for a more humane
treatment of the Aleuts, but since no control measures were
ever adopted, the situation remained unchanged. The illusions
that the Aleuts nourished every time a government expedition
visited the colonies, that government aid might be forthcoming,
were of short duration. Thus, in 1791, Baranov wrote to
Shelikhov:

"Billings has apparently told them many things. They
have been spoiled, and, since bringing in the food involves
great difficulties, they demand to be paid for every step
they make. I was compelled, first of all, to work on their
prejudices. Not the slightest harm has been done to them,
but they have been brought back to obedience."[7]

On one occasion the Aleuts even managed to get an audience
with Paul I himself. That was shortly before the franchise of
the Russian-American Company was approved, and when the
competition among the rival companies in the colonies was
especially intense.
The merchant Kiselev, who was gradually being pushed
out of the islands by the company of Shelikhov's heirs, decided

to make use of the Aleuts in his contest with his rival. His
plan was a very simple one. The Aleuts, whom he was to
bring to St. Petersburg, were to tell Paul how they were being exploited by the merchants, especially by Shelikhov's
company, and, by contrast, put his company in a very favorable light for the way it treated the Aleuts. The fact that
Kiselev helped the complainants to make their way out of the
islands was to serve as proof of his being their protector.

And so in the summer of 1796 six Aleuts together with the
priest Makary secretly left Unalaska and proceeded to St.
Petersburg with a letter of grievance, signed by all the
Aleut chieftains. They spent the winter in the Kuriles. Here
one of the Aleuts died, and two fell ill and were forced to turn
back. Finally, in May, 1798, almost two years after they had
left the Aleutians, two of the Aleuts (the third died in Moscow)
arrived in the capital.

The Aleuts were given a friendly welcome, but their audience with the Tsar did not bring any positive results. Paul's
ukase of June 4, 1798, ordered "the Aleuts who have come...
here to be allowed to return home, after they have been
rewarded with raiments proper to their custom."

The letter of grievance submitted by the Aleuts bore no
fruit, but the governor of Irkutsk was ordered "to go into
the circumstances presented to him and to try to settle everything, so as to bring about mutual satisfaction [i.e., between
the Aleuts and the merchants.-Au.] and to eliminate abuses."

Priest Makary, who had come with the Aleuts, was to be
punished for his wilful absentation from the islands by doing
penance according to the tenets of the Church. Only after
much trouble was he forgiven "his action, out of Imperial
indulgence to the entreaty of the Aleuts."

The Aleuts went back to their homeland, escorted by a
Senate courier. In January 1799 the two Aleuts reached
Irkutsk where they remained to spend the winter. And here,
in Irkutsk, a singular thing happened. Almost on the eve of
their departure from Irkutsk, the two Aleuts died suddenly.
Nikolay Lukanin died on March 6, and Nikifor Svinin on the
16th.

It is beyond debate that, if these delegates had returned
home, it would have been very embarrassing to the company
of Shelikhov's heirs. By that time the question of organizing
a monopolistic Russian-American Company had been definitiv
decided, the battle among the rivaling merchants was over,

and the return of the delegates with the news that it was useless to complain against the abuses might have provoked the
natural indignation of the natives.

In fact, the representatives of the Aleuts allude to this
circumstance in their memorandum to the Metropolitan of
Moscow while they were still on the way to Siberia:

> "Do not bring matters to such a dangerous pass that, be-
> cause of the intolerable condition of our kinsmen, due to
> abuses on the part of the Russians, there may not result
> internecine strife leading to great bloodshed on both sides,
> between the new Christians and the old."[9]

It is clear, then, that the Irkutsk merchants, who were on
the point of becoming stockholders of the Russian-American
Company which enjoyed the patronage of the Tsar, were not
interested in the return of these two Aleuts to the islands.

Legally, let it be noted, the Russian-American Company
had no authority whatsoever at the time of its formation over
the native tribes and particularly over the Aleuts. As early
as 1779 a ukase forbade the further exaction of the fur-tribute
from all the inhabitants of the Aleutians, and in return, the
government imposed no duties on the Aleuts. At any rate,
there was nothing in the charter and franchise of the
Russian-American Company, as confirmed by Paul on July 8,
1799, on the relationship of the Aleuts to the Company. Only
the statutes confirmed on September 13, 1821 contained a
section entitled "Concerning the Islanders," which endorsed
the right of the Company to use the labor of the natives in case
of utter necessity. This question was most fully worked out
in the statutes confirmed on October 10, 1844.

Actually, however, these rules merely gave permanent
form to an order of things that had developed over a long
period of time, since, from the very first, the Company
followed the course of exploiting the native population as slave
labor .

The Aleuts, by the provisions of the statute, were governed by their own "Toyons" (chiefs) but under the supervision
of elders, foremen, and supervisors all with the approval of
the governor of the colonies. "The Aleuts are forbidden to
absent themselves anywhere without special permission of
the authorities, but in the time they have free from the Company's work they are allowed to engage in fishing along the

shores they inhabit, and that only for their own subsistence
and for that of their families." "The Aleuts between the
ages of 18 and 50 are under obligation to serve the Company
as hunters, it being understood that the Company had the
right to call up for service no more than half of the workers
within the aforenamed age groups." "The Aleuts are forbidden
to sell as well as to give away furs except to the Company."
"The Aleuts are under obligation to sell to the Company the
animal skins processed by them at a price fixed by the
Governing Board. In place of cash, they are under obligation
to accept from the Company either merchandise at the Company's price or Company stamps." "The Aleuts are forbidden
to enter into any barter or commerical relations with anyone
except the Company, even though the object of those relations
is not the fur-trade at all." "The colonial administration has
the right to utilize the Aleuts to prepare the provisions of fish
and fowl both during the hunting season and the rest of the
year, and does not have to pay them any special remuneration.
And finally, "the Company has the right or obligation to prevent the growth of luxury among the Aleuts, such as the use
of bread, tea, and similar items."

In these articles of the statute "Concerning the Islanders"
only two points call for further elucidation. First, there is
the question of the degree of independence enjoyed by the native chieftains, in their administration of the internal affairs
of the Aleuts and secondly, there is the question of the proportion of Aleuts employed on the Company's concessions as
compared with their total number.

For a long time the Russian-American Company had been
playing for the favors of the upper stratum of the Aleutian
tribes. The moment the merchants began to exploit the animal resources of the Aleutians by establishing new settlements, they attempted to utilize the esteemed elders, whom
the Russian called "Toyons," in influencing the Aleuts. As
early as 1791 Baranov wrote in one of his letters to Shelikhov:

> "Do not forget to send over for the toyons twenty of the
> best suits of clothes with flashy trimmings; you may risk
> two or three hundred rubles at the expense of the Company.
> We must attach them to us; for since it is sometimes pos-
> sible to proceed by political means and not necessarily by
> force, we are compelled by the conditions in Europe and
> the situation of the Company in Kenai to make the tribes

that are in our employ industrious and devoted when we
draft our plans for the future."[10]

Soon the toyon became practically a clerk of the Company.
By the terms of the instructions, as Kostlivtsov testifies,
the toyons were usually chosen from "a family that was distinguished by high birth, good management, and proficiency
in hunting." Those selected were approved by the general
manager of the Company, and were directly subordinated to
the heads of the divisions. There was no definite time-limit
on the position of toyon and it often continued for life.

"During the period of service each of the toyons receives
an annual salary of 250 rubles in banknotes, various allowances
in the form of provisions and gifts, and sometimes he will be
rewarded by the general manager with a medal bearing the
inscription 'For Diligence.' When he leaves the service on
account of old age or illness, the Company always gives him
enough aid to secure his existence. The toyon, who is a
functionary and enjoys the various privileges which the Company grants him, lives much better and more comfortably
than the other Aleuts."[11]

The duties of the toyons were described in a special order.
The "Rules for Toyons Elected as Elders" imposed the following duties upon them: "The elder assigns the Aleuts to
workers' detachments, in the summer to the hunting of sea-
otters and in the winter to staving and shooting; also to whaling and bird hunting."

In choosing the Aleuts for service in the hunting-stations
and in issuing to them the necessary tools received from the
foreman, the elder was duty-bound "to exercize strong supervision over the fur-hunters and to see that they tend carefully
to the work at hand and exert themselves to the full for the
benefit of the Company, which is really their own benefit, and
that they do not lose any time in idleness and inactivity."[12]

All Aleuts were obliged to work both on the hunting-posts
and on the preparation of provisions for the Company, and
so forth. For this type of work "old men, women, and juve-
niles of both sexes may be utilized, and they are to carry out
without subterfuge the commands of the elder for the common
benefit of the settlement."[13]

Furthermore, the elder was also charged with purely police
functions: "The elder must see to it that none of the Aleuts

committed to his charge ever loafs about doing nothing, or
dares absent himself from the village without obtaining permission from the elder."

Such were the obligations of the toyons, or elders, in the
Aleut settlements. Hence, the toyon was nothing but a Company clerk. As Davydov writes, "the chief...of the savages
is almost indistinguishable from the others except by the
title of toyon, or worse still, he is being converted into the
mainspring of oppression for the other islanders."[13]

As to the number of natives who were actually engaged in
Company work, it in no way corresponded to the norms indicated in the statutes. While Kostlivtsov was in the American
colonies, a complaint was lodged with him, in the name of
the Aleuts, against the Company for disregarding the statute.
It said that when otter parties were being fitted out, "almost
all of the adults are sent out to the hunting-stations, and only
the old men, women, and children are left at home, wherefore their families are suffering of a shortage in provisions."
The representatives of the Aleuts pointed out "that they spend
the best part of the year hunting sea-otters and return home
when all of the periodic fish have gone out to sea. Thus they
have no opportunity to lay in betimes sufficient provisions for
their families for the winter, which provisions consisted
chiefly of 'yukola,' that is dried or sun-dried fish."[15]

Even Kostlivtsov, who tried to defend the Company, could
not deny that the Aleuts were held in a state of slavery. But
he attempted to shift the blame from the Company to purely
natural causes: "Personally he is not a slave, not a serf
belonging to some master, no one forces him to do anything--
but, if one looks more closely into his condition, one must
admit that the Aleut is a slave of circumstances, in the full
sense of the term."

At the same time Kostlivtsov observes that the Aleut is
never idle: "Laboring hard and constantly all his life, and--
in the nature of his pursuits--at the risk of his life, it was
to be hoped that the Aleuts, if they are not all rich, would
at least be living in a state of contentment, well provided
with all the necessities of life. But, I regret to say, in
reality, their situation is quite opposite."[16]

Essentially the relationship between the Aleuts and the
Company recalled in many respects the so-called "mita"
system, which was in effect in the gold and silver mines
of Peru and Mexico. At the colonists' demand the Indian

villages in Peru were obliged to send one seventh of their
population to work in the mines, and those in Mexico, one
fourth. The workers received a beggarly wage, which was
paid out to them at the end of the period of forced "hired labor." Here in the Russian colonies, the proportion of those
impressed into working for the Company was considerably
higher, and comprised, at certain periods, the whole able-
bodied population.

When the Company was in its prime, in the first decades
of the nineteenth century, the system of forced labor for the
native population was organized in the following manner: the
main party, consisting of some 500 canoes, would be sent in
April from Kodiak along the American mainland as far as
Beaver Bay, returning only at the end of August. Only the
youngest Eskimos were selected for this party, since during
the hunting season it was often necessary to put up a defense
against attacking Tlinkets. The second party, comprising
some 200 canoes, would set out about the beginning of April
and would sail along the islands lying north of Kodiak until
the end of August. The third party, numbering forty canoes,
would engage in hunting on the islands north of Kodiak and
would also transport the necessary provisions from one island to the next. The fourth party of fifty canoes would set
out in a westerly direction from Kodiak.

Everyone leaving on a hunting expedition would make himself a new canoe which, in the case of the natives, represented
a considerable investment; for the canoe could not be used
again when it was brought back. The old men and the children
who remained in the colony would be sent out in Company
canoes to hunt birds. Each of them had to catch enough
birds to make seven parkas,[17] or about 300 birds. "If anyone
is unable, on account of old age or illness, to procure the
prescribed number, he is to make it up from the surplus
procured by someone else. The Company does not pay anything for the official number of seven parkas. Bird-hunting
is quite dangerous, especially for old men.... Anyone procuring seven parkas is given one in return, for which he is
to pay five black foxes, or eight dark-grey or red ones."[18]

The women were sent out to clean the fish, sew the parkas,
pick berries, and dig martagon.[19] Says Davydov: "It is
very difficult to procure martagon and it has a very short
season. Since pregnant women and those having infants were
unable to dig up the fixed amount, they would be obliged to

buy some from the others. When the berries are ripe, the women are again sent out to pick a specified amount, depending on the crop, ranging from 4 to 8 ishkat.[20] This continues until late in the fall--and there is no pay for it."[21]

At first the Company distributed the natives throughout all the little islands. Altogether the Kodiak Eskimos were scattered in sixty-five different places. Later on, however, when the animal resources had been depleted, all the natives were concentrated, beginning in 1841 and over a period of three years, in seven settlements.

As was observed by Kostlivtsov and Golovnin, who made an inspection tour of the colonies, "the Aleuts, by order of the authorities of the colonies, are now gathered in large settlements. In some places they have been brought together in too large numbers, which makes it difficult to prepare sufficient stocks of fish and other victuals for the winter. For the most part they live in small houses made of some kind of wood, half dug into the ground, covered with earth on top, and without windows or stoves."[22]

In the reports of the Company there is frequent reference to a fixed price according to which the Aleuts were paid for the animal-skins they processed. This was regarded as proof of the "independence" of the natives.

The statute read that the natives "wishing to sell any of the peltry procured by them are not allowed to do so except to the Company exclusively, according to the set rate which the management is to submit to the government." Such a rate actually existed and was even raised at definite intervals. In 1804 a sea-otter skin brought in 10 rubles,[23] in 1827--20 rubles, in 1836--30 rubles, and in 1852--50 rubles. Dark brown foxes brought in 2 rubles a piece in 1804 and 9 rubles in 1852. A white polar fox brought in 8 kopecks in 1804, 20 kopecks in 1836, and so forth.[24] However, as the Company itself stated, "this business, namely, the purchase of animals from the dependent Aleuts, is practically of no account to the Company by reason of the extreme laziness and indifference of the Aleuts. If the Company...continues to buy animals from the savages, it is doing so not from its own islanders but from tribes that are almost completely independent of the Company."[25]

It was a favorite device of the Company to allege that the natives were lazy, every time it felt that it needed new justification for applying compulsory measures to them. The

truth is that under the system of exploitation that was in vogue
in the possessions of the Russian-American Company with
respect to the natives, these natives did not even have time
to store away any provisions for the winter, let alone do any
hunting on their own. Summarizing his impressions of the
life of the native population Davydov says:

> "If the colonists in America have until now and because
> of their laziness been suffering from a lack of food, the
> reason for their suffering today is very different, namely,
> that the women are laying in a supply of fish, berries,
> martagon, and other things for the Company during the
> whole time that the fish continue to run into the rivers. As
> for the men, they spend the whole summer hunting sea-
> otters and birds and return in the fall shortly before the
> fish go out to sea. So, working for others during the best
> time of the season, they hardly have any time to dry fish
> and to store it away for their own future consumption."[26]

By the provisions of the statute, the Aleuts had the right
to complain to the Governing Board against abuses on the part
of the local authorities, or of any official of the Company.
The commandant of the port of Irkutsk, in his report to
the civil governor of Irkutsk in 1815, pointed out quite correctly that if the Aleuts "had turned" with all their complaints
"to the Governing Board of the Russian-American Company
in St. Petersburg and had expected satisfaction from that
quarter, it may be said most assuredly that such complaints
would never reach the Governing Board, even though the
Company were to exist several more centuries."[27]

"Under these circumstances," wrote the commandant of
the port of Irkutsk, "the Aleuts will forever remain in a state
of oppression and will always be suffering at the hands of the
Russian fur-hunters what they have frequently endured until
now; for the Aleuts, being a most peaceful and docile people,
not knowing Russian habits and not having anyone among their
own countrymen who knows how to read and write Russian,
nor anyone on the islands who would act in their defense,
never even make an attempt, in spite of all the abuses they
have endured, to ask one of the Russian hunters working for
the Company on the island of Atka and on the other islands of
the Andreanof chain to write a petition to the Governing Board
and expound all the wrongs suffered by them; since it may be

supposed that it would be a rare worker indeed of those found
in an artel of that division who would put down on paper anything unfavorable to a fellow-worker, whatever the Aleuts
may decide to complain about."[28]

The single instances of individual Aleuts coming to Okhotsk
on Company vessels did not change the situation in the main.
In three years, only one complaint reached the commandant
of Okhotsk, and not because there were no grounds for com-
plaining. In 1812 the Aleut Gilev arrived in Okhotsk on the
Company·vessel "Finlandia" to enter an oral complaint with
the commandant of Okhotsk against the various "abuses and
outrages" committed by employees of the Company. These
abuses "consist mainly in that many of the workers on the
hunting-stations living on the islands have made it a practice
to abduct the wives and daughters of the Aleuts, carry them
off as hostages, and live with them on the islands. Then,
when they are sent back to Okhotsk, some of the hunters
take their women along, while others leave theirs on the islands to become a public charge."[29]

The commandant of Okhotsk did only one thing: he forced
the fur-hunters who brought along their Aleut women to marry
them. One assistant pilot by the name of Dubinin, "was
forced to marry legally the wife he had snatched...as a hostag
on Atka. The same was done with the workers who brought
Aleut girls to Okhotsk from the Andreanof chain. All of
them...were married according to the laws of the Church in
the winter of 1814."[30]

As a result of the condition of servitude in which the Aleuts
were forced to live they were rapidly becoming extinct.

It is doubtful if the question of the size of the native population at the start of the Russian colonization can be answered
with any degree of certainty. The information supplied by
Shelikhov to the effect that there were some 50,000 people in
the Russian colonies was "highly exaggerated"; it was his purpose to attach the greatest importance to the incorporation of
the American colonies in the Russian empire.

In the early period of the occupation of the colonies there
was no question of taking census, and later on, the administration of the Company preferred not to make public the information it undoubtedly had at its disposal. Thus in 1824,
when, in-spite of the repeated requests by the Minister of
Finance for comparative figures on the births and deaths in
the colonies, such information was, for various reasons, not
submitted.

But even the summary report covering a period of several
months in the colony of Ross and a year at the Novoarkhangelsk
and Kodiak offices showed that the number of deaths was in excess of the number of births. Kankrin even made this anno-
tation in the margin: "More are dying; it must be hard for
them to live."[31]

As for the rest, the government preferred not to draw any
further conclusions from the information it had gathered on
the condition of the natives in the American colonies.

But even though we have only inexact information as to the
number of natives in the American colonies, we can still
speak of them as dying out during the rule of the Russian-
American Company. According to Khlebnikov, 2,195 out of
6,510 natives died between 1792 and 1817 on Kodiak alone.[32]
In 1824, according to the Governing Board, the total number
of Aleuts of both sexes was 8,403,[33] and by 1859, shortly
before the Company was liquidated, the number of Aleuts
had diminished to 4,363.[34]

While they were actually slaves of the Company, the "completely dependent" natives did not constitute the "property" of
the Company. There were in the colonies, however, not only
slaves who belonged to the Company in fact, but also those
who belonged to it legally. The latter were ordinarily employed in the capacity of personal servants to members of
the Company administration, and in a number of other tasks.

In its reports the Governing Board pointed out repeatedly
that with the coming of the Company to the islands and to the
American mainland, slavery, which had prevailed among the
native tribes, was completely eradicated. To a certain degree this assertion was in conformity with reality. The
slaves were taken away from all the native tribes, with the
exception of the Tlinket, but they did not, for all that, become free men; they merely became the property of the
Company. These same "Kalgi" or, as they later came to be
called in the colonies, "Kayury," were considered "to be in
the permanent service" of the Company. Furthermore, even
individual fur-hunters such as Company clerks and others,
had their own "Kayury."

However, with the advent of the Russians, the wars among
the native tribes came to a halt and, consequently, the main
source of slaves was also dried up. At the same time, the
number of "Kalgi" or "Kayury" was constantly on the decrease.
Then the Company found the following way out, as Davydov
reports:

"When the number of 'Kayury' had diminished as a result of hard labor and of various mishaps, they started to
impress into slavery those among the islanders who had
committed certain offences; and it is understood that from
then on the number of criminals on Kodiak was always on
the increase."[35]

The "Kayury" were employed in various capacities. They
caught fish in the shallow waters along the shore, processed
foxes with sharp-edged hammers, worked in the salt-mines
and brick-yards, felled trees, were employed as oarsmen.
In the wintertime, not needing so many "Kayury" and wishing
to save some unnecessary expenses, the Company put them
up with the natives. According to Davydov, the "Kayury"
"were forced to work for the Company until they were too old,
or until such time as their relatives had an opportunity to
redeem them." Even physical disability did not save them
from hard labor. "If a 'Kayur' grows lame or loses an arm,
or is incapacitated for work in some other way, he is assigned
the job of scaring away the crows with a suspended scarecrow
or something like that."[36]

In its reports the Company evaded the problem of its slaves
or "Kayury." Therefore it is impossible to ascertain how many
of them there were. Only in one report, that for 1810, does
the Governing Board write about the "Kayury" that it is utilizing their labor because "the friendly islanders have voluntarily loaned out the 'Kayurs' of both sexes to the Russians to help
with the tasks and the labors with which the Russians are unable or have no time to occupy themselves."[37]

The number of "Kayury" as given in that report was 500.

The native tribes, the Kenai people, Chugaches, and others
which the Company called "semi-dependent," were not dependent on the Company in any way. The relations between them
and the Company were more or less normal. The Company
rarely bought furs from them or hired them to work for it.
Yet in the reports, in order to enhance the importance of the
Company, they are designated as "semi-dependent."

The category of natives who were "not completely dependent" upon the Company comprised the Tlinket (Kolosh) who
lived in the territory of the Russian colonies in America.

Paragraph 280 of the statute stipulated that the Company
had the right to offer these people its "protection." But,
State Councillor Kostlivtsov, who made a tour of inspection

of the colonies in 1860, remarked, not without wit, that the
paragraph in question dealt only with a "pleasant illusion" of
the Company and did not at all conform to things as they were.
This is what he said:

> "Although, both in the Company statute that is now in
> effect and in the one that is being drafted these natives
> are designated as 'not completely dependent' of the colo-
> nial government and as merely living in the territory be-
> longing to the colonies, I, for my part, should suggest
> that they be more correctly called 'completely indepen-
> dent.' The Kolosh cannot in any respect be regarded as
> dependent on the Company, rather it may be said that, in
> turn, the Company's colonies on the American coast de-
> pend on them; for the Kolosh have only, so to speak, to
> begin to make a little noise to deprive the port of Arkh-
> angelsk and its entire population of all fresh food and even
> of the opportunity to show their faces a few yards outside
> the fortifications."[38]

Rear-Admiral M.D. Tebenkov, who was Governor of the
colonies from 1845 to 1850, said frankly in one of his reports
that "only the disunity among the Kolosh and their lack of
leadership have saved us from their attacks. While we have
very many reasons for being indulgent with them or directing
their insolent activities into other channels, I still am not
convinced that sooner or later, with things going as they are,
Sitka will be able to avoid a bloody catastrophe."[39]

The colonial authorities, without an armed force of sufficient strength, were always afraid of aggravating their
relations with the Tlinket. In the event that the Tlinket were
discontented, Sitka was doomed to an existence of semi-star-
vation. The whole population would be forced on a diet of old
salt meat and salted fish, for it would not be safe to venture
beyond the confines of the fortifications.

As for arousing the interest of the Tlinket in the economic
advantages of trading with the Company, that, too, was not
feasible; the Company always had difficulty in delivering the
goods.

It is possible to judge from the letters of the colonial administration the extent to which the Company was dependent
upon the Tlinket. In one of his letters, Governor Muravyov
said that in 1823 "the hunting season for sea-animals, with

the exception of seals, was a failure, and had been rendered extremely difficult because of the danger from the Kolosh who were trying in every way to interfere with all hunting. Since the Kolosh themselves process sea-otters, it would have been considerably more advantageous to the Company to buy these otters directly from the Kolosh than to hunt for them. But in the colonies there were none of those articles for which the Kolosh usually barter their sea-otters, and, therefore, there was nothing with which to buy them."[40]

From the very first years that the Russians made their appearance in that area the opposition of the Tlinket was tenacious and stubborn. Baranov, describing in a letter to Shelikhov one of his clashes with the Tlinket in 1792, said that "the resistance offered by the Russians with rifles and by the Americans[41] with bows-and-arrows and in hand-to-hand fighting with pikes, was very stubborn, to be sure-- but it was of no avail, for the attackers were all dressed in three or four coats of plaited wooden armour, and over these they wore thick elk-skin cloaks, and on their heads they wore extremely thick wooden helmets with figures of various monsters painted on them, wherefore neither bullets nor bricks nor arrows nor pikes were powerful enough to defeat them, and had the Russians not chanced to have a one-pounder with them they would certainly have been worsted; for the attackers fought with great ferocity until daylight, being given orders by the voice of one man, something that had not been seen before in the case of these savages, and bravely stepping forward to take the place of their dead."[42]

In the year 1801 the Tlinkets laid waste to so-called Fort Mikhailovsky on the island of Sitka, and in 1805 they did the same to the colony of Slavorossiya on Yakutat Bay. The struggle with the Tlinket was further complicated by the fact that these remarkable sharpshooters were armed with rifles which they had bartered from the foreigners. In his report for the year 1860 Captain Golovin wrote, that "it is not so long ago that not one Russian dared to venture unarmed fifty feet outside the Novoarkangelsk fortifications. At the present time such animosity no longer exists, but trade relations are being maintained only with the Kolosh of Sitka, who live within some seventy feet of Novarkangelsk."[43]

People in the colonies were living in the shadow of a constant menace. The naval officer A. Markov, who visited Novarkhangelsk in the mid 1840's, relates that "guns from all directions, both from the fortress and from ships dropping anchor in a row opposite the Tlinket colonies" were always pointed at the Tlinket villages.

But these precautions were of little avail. The attacks on the Tlinket on the Russian settlements, and even on the center of those settlements, continued down to the time when the Russian-American Company was liquidated. In 1852 the Tlinket destroyed a small Russian settlement, some thirteen miles from Novoarkhangelsk, and in 1855 they even launched an attack on that town itself. Seizing a church on the edge of the town, the Tlinket opened intense fire on the center of the town. The situation of the besieged Russians was very critical; they were outnumbered many times over by the besieging Tlinket. Only through negotiations were the Russians able to have the siege of Novoarkhangelsk raised.

The tribal chiefs of the Tlinket were ceremoniously received on their visits to the Russian fortresses. They were showered with presents of all kinds, but it was still impossible to feel safe from a sudden Tlinket attack; nor was it possible to buy from them all the peltry they could procure.

To be sure, as early as at the end of the 1830's the Russians succeeded, through various gifts and by protracted hard drinking, to make a convinced "Russophile" out of Chieftain Kuatka of Stakhine. As a token of his devotion to Russia, Kuatka, following the admonition of the local priest, refused to bring the customary human sacrifice during the commemoration ceremony in honor of his deceased relative, and showed in every way his complete loyalty to the colonial administration. In response to the Company's solicitation, Nicholas I "in February, 1839 authorized the bestowal upon the Kolosh chieftain Kuatka of Stakhine of a brocaded caftan with the proper sash and cap."[45] But even before the presents reached the colonies, Kuatka was declared to be "unworthy of His Majesty's most gracious reward." Then another chief was found, by the name of Kukhkan, whom it was decided to raise to the rank of "head chief of the Kolosh living in the Russian colonial possessions." At the same time he was given the caftan, sash, and cap that had been intended for Kuatka.

The Company regarded its attempts to utilize the Indian chiefs as of vast importance. In the opinion of the governor of the colonies, in view "of the great importance and influence that the head chief of Sitka is exercising not only over the

Kolosh but also over the Russians, it would be useful to have that honorary title bestowed by authorization of His Majesty," and the Governing Board added that such chiefs would not only be useful but, "considering the close proximity of the English, would also be indispensable not only to the Company but, in general, to the strengthening of our influence over the Kolosh living in the Russian possessions."[46]

In 1842 the office of head chief was approved by the Tsar, and, in conformance with an especially composed oath, Kukhkan pledged himself "to serve faithfully and honestly and to obey in everything, without sparing his life, to the last drop of his blood."[47]

In concluding our description of the Company's policy towards the native population we should say a few words about its attitude towards the baptism of the Aleuts and the activities of the Church in the territory of the Russian colonies in general.

When the Russian-American Company was established, Shelikhov and later his heirs took great pains to point out that there were unlimited possibilities for the propagation of the "faith of Christ" throughout the breadth of the Russian colonies in America. As a result of their efforts and at their own expense, a religious mission, headed by Archimandrite Ioassaf, was dispatched to the American colonies in 1793. Immediately upon his arrival, however, Ioassaf met with unconcealed opposition on the part of the Company clerks. In 1795 he wrote in one of his letters to Shelikhov: "I am busy baptizing the Americans without hampering the Company in any way, for the 'kayury' remain 'kayury,' the hostages remain hostages and every trapper continues on his job, and the fact that he is baptized is not, it seems to me, an encumbrance. Yet, I am always being thwarted in carrying out my duties."[48]

Still, this opposition did not keep Ioassaf from being able to report in 1796 that he had baptized 6,740 persons on Kodiak and on the adjacent islands.

In 1799 he was recalled from Kodiak, raised to a bishop, and sent back. But the Company vessel "Phoenix" with him on board, was wrecked.

In 1803 the question arose of sending a new bishop to the colonies. The Company, however, was very reserved in its attitude; it had already received the franchise, and it no longer saw the need for any zeal in spreading the "faith of Christ."

The Governing Board replied to the Synod that there was no need, for the present time, of a new bishop, and that "the presence in the colonies of a bishop brought over for the single purpose of ordaining some of the natives into the priesthood, was premature, since no general gathering place had as yet been designated where the Company's settlements would be so secure as to good climate and fertile soil to be able to engage in farming and in other pursuits."[49]

But the Company not only opposed the establishment of an episcopate in the colonies, which would have entailed considerable expenditures on its part; it bent all its efforts to discredit the activities of the priests who were already there. Thus it reported, on one occasion, that the clergy in the Russian colonies "through an easily pardonable error, had exaggerated the number of newly baptized Christians" and that it was no secret to anyone that "the very same Aleut families were entered in the rolls of the newly baptized twice or even three times, under different names and by different missionaries."[50]

On another occasion the Governing Board of the Company requested the government for protection against the continual visits paid to the Kuriles by Kamchatka county officers and by members of the clergy. The former, said the administration, were coming around "ostensibly to survey the colonies for any needs that the inhabitants might have, and the latter, purportedly to preach; and all of them are really here to barter fur goods for tobacco and vodka." The Company asked, therefore, "that these islands be freed of such visitors."[51]

As for the ecclesiastical authorities, they retaliated in kind. Having received a memorandum from some member of the clergy on the decrease in the population of the islands, the Synod submitted it to the proper authorities. This started off an exchange of letters, filled with stinging remarks at each other's expense, that continued for many years. As a result, certain facts came to light which the Company would hardly have wanted to make public.

To the very end of the Company's existence, the Governing Board opposed any increase in the number of missionaries in the colonies. When in 1850 the Synod broached the question of increasing the number of missions in the colonies so as to be able to continue the conversion of the native population on a more extensive scale, the Governing Board protested again.

It contended that such a step was inopportune, and proposed
that the conversion of the Chukchi be completed first, a task
which the Synod had not been able to accomplish in more than
a hundred years.

"An increase in the number of missions for converting the
native tribes to the true faith," wrote the Governing Board
to the Head Procurator of the Synod in 1850, "can hardly be
conducive to the desired lasting results that would come first
from attenuating, in those territories, the hostile influence
of the English and their native subjects in the east, and of the
Chukchi in the west. For the firm establishment of the true
faith among the natives in the Kamchatka eparchy it would be
very helpful to have the missionaries concentrate, if possible,
their first efforts on the territory of the Chukchi bordering
on Kamchatka, since only after these people have been converted to Christianity, will it be possible to expect sure success in the propagation of the faith among the coastal tribes
of North America."[52]

There were solid grounds for the protracted battle which
the Company was waging against the Synod. In the first place,
the maintenance of the clergy and the churches in the colonies
entailed large expenditures on the part of the Company. For
instance, between 1849 and 1859 the Company spent 345,856.3
rubles on the clergy and 71,723.18 rubles on the churches.
In one decade, then, the Company expended on this one purpose more than 400,000 rubles, or about 10 per cent of the
total amount paid out in salaries to all the officials and
workers in the colony during the same period. At the same
time, the activities of the clergy among the conquered Aleuts
not only were of no benefit whatsoever to the Company, but
they even interfered with its functions. The priests meddled
with the orders of the administration and continually sent de-
nunciatory reports to St. Petersburg. On some occasions
the clergy brought actual harm to the good relations with the
natives, even to the extent of arousing their active indignation,
which, in the final analysis, was vented on the Company.

As for the activities of the Church among the unconquered
Tlinket, here, too, the clergy manifested its utter incapability
of securing results desirable to the Company. It limited its
efforts to baptizing the Tlinket and seeing that they observed
the rites and ceremonies of their new faith.

Rezanov wrote as early as 1805 in a letter to the directors
of the Company:

"I should like to tell you of the clerical mission that it
has baptized a few thousand souls here, but only literally
'baptized.' When I see how the habits of the people of
Kodiak have indeed been somewhat softened, I do not attribute it to the efforts of the mission but to time and to
their own capabilities. Our monks have never followed
the course pursued by the Jesuits in Paraguay, have never
sought to develop the intelligence of the savages, and have
been incapable of comprehending the broad purposes of
the government or of the Company. They immersed the
Americans and when these savages by imitating the
monks, succeeded after half an hour in making the sign
of the cross, the monks would boast of their successes
and, making no further use of the natives' capacities,
they would return triumphantly, believing that once they
have gone through the motions, they have accomplished
their aims."[53]

Rezanov, by demanding that the sermons to the natives
be given in their native tongue, forced the clergy in the colonies to set to compiling a dictionary of the Tlinket language.
But this project came along very slowly, for, in the words
of Rezanov, "any new task seems insurmountable" to these
representatives of the clergy.

Rezanov relates further how the clergy actually harmed
the interests of the Company:

"On the Alaska Peninsula, on Lake Ilyamna, which is
called Lake Shelikhov, trade had developed with the mountain tribes, which opened up great possibilities. The monk
Juvenal at once rushed off there to preach. He baptized
them by force, married them, took away the girls from
some and gave them away to others. For a long time the
Americans endured his violence and even the beatings he
gave them, but finally it occurred to them that it was
possible to get rid of that monster, and, taking counsel
among themselves, they ended by killing him. To be sure,
he himself was not to be pitied, but they sacrificed to his
cruelty the whole artel of Russians and Kodiakians, not
leaving one of them alive."[54]

The condition of the so-called Creoles was little different
from that of the Aleuts in the colonies of the Russian-American

Company. Not being able to establish a sedentary population
by using the Russian colonists, and not being given the right
to acquire any serfs, the Company attempted to create a
special class of "colonial citizens" out of the Creoles. From
the very beginning of its existence the Company upheld the
seizure of native women by the fur-hunters, justifying this
violence by considerations of a "higher" order. The Governing Board said:

> "If one looks at all this from the political point of view,
> one must admit that contacts between the Russians and the
> Aleutian women are indispensable, both in order to discover
> any injurious designs that the natives may harbor and also
> to establish firm relations between them since the children
> born from such unions will perforce bring about a union
> between the Russians and the Aleuts who are related to
> them, and the children themselves, being all baptized,
> will become accustomed to being Russian and not Aleutian,
> and such a regeneration spells stability for the Russians."

In 1818 the Governing Board submitted to the Minister of
the Interior, Kozodavlev, a plan, previously formulated by
Rezanov, for the establishment of a "class of colonial citizens" from the Creoles. The plan proposed "to utilize the
Creoles for the benefit of the fatherland and of the Company
in such a way as to constitute of those who are capable of
bearing arms a Company garrison for the defense of the local
ports and fortresses, and to send some of them to Russia to
learn the various ways of serving at the front, beating of the
drum, and the like; and to employ the others, who are qualified, in navigation, in office work, in trade, or in some
necessary craft, or in tilling the soil."[56]

There were about two hundred adult Creole males in the
colonies at that time. Unlike the Russian trappers, the
Creoles, being employed on Company projects, were allowed
to have their own household.

However, in its attempt to set up a manpower pool, the
Company itself reduced the Creoles to the level of slaves.

The status of the Creoles in the Russian colonies in
America was first formulated in the Charter of the Russian-
American Company that was approved in 1844, when the
Company's franchise was extended for another regular twenty-
year period. A special section, entitled "On the Creoles,"

gave them formally the same status as that of the free class
in the Russian empire, the lower middle class, but actually
this independence was reduced to naught by a series of reser-
vations in the charter.

Thus, for instance, the Creoles who had studied at the Company's expense even for a very short period, became dependent on the Company for a period of from ten to fifteen years,
while those who studied in the colonies, had to pledge themselves to serve no less than fifteen years, or five years
longer than those studying in Russia.

In his report on his inspection tour of the colonies in
1860-1861 Kostlivtsov rightly observes that in the Charter--
not unintentionally--no mention is made of what the Creole,
who paid so dearly for his right to study, was supposed to
learn. And Kostlivtsov asks, "Can it be that, in return for
learning to read and write and how to wield an axe as a plain
woodchopper, he has to serve the Company for such a long
time?"[57]

Under these circumstances the direct purpose of building
schools for the Creoles was to impress them into the service
of the Company. Even though all the Creoles under age
attended those schools only for a short time, the whole Creole
population gradually came into a lasting state of dependency
upon the Company.

After the expiration of the term of service agreed upon,
the Creoles were to be released from their condition of dependency, "unless they were in debt to the Company." It
was this reservation that constituted the chief obstacle to
the liberation of the Creoles after their fifteen-year period
of bondage; for the conditions of life in the colonies, as we
have seen in the case of the workers on the hunting-posts,
led inevitably to a state of general indebtedness.

As of January 1, 1861, a short time before the affairs of
the Company were liquidated, there were as many as 1,896
Creoles in the colonies, of whom 783 constituted the male
population that was able to work. Not unlike all the other
natives, they were in a state of servile dependency upon the
Company.

In summarizing our findings let us point out once more
that the policy of the Company was identical with that of the
government, and that it was actually the government which
handed over the original inhabitants of the colonies to the
Company in absolute bondage. And only when the question of

liquidating the Company had been decided, did the government assume the attitude of a disinterested defender of the natives and utilize facts, that it had known for decades, to accuse the Company of the illegal exploitation of those natives.

Chapter X

THE FINAL PERIOD OF THE RUSSIAN-
AMERICAN COMPANY

THE CONVENTION of 1825, which granted the English the right of free navigation of the streams flowing from the English possessions across Russian territory and out to the sea, actually made the English masters of the whole territory along the lines of the river communications. In its efforts not to let those regions slip out of its hands, the Russian-American Company constructed a number of fortified settlements on the mainland with the view of hampering the development of barter operations between the English and the native population by entering into trade with them on its own.

The southeast frontier of the Russian colonies in America was contiguous with the possessions of the English Hudson Bay Company. This company held the rights to monopolistic trade with the Indians in North America, both north and west of the boundary of the United States. In contrast to the Russian-American Company, the Hudson Bay Company did not engage in fur-hunting, but limited its operations primarily to bartering furs with the natives. When the English had been granted the right of navigation of the rivers flowing through Russian territory, the agents of the Hudson Bay Company became most active among the Indian tribes living in the Russian colonies. It was beyond the strength of the Russian-American Company, which also bartered a part of its furs with the natives, to engage in competition with the English. The latter paid higher prices, and selected their wares with a view to meeting the needs of the Indians, whereas the Russian-American Company was striving to pass off on them all kinds of substandard merchandise.

The relations between the two rival companies had been so aggravated that in 1834 agents of the Russian-American Company ran the risk of openly violating the Russo-English Convention by refusing passage past the fortress of St. Dionysius (at the mouth of the Stakhine River) to a ship belonging to the Hudson Bay Company. As a result of this

217

clash, the Hudson Bay Company sued the Russian-American
Company for the amount of £22,118 (about 135,000 silver
rubles).

Suddenly, however, these unfriendly relations with the
Hudson Bay Company changed to ardent friendship. In 1839,
"with the approval of His Majesty," an agreement was signed
between the Russian-American Company and the Hudson Bay
Company by which certain portions of the Russian possession
on the northwest coast of America were leased to the British
company. The Hudson Bay Company received for a term of
ten years, beginning on July 1, 1840, the territory running
northwestward from latitude 54°40′ N. to a line drawn between Cape Spencer at Cross Sound and Mt. Fairweather.

The leasing, or rather the cession to the Hudson Bay Company of a section of the coastline, which had until then been
exploited by the Russian-American Company, was not the
result of a commercial deal for the benefit of the Company.
Rather it was an attempt on the part of the Russian government to eliminate one of the causes that might in any way
lead to a further aggravation of the relations between Russia
and Great Britain. Any deterioration in the relations between
the two, at that juncture, would have been decidely disadvantageous to Russia. For it was precisely during that time,
between August, 1839 and July, 1840, that the Russian Ambassador in London, Baron Brunnow, was conducting negotiations concerning the government of the Straits.

There were two points of view on the problem of the Straits
a problem that had become very acute as a result of the defeat
inflicted on Turkey by the pasha of Egypt. There was the
Austrian point of view as proclaimed by Metternich, which
envisaged a joint guarantee of the territorial integrity of
Turkey by all the European powers, and there was the British point of view as upheld by Palmerston, which, though it
aimed to put certain restraints on Russia in the Near East,
did not call for a full-fledged guarantee of Turkey's inviolability. Russia found England's position much more suitable
and there was no sense in her doing anything at that time that
might aggravate the relations between the two powers ever so
slightly, just for the purpose of strengthening its position in
the competitive struggle with the Hudson Bay Company.

By leasing a portion of its territory to the British company the Russian government was aiming at the same time
to set a limit to the claims made by the Americans. The

latter insisted on the renewal of Article 4 of the 1824 convention as to the right of free navigation in the territory belonging to the Russian colonies in America. Not without cause
did Bodisko, the Russian Ambassador to the United States,
regard that agreement with a good deal of apprehension. He
said in a dispatch to Nesselrode, dated August 10, 1839, that
the plan "to lease the northwest coastline to the Hudson Bay
Company to be exploited by it has impelled me to call the
attention of His Majesty's Ministry to the unfavorable impression which such a decision is bound to produce, and to
the consequences to which it might lead, as soon as it has
become known to the American shipowners."[1]

Nesselrode believed, however, that, in view of the alliance between Russia and Great Britain, the claims put forth
by the United States were of no material importance. On
January 4, 1839, he wrote to the Minister of Finance as
follows:

"From the political point of view, the desire for ef-
fecting a rapprochement with the Hudson Bay Company by
leasing to it the aforementioned territories should, in my
opinion, meet with the fullest approval. The execution of
such a plan would offer us the immediate advantage of e-
liminating not only competition in the fur-trade with the
natives, but also the very circumstances that have often
been the cause of friction with the English and the citizens
of the United States. Certain of these incidents have again
and again been the cause of disagreeable exchanges with
their respective governments. This deal in particular
would obviate all further explanantions on our part with
the government of the United States on the subject of...the
efforts made by that government to obtain a renewal of the
right of free navigation, granted by the Convention, of the
lakes and sounds adjoining our possessions in America--
efforts that would not be to our advantage at all."[2]

According to the terms of the agreement, the Hudson Bay
Company withdrew its lawsuit against the Russian-American
Company and paid rent of 2,000 sea-otter skins annually.
First concluded for a period of ten years, the agreement was
renewed several times, remaining in force down to the final
liquidation of the Russian-American Company.

The course that the conflict with the Hudson Bay Company

took and the way in which it was solved by direct orders
from the government, are symptomatic of the position that
the Russian-American Company occupied in the early 1840's.
Its colonies in America were beginning to lose the importance
they formerly had for the tsarist government. They were
essentially being converted into a form of exchange money
to be paid out in return for any benefits and advantages that
might be secured in the Near East. But, in spite of this, the
existence of the Russian-American Company had not yet lost
its significance in the eyes of the government, since at that
very time, in the 1840's, it was being almost wholly transformed into a government institution, to be confronted with
entirely new problems.

Article 1 of the Charter of the Russian-American Company as approved in 1844 declared that the Company was organized "for the purpose of engaging in hunting and fishing
on the mainland of northwest America and on the islands,
both the Aleutians and the Kuriles, as well as throughout the
extent of the Northeastern Sea." But such a delimitation was
even then only in slight agreement with the facts; for by that
time the hunting activities of the Company had yielded first
place to the immediate functions involved in the administration
of the American territory under Russian control. These
problems facing the Russian-American Company were formulated with great clarity in the draft for the new charters, which
was submitted to the government for examination in 1861.
Here nothing was left unsaid. Article 1 of the draft defined
the functions of the Company and pointed out that it was organized "for the purpose of administering the Russian colonies in America."

This idea was not new to certain circles of the Russian
government. As early as 1841, before the charter for the
preceding twenty-year period had been approved, it was said
in the State Council that "the Company is not only a commercial corporation, but also, to a certain extent, a government
institution, and that the privileges granted to it comprise not
only rights but also obligations."[3]

N.N. Muravyov, Governor-General of Siberia, who, at
that time, was charged with investigating the condition of the
Company, wrote in a report to the Tsar that "the Company
is in a difficult situation, that the Kiakhta trade no longer
offers it a secure market for its products...that as a result
of the high prices prevailing in California, the colonies have

been deprived of the means of obtaining bread for their sus-
tenance at reasonable prices, and are compelled to procure
it from the Baltic, since it would cost them even more to do
so from around the shores of the Sea of Okhotsk."[4]

The picture of the economic situation of the Company as
given by Muravyov was, as we have seen, a rather gloomy
one. To all intents and purposes the Russian-American Company was already on the threshold of complete economic collapse. If it had been an ordinary commercial undertaking,
the question of liquidating it would naturally have come up
for discussion. But Muravyov insisted that the Company be
retained and that the necessary material assistance be extended to it. He only refelcted the attitude of the government,
which believed that the part played by the Russian-American
Company in opening up roads for tsarist expansion in the
East was not yet finished, and that it might still be useful to
the government to cloak that expansion behind private initiative . Of no little imporatnce, too, was the question of
administering the territories in America which were as yet
far from being subdued.

"In my opinion," wrote Muravyov, "the existence of the
Russian-American Company is necessary for the government--
for a time, at any rate; for to assume the administration of
our North American possessions would entail very considerable expenditures, both in the form of single subventions and
of annual subsidies, and in the meantime our administration
and our strength in the Sea of Okhotsk and in Kamchatka are
still such as to render premature any further expansion along
the American coast. I dare say, on the other hand, that to
abandon our possessions in North America, in the event the
Company should not be in a position to administer them, would
not be in line with the aims of the government. Both these
considerations lead one to the conclusion that the government
will have to lend the Company its assistance in the difficult
situation in which, as I know, it finds itself at present."[5]

But the most important reason for trying to keep the Company were the aggressive moves that were being prepared in
the region of the Amur. And it was not by sheer accident
that Muravyov, fearing that the Company might, as a result
of the difficult financial situation in which it found itself,
want to reduce its fleet proposed that the Company fleet be
fully manned with officers and seamen in active service, and
agreed to do it at government expense.

By way of proving the utter necessity of retaining the Russian-American Company Muravyov cited the case of similar companies in other countries, maintaining that "the rapid progress made by the English East India Company, supported and, it may be said, directed by the government, may serve as an example of some sort for us, with this favorable difference, that the whole expanse from St. Petersburg to the Eastern Sea is one continuous stretch of vast empire belonging to Your Majesty."

And indeed, towards the end of the 1840's and during the first half of the 1850's the Company played an exclusive part in the Russian eastward advance and in the recovery of those regions on the Amur River which the tsarist government had at one time relinquished.

Having set for itself, in the second half of the 1840's, the task of recovering these regions on the Amur, the government had, first of all, to solve the question of the navigability of the mouth of the Amur River and of the existence of a passage from the Amur to the sea. To carry out an open exploration of this region was an impossibility for the tsarist goverrment. China had just been defeated by Great Britain in the so-called Opium War. In 1842 China signed the Treaty of Nanking, which laid the foundation for a whole system of unequal treaties that China was to sign with the capitalistic countries. However, the Treaty of Nanking still did not satisfy all the demands made by the English middle class on China. The treaty was regarded as "moderate" in English bourgeois circles, where it was emphasized that the total of the losses incurred in the war were not made good by the advantages gained. The "moderation" of the English in concluding the Treaty of Nanking was attributable to the fact that the English government was afraid that excessive pressure on China would arouse the opposition of the other powers which also claimed the right to consolidate their position in China.

In these conditions any open exploration of the Amur region by Russia would have served as a special incentive to England to continue with her own activities in China, and might even have precipitated new demands on her part to the Chinese government. But any further attack by England on China did not enter at all into the calculations of the tsarist government. On the other hand, the period following the Opium War was most propitious for obtaining from China the return of the Amur region by peaceful means.

At any rate, it was necessary to act vigorously, but at the
same time most cautiously. And in circumstances like these
the Russian-American Company was truly irreplaceable; for
according to the declaration of the Governing Board, the
Company was the most faithful, reliable, and conscientious
agent of the government, "one that was indispensable to the
government in all special cases where the government found
it inconvenient to act in its own name."[6]

In 1844 the Ministry of Foreign Affairs informed the Governing Board of the Company that, by Imperial decree, the
Company was to take over the exploration of the Amur river.

In the spring of 1846 the Company vessel "Constantine,"
under the command of Gavrilov, began the task of exploring
the estuary of the Amur. In spite of the fact that the expedition was given only a short time to carry out its task, and
could not produce a definitive answer as to the conditions
prevailing in the area of the estuary, it did contribute in the
highest degree to the knowledge of the region.

In 1849, Muravyov commissioned Lieutenant-Commander*
G.I. Nevelsky to continue with the exploration of the estuary
of the Amur. At the same time he ordered the Russian-
American Company to dispatch a commercial expedition over-
land to the mouth of the Amur, with the dual objective of
establishing Russian colonies and of winning over the native
population, or the Ghiliacks, to the Russian side by entering
into profitable commercial deals with them. The Ministry
of Foreign Affairs in its memorandum to the Governing
Board justified the necessity for such an expedition by pointing
out how especially important it was for Russia to establish
relations with the Ghiliacks, "living near the mouth of the
Amur, on its north bank, who, life their fellow-tribesmen,
apparently consider themselves independent of China."[7]

In the course of the summer months of 1849, the Company's
trading expedition did some bartering with the Ghiliacks, obtained valuable information as to their needs, and drew up a
description of the region. In 1850 another trade expedition
of the Company was active in the Amur region, parallel with
the expedition of Lieutenant-Commander Nevelsky. The first
Russian settlement on the Amur, called Petrovskoye, was
established in June 1850 by Lieutenant-Commander Nevelsky

*In Russian "Kapitan-Leitenant." --Ed.

and by the leader of the expedition, Orlov. The latter, who
was in the service of the Company, was left as head of the
colony, and continued to engage in active bartering with the
native population.

That same year, an especially appointed committee adopted a decision on the subject of the colonization of the Amur
region, which placed particular emphasis on the requirement
that the future Russian colonies should be set up as trading-
stations of the Russian-American Company.

The Company fleet, as well as the main body of its employees, were thrown into the attempt to gain possession of
the Amur region. In 1851 a number of persons in the Company's employ were already colonized at the trading-post of
Nikolayevsk. The several expeditions sent out from these
posts continued to advance ever deeper into the interior.
They explored the vast territory of the Amur region, opened
up new roads, and founded new colonies.

This continued until the year 1858, when the Treaty of
Aigun was concluded with China, according to which Amur
was returned to Russia. Any further activities in that region
on the part of the Company were thus   rendered superfluous.

A great deal of energy and a large amount of money were
expended by the Company in the construction of a harbor in
Ayan Bay to take the place of the unsuitable port of Okhotsk.
The new port, joined by means of a two hundred-verst highway to the natural boundaries along the Ma-Yen and the Aldan
was of great importance as a base for further advances up
the Amur.

The governor-general of Eastern Siberia, in a special
memorandum to the Siberian Committee in 1859, noted that
"the part played by the Russian-American Company at the
very beginning of the Amur undertaking was the more important as it laid the foundation for an enterprise that was to have
important consequences. It is well known that the first decisive steps we took on the Amur in 1850, when the government
considered it necessary to keep them secret, were achieved
under the auspices of the Company. Thus were founded our
first trading-posts at the mouth of the Amur."[8]

It is clear, then, that up to the middle of the 1850's the
government was very much interested in continuing the activities of the Russian-American Company. During that period
all measures were taken to free the Company from its difficul
financial situation by granting it a monopoly not only in the fu
trade but also in the tea-trade as well.

Not long before the fiftieth anniversary of the Russian-American Company the Governing Board, in drawing up the account of its activities, divided the history of the Company into three periods:

"The first period, marked by confusion and by the irresponsible utilization of the means and resources of the Company, lasted until 1821. The second period, distinguished by the gradual introduction of order and accountability, concurrently with the drying up of the sources of wealth in the colonies, may be said to have continued until 1838. And finally, the third period, characterized by the thorough organization of the administration of the Company, began in 1838 and has continued until now. However, the gradual decline of the tea-trade and the obstacles encountered in the attempt to sell the furs at a profit in the Russian market, are a manifest threat to the further success of the Company."[9]

In other words, in the first period of the Company's existence there was peltry but no order. In the second period, there was more order but less peltry, and, finally, in the third period, there was perfect order but the treasury was empty. It must be admitted that this picture of the evolution of the Company was very close to the truth.

Outwardly the situation of the Russian-American Company was quite favorable even during the second and the third periods. Every year, as in the past, the Company would declare a dividend, which was, moreover, considerably in excess of the rate of discount. Altogether the Company paid out in dividends between 1797 and 1859 inclusive a sum equivalent to 5,734,308.99 rubles, silver. Figuring that the Company during that period had an average of 7,484 shares, it appears that in sixty-two years the stockholders received 766.20 rubles on an investment of 150 silver rubles.[10] The annual dividend for 1826 to 1861, converted into silver, fluctuated between 13 and 20 rubles, which amounted to between 8 and 13 percent of the annual income.[11]

However, our study of the activities of the Russian-American Company for the first two decades of its existence has shown that the payment of dividends did not at all signify that the company was doing successful business. The total amount that the new management disbursed was many times smaller than it should have been according to the balance-sheet, since a considerable portion of the shares did not actually exist.

But behind the external soundness of the Company, there lurked a very difficult economic situation which was growing worse from year to year. This becomes most apparent from an examination of the figures on the amount of peltry procured by the Company. When we compare the quantity of peltry processed during the first two decades of the Company with that processed during the final two decades we necessarily arrive at the conclusion that the fur-resources of the colonies had been depleted in the meantime as a result of the predatory methods which the Company used in its operations.

Between 1797 and 1821 72,894 sea-otters were procured, and between 1842 and 1861, 25,602, showing a drop of 47,292. The same is true with regard to fur-seals. Between 1797 and 1821 the Company exported from the colonies 1,232,374 seal-skins, and between 1842 and 1861 only 338,604, showing a drop of 893,770.

But the situation of the Company took a turn for the worse not only because the fur-resources had been depleted; there were a number of other causes for the economic plight of the Company towards the end of the 1840's. Primary among these were the loss of the chief market for peltry, such as China had been over many years, and the difficulties involved in supplying the colonies with bread.

The decline in the purchasing power of the Chinese consumer, caused by the penetration of the capitalistic powers into the Celestial Empire at the end of the first half of the nineteenth century, the discount of silver resulting from the large-scale importation of opium, the destruction of the artisan class and of the small merchants by reason of their inability to compete with the foreign merchants, and, finally, the appearance of Canadian furs on the Chinese market--all this contributed to the drastic curtailment in the sale of Russian peltry in China, It was precisely the ruin of the small and the medium class of consumers that dealt an especially grievous blow to the Company, inasmuch as the furs it imported into China belonged to the cheapest varieties.

Of the average annual catch of 18,000 fur-seals, 8,000 went to China by way of Kiakhta. Since the opening up of Shanghai, another part of the catch was usually dispatched to that port, and only a small percentage made its way to the domestic market in Russia. The greatest quantity, then, of river-otter-skins, about 2,000, went to China, and only the expensive furs, such as sea-otters, sold in China in small numbers. Prior, then, to the rise of foreign competition almost all peltry, with the exception of sea-otters, met

When Russian trade with China had declined, it became necessary to look for new market, first of all in Europe. But the winning of new markets proved to be too difficult a task for the Company.

Notwithstanding the high quality of the raw skins, the furs that the Russian-American Company put on the market were of medium and sometimes even of poor quality, because of the shoddy processing. These low-grade varieties were acceptable on the Chinese market, but not at all on the European and American markets. Whenever it sent some of its furs over to New York and, especially, to London, which was then the center of the fur-trade, the Company was compelled to sell them very cheaply because they had been poorly processed.

In 1865 one of the employees of the Company by the name of Rutkovsky was sent to London to make a study of the system used at the firm of Oppenheim and Co. which was in the business of dressing fur-seal skins. "Here I had the opportunity," Rutkovsky reported, "to see some of the seal-skins from the colonies and from the islands of Lobus and Castillas. The latter variety is very much preferred on the London market, and I was indeed able to convince myself that the fur and the fluff of those skins are much longer and thicker. The salting of the skins is done very carefully and there is no brine left in the barrels. A number of the skins, to wit some five hundred , of those recently received from the colonies, had fluffy red spots where the fur could easily be pulled out with the fingers without disturbing the fluff. Mr. Sherster showed me similar skins that had been processed which had a number of bare spots on them. A few skins on the bottom of the barrels were stuck together and turned black because there was no salt on them."[12]

The Russian-American Company had supposedly intended to set up the dressing of skins in its colonies according to the very latest methods, but was prevented from doing so by the lack of qualified specialists. An attempt was made to entice some expert workmen over from the firm of Lempson in London, but it did not succeed. The English owners would not let go the workers they needed themselves and, furthermore, English law prescribed severe penalties for revealing industrial secrets.

While the slump in the trade with China was reaching an acute stage, a decline also developed in the sale of furs in

Russia, where the Company sold the most expensive varieties
of fur, especially sea-otters. As was pointed out by the Governing Board in 1845, "the wholesale buyers, seeing that the
best Company furs for which they paid good prices could be
sold only with great difficulty, and that the demand for them
had considerably relaxed, have been trying to replace them
with cheaper varieties. These latter, gradually coming into
use, have contributed to reducing even further the public demand for the more expensive varieties."[13] Neither was it
feasible to count on selling in the Russian market the cheaper
furs which could not readily be sold in China. Sealskin, the
chief product of the Company, used by the "third estate,"
was not yet worn by a sufficiently wide circle of people.

As we have pointed out, the Russian-American Company
was having great difficulty during that same period in keeping
the colonies supplied with grain. The discovery of gold in
California brought forth an unprecedented influx of immigrants.
As a result of the sudden increase in population, the prices
on agricultural products soared so high in California, that
it was cheaper for the Company to import these products into the colonies almost from as far away as St. Petersburg.

As for the deficit that had developed as a result of the decline in the trade with China and of the depletion of the most
valuable varieties of peltry, the Company had two ways of
meeting it. One was to utilize new varieties of furs, which
until then had not occupied an important place in the Company
budget, the other, to develop the sale of consumers' goods
in the borderlands of Russia, such as Kamchatka, Amur, and
so forth.

During the last period of the Company there was a considerable increase in the quantity of certain varieties of peltry.
There was also a rise in the catch of sea and river-otters,
and so forth. A much larger quantity of walrus tooth and
castoreum was procured. These were all very valuable export articles which went to England and to other countries.
But in spite of this increase in several of the categories of
trade, the Company was still not in a position to take advantage of all the opportunities open to it to make up for the ever-
growing deficit. The Company was even unable to organize
the process of the melting down of whale fat, of coal-mining,
or ice-cutting--ice was being exported to California.

The attempt of the Company to meet its deficit by expanding its commercial operations within the country itself also

met with failure. This task called for a change in the methods of work, but the monopolistic character of the Company rendered it incapable of entering upon any such activity. Wherever the Company encountered the competition of other commercial enterprises on an equal footing it was unable to withstand such competition and had to yield to the pressure. As was noted in the memorandum on the Russian-American Company that was prepared in the State Council when the question of renewing the Company's franchise was under discussion, "the Company's trade with the Siberian natives, which was expected to develop upon the establishment of the port of Ayan, has been curtailed, as has also the trade on the Amur and in Kamchatka. The reason for this decline in trade was that the Company did not have a monopoly on trade either with the Tunguses or in the Amur region. Without such a monopoly the Company was unable to stand up against the competition not only of the foreign merchants on the Amur but even of the Siberian traders in the Ayan region."[14]

Being a government agency, the Russian-American Company tried to strengthen its economic position by non-economic means, in the hope that they would help to place it in an especially favored position with relation to its competitors. The government, upholding the Company in its own interests, not only granted it a monopoly in those places where the fur-bearing animals were procured, namely, on the American mainland and on the adjacent islands, but also on the markets where the peltry was sold. The preferential position that the Company enjoyed in the fur-trade was planned as a preventive against new rival enterprises, as well as a means of actually taxing the other fur-dealers for the benefit of the Company.

As early as 1834 the Chaplins, largescale furriers of St. Petersburg, petitioned the Ministry of Finance for permission to trade with the United States and to export furs from there, especially sea-otters, to the Kiakhta market. It was a proposition that would no doubt have been profitable to the government, since the Chaplins also intended to export Russian manufactured articles to China. But their request was denied, because the government saw in the plan the possibility of doing injury to the Russian-American Company. The letter of the Governing Board written on this occasion to the Minister of Finance reveals quite unequivocally the motives which impelled the government to reject the profitable proposition of the St. Petersburg furriers.

That letter reads partly as follows: "In the first place,
as a result of the increase in the quantity of sea-otter-skins
by the importation of foreign skins, the furs of Russian production will drop in price and, consequently, those trading
in them will incur losses, and in the second place, since
Canadian sea-otters are superior in quality to the Russian
and Norwegian varieties, the Chinese, who always barter
for the better varieties, may stop buying the cheaper ones
altogether in the expectation that they may be able to procure
both kinds in Russia. Should this be the case, the trade in
Russian sea-otters may become a totally losing proposition,
to the detriment of the merchants and the fur-hunters, and
may even spell the ruin of the Russian-American Company." 1

The government actually made the Russian-American
Company master over the entire domestic fur-trade. Dic-
tating its own terms and not allowing anyone to trade in those
varieties which it considered within the scope of its monopolistic privileges, the Company, with the aid of certain of the
government departments, cut off any incipient competition
at the root.

At the beginning of the Company's activity, when the fur-
trade constituted the main source of its income, a ban was
placed on the importation of sea-otters, river-otters, and
fur-seals into Russia. In this way the Russian-American
Company secured a complete and unlimited monopoly in these
varieties of fur. But along about the 1850's, when the main
source of the Company's income was not the fur trade, but
the tea trade, the policy of the government with respect to
the importation of a few of the formerly banned varieties of
fur underwent a change. The importation of these same furs
into Russia was allowed, but only upon payment of a customs
duty that went partly to the Russian-American Company.

By the tariff of 1857 the ban on the importation of fur-seals
and river-otters was lifted, but the ban on sea-otters remained
in force, since almost the whole catch of the latter was disposed of by the Company in Russia. The tariff fixed the duty
on river-otters at 1.20 rubles a pound and on fur-seals at 60
kopecks, with 25 per cent of the revenue going to the Russian-
American Company. In the guise of remunerating the Company for its renunciation of the privileges that had been granted
to it, the government gave it new, and considerable subsidies.
Henceforward the Company was to add to its profits by allowing the importation of certain varieties of fur, just as it had

recently been profiting by banning such importation. This
was the way in which the life of the "private" enterprise was
being sustained by artificial means, only because, although
it had long been on the brink of economic collapse, it was still
necessary to the purposes of tsarist foreign policy.

No less interesting in this respect was the granting of
special privileges to the Russian-American Company in the
trade with Chinese tea. The tea trade in which the Company
was engaged by exchanging tea for furs in Kiakhta also began to run into difficulties along about the 1840's. The slump
in the tea trade was brought about not only by the changed
situation in China, which developed when that country's ports
were opened to foreign commerce and goods of foreign origin
began to make their appearance on the Chinese markets, nor
by the rise in the price of tea; it was the result of the changed
trade situation in Russia itself.

In one of its memoranda the Governing Board pointed out
that beginning with the year 1841 the Company "in its attempt
to dispose of its teas, became conscious of the very same
disadvantages to which the tea trade as a whole was subjected,
and for the following reasons: 1) the increase in the capital
of the Kiakhta traders, as a result of which the quantity of
merchandise bartered rose to almost 30 per cent, and the
wholesale price dropped correspondingly; 2) the rise in the
cost of transporting the tea, resulting from the increased
quantity of merchandise that was offered for exchange, and
the development of gold-mining in Siberia."[16]

In its search for ways to combat its rivals who were bringing in tea by way of Kiakhta, the Company made several attempts to import tea into Russia directly through Shanghai.
In addition, the government granted the Company the right to
sell its tea at prices "most closely approximating those of
the Kiakhta tea," which really made it possible for the Company to sell its tea below the average price prevailing in
Russia.

The permission granted to the Company to carry on its
tea business not through Kiakhta but through Shanghai was
of added significance to the government in the sense that
these trade expeditions could be utilized to survey the sea-
lanes into China. In this the Russian government would
simply be following the example of the other powers. Nesselrode, in supporting the Company's petition for the permission
to trade in tea through Shanghai, adduced the following reasons
for his stand:

"Allowing the Company to export from the Chinese ports a specified quantity of tea might also be of use in helping us to clarify the problem of sea-trade with China in general. It is even possible that in this way, and without official sanction by the Chinese government, a new form of trade intercourse may imperceptibly be established with that government, in the same way as our merchants have, without official sanction on the part of the Chinese, been trading on the western frontier of that country, in Chuguchak and Julja."[17]

It is clear, then, that in granting the Russian-American Company the right to engage in sea-borne commerce in tea, the government was pursuing a dual purpose. On the one hand, it used the Company to cloak tsarist expansion, and on the other hand, in the name of the very tasks that the government was aiming to achieve, it placed the Company in a favorable position with relation to its rivals.

Beginning in the 1850's, the Russian-American Company imported by sea an average of about 8,000 poods of tea annually, or 30 per cent of all the Chinese tea imported into Russia. In the last years of the Russian-American Company the tea trade became its chief source of income. The gross receipts of the Company between 1857 and 1861 averaged 952,275 rubles, silver, annually, of which 421,912 rubles came from tea, and 301,030 rubles from the so-called "increments," or additions to the price of merchandise imported into the colonies to be sold to the hunting-station workers and to the natives, 20,651 rubles from other trade, and only 208,682 rubles from the sale of furs. On the imported tea the Company was supposed to pay the treasury 210,658 rubles annually in customs duties. But the government did not require the payment, actually giving the Company a new subsidy in disguise. By 1867 the Company's indebtedness on its delinquent custom duties had risen to more than 700,000 rubles.

But at the end of the 1850's and the beginning of the 1860's, when the tsarist government, as we shall see, had no further use for the Company, the attitude in government circles towards the Company underwent a drastic change. During the last three or four years of the Company's existence, when the only thing that held up its liquidation was the search for a buyer for the colonies in America, its activities were subjected to fierce criticism on the part of individual ministers and of special committees. The deterioration of the Russian-American Company, about which everyone had been keeping silent, had now become a topic of discussion in all the memoranda dealing with the Company.

The Minister of State Property in a letter he wrote to the Minister of Finance towards the end of 1862 describes the condition of the Company in the following words:

"The main pursuit of the colonies--the hunting of sea-otters--has been continually on the decline. Generally speaking, the fur business has begun to yield first place to Canada and Great Britain. These two countries have been sending furs to Europe in vast quantities and at incomparably lower prices. Whaling in the colonies has passed into the hands of the Americans. Fishing has been done on a scale which barely meets the needs of the colonies themselves, in spite of the extraordinary abundance of various good stocks of fish in the lakes and rivers of the colonies. Nothing has been done with respect to farming and cattle-breeding. The mineral resources of the region have hardly been tapped. All the commercial relations that the Company has maintained have been seriously impaired and are falling into decay. Its merchant marine has been allowed to be reduced to negligible proportions, and it is compelled to charter foreign boats to meet its own requirements."[19]

A committee comprising representatives of the various government departments examined the report of the inspection that had been made in the colonies, completing its task in May, 1863. In its conclusion the committee remarked that the Russian colonies in America "are at a perfect standstill as regards colonization, hunting, trade, and civic development, and that, generally speaking, the Company has far from justified the expectations which the government had placed in it. On the one hand, the decline was the direct result of the policy of unmitigated monopoly which destroys every opportunity of competition and takes away the incentive to vigorous action, but, on the other hand, it was the natural climatic and geographical conditions in the region in question that were the main cause of the low state in which the Company now finds itself."[20]

Chapter XI

THE SALE OF THE RUSSIAN POSSESSIONS IN AMERICA

THE OUTCOME of the Crimean War which "...demonstra-
ted" to the whole world "the rottenness and impotence of en-
serfed Russia,"[1] brought about a change in the position of
the Russian empire as a colonial power in the Pacific. Actually the problem of further expansion on the American continent had been solved, so far as Russia was concerned, in
the middle 1820's. Yet, it was the war that posed before the
tsarist government in all its acuity, a problem that had
arisen more than once before, the problem of defending and,
consequently, of retaining Russian colonies in America.

At the outbreak of the Crimean War the Russian-American
Company was almost without any armed force that was capable of making a stand against foreign invasion. As the colonial administration reported to the Russian ambassador in the
United States, "all the settlements in the Russian-American
colonies have, to be sure, some sort of fortifications, but
these may be relied upon to stand up only against savages and
are almost useless in the event of real warfare."[2]

Even Novoarkhangelsk, the very center of the colonial
government, though it did have, according to the administration, "some more effective means of defense, still was not
in a condition to withstand any serious attack."

For the purposes of defense the Administration divided
the colonies into three groups. The first comprised the
region around Novoarkhangelsk itself, where "the local means
of defense are insufficent and could hardly be reenforced
later on by the Company's own resources." The allies, as
a result, let it be noted, of a visit paid to Novoarkhangelsk
by an English frigate in August, 1853, were perfectly aware
of the complete indefensibility of that port. The second group
included the settlements on the Aleutian chain and on the
American mainland, which, in the opinion of the Company,
it was not necessary to defend at all, inasmuch as they were
"little known to foreigners." Finally, the third region comprised the Company's colonies on the Asiatic coast, including

Sakhalin. These points were regarded as belonging within the general frontiers of Russia, and it was therefore incumbent upon the government to look after their defense.

It would seem, then, that out of the whole vast territory belonging to the Company, the administration considered as most vulnerable the center of the colonial government, Novo-arkhangelsk, where the greater part of the Company's property was concentrated.

Being well informed about all the diplomatic machinations and having secret and open agents everywhere, the administration of the Russian-American Company knew all about the general feeling prevailing in London that England would inevitably intervene in the Crimean War. Knowing this, it was preparing in its own way to defend it possessions.

While it hastily purchased a number of screw-steamers for the colonies and sent some troops on the ships that had been provided "with the neutral flag of Hamburg and the proper documents," the Russian-American Company had no intention whatsoever of setting up an active defense of its possessions.

On January 14, 1854, when the first news was received in St. Petersburg of the appearance of the allied fleet in the Black Sea, the Governing Board of the Russian-American Company submitted to the Ministry of Foreign Affairs the draft for a plan of action that was to assure the complete security of the Russian colonies.

The plan had been worked out in England, the very country against which it was intended to defend the Russian colonies, and had the unofficial approval of the leaders of British foreign policy who, at the same time, were preparing for a break with Russia. According to Bancroft, "as soon as war between England and Russia became a certainty, representatives of the Russian-American and Hudson Bay Companies met in London to consult on the exigencies of the case."[3]

Starting with the premise that "it is only England, without the cooperation of the Americans, of whom the Company may be in fear of hostile action against the colonies," the administration, by January, 1854, had with the aid of the Hudson Bay Company, obtained a guarantee from the British government of the inviolability of the Russian colonies. This guarantee was to be expressed juridically in the form of a neutrality pact between the Russian-American and the Hudson Bay Companies.

Upon giving the Russian-American Company a guarantee of absolute inviolability not only on the part of the British fleet but also on the part of the whole allied fleet, the Hudson Bay Company was to receive an extension of the lease on the comparatively insignificant strip comprising the Russian possessions in America.

A favorable answer was received on January 25, 1854, that is, eleven days after the Russian-American Company had petitioned the Russian Ministry of Foreign Affairs "that the Governing Board be authorized to enter into direct negotiations with the directors of the English Hudson Bay Company ...and that the latter should be asked to obtain from its government the recognition of the neutrality of the possessions and ships of the two companies."[4]

The director of the Ministry of Foreign Affairs, L. Sinyavin, informed the management of the Company that "it has pleased His Imperial Majesty to give his most gracious assent to the petition on condition that when a mutual agreement has been reached between the two companies it would be submitted by them for the approval of the two respective governments."[5]

There were many people, however, who did not believe in the possibility of such an agreement. Even to persons close to the Company but not completely initiated into the preceding negotiations such a result seemed paradoxical. The consent of the English government to enter into negotiations was regarded as a trap.

The Company's agent in Hamburg hastened to inform the management that "certain arrangements are being concocted in London that are highly detrimental to the interests of the Company." He insisted on the necessity of sending a representative to London "without the slightest delay," who would have the authority to act on his own "in all circumstances, even in the event it should seem necessary to sell the possessions to one of the neutral powers."[6]

"I do not believe," wrote the same agent, "that the English government is actually interested in the proposals which you may decide to make with relation to your territory." And this opinion was shared by all. Even some of the members of the Council of the Russian-American Company, upon learning in executive session of the negotiations between the management and the Hudson Bay Company, espressed the apprehension that "the dealings" between the two companies on the

neutralization of their possessions "can only serve to turn
the attention of the English government to Novoarkhangelsk
and to prompt it to adopt certain measures which perhaps the
English would not have thought of doing, if there had been no
such negotiations."[7]

However, in this particular case there were no grounds
for pessimistic suppositions. The neutrality pact between
the Russian-American Company and the Hudson Bay Company
was approved by the English government and, subsequently,
also by Nicholas I, as indeed the administration of the English
Company in London was duly informed on March 31, 1854.
Thus when the war broke out, the Russian colonies were
completely out of danger.

The preliminary negotiations between the two companies
were naturally cloaked in deep secrecy, and the administration of the colonies, remote as it was from the capital, was
not even in a position to expect such a happy ending to the
long-standing conflict between Russia and England on the
American continent.

The administration of the colonies, having been informed
by the Russian ambassador to the United States of the intention of the English and French governments to dispatch a
naval squadron "to blockade the ports of the Imperial colonies
in North America, immediately war--now become inevitable
--is declared on Russia, and even to seize those colonies, if
possible,"[8] hastened to work out its own plan of action to assure the safety of the Company's property. But this plan was
based not on the pact with the English Hudson Bay Company,
whose representatives in the colonies, either because they
had not been informed of the negotiations taking place in the
mother country, or else because they wanted to intimidate the
Russians, were even then attempting to start aggressive action against the Russian-American Company. The colonial
authorities based their own plan upon a pact with the American
merchants.

Kostromitinov, the agent of the Russian-American Company,
who was also vice-consul in California, came into possession
of information to the effect that "the Hudson Bay Company is
already taking steps to seize everything it possibly can."[9]
He communicated first of all with the Russian ambassador
in the United States and quickly set about drafting the text of
a fictitious agreement that provided for the transfer of all
the property and of the franchises of the Russian-American

Company to the "American-Russian Company of San Francisco," with which the Company had already concluded a
number of commercial agreements. The agreement was for
a term of three years, from May 1, 1854 to May 1, 1857.

Drawn up and signed by the two parties as Novoarkhangelsk
the agreement was quite outspoken as to the basic purpose
for which it had been drafted. That purpose was, if not exactly to force the English to give up entirely the idea of attacking the Russian colonies, then, at least, to give the Company the opportunity, by accusing the English of having en-
croached upon the possessions of citizens of a neutral power,
to demand satisfaction of England for all losses incurred.

Not without reason was Article 9 of the agreement, with
just such a situation in view, made to read as follows:

> "All contingencies and circumstances of whatever sort
> or class they may be, as long as they are independent of
> the commercial management of the Russian-American
> Company or are beyond the scope of its functions, shall
> not be regarded as a violation of this contract by the
> party of the first part [the Russian-American Company. --
> Au.]; and the party of the second part [the American-
> Russian Company. --Au.], having now purchased the proper
> ty and the franchises of the party of the first part, is ac-
> cepting the same on its own account and at its own risk,
> ...and will, under no pretext whatsoever bring claims,
> in the aforementioned case, against the Russian-American
> Company, that is, the party of the first part."[10]

The American-Russian Company pledged itself, as it
were, to pay the Russian-American Company seven million
dollars for the property and the franchises. "This document,
wrote Kostromitinov with regard to the fictitious agreement,
"would indeed have been produced, in case of necessity."

At the same time another plan was being worked out at the
initiative of the Russian ambassador to the United States,
Stoeckl, which was calculated to undermine British trade in
the Pacific.

Kostromitinov informed the Governor of the Russian Colonies, Voyevodin, that he had received a dispatch from Stoeckl
"deeming it very likely that the colonial administration had the
authority to issue written permits (letters of marque)[11] to
those desiring them." In Stoeckl's opinion, there is "many

a freebooter along the Pacific coast who will be willing to take advantage of the propitious occasion of a war between Russia and the Western powers to fit out a so-called privateer under the Russian flag, and chase after French and English trading-vessels."[13]

Privateering was regarded, it would seem, as the only possible method of preventing the English from seizing all the Pacific trade. "Russia does not have the fleet to control the Pacific," wrote a certain "American citizen" who expressed the desire to assume the leadership in organizing the privateering venture, "therefore, all her ships will be captured. The colonies, too.... It is clear that Russia must use all means at her disposal to destroy the vast Pacific trade of France and England with China, Australia, North and South America, and the East Indies."[14]

San Francisco was to become the center of Russian privateering. It was intended to buy the ships there and provide them with letters of marque. In Sitka, or in some other Russian port, these ships were to be fitted out and manned with Russian officers and sailors. The size of the privateering fleet which Russia would be able to organize at San Francisco--it seemed feasible at first to use that city as the base--was limited only by her buying capacity of ships. It was thought possible to send out between six and eight well-armed privateers against the English and French at the cost of two million dollars. Success seemed to be assured by the fact that the allies would not be able to concentrate a squadron of any considerable strength in the Pacific waters, since they would be compelled, by sheer necessity, to scatter their naval effectives in the Atlantic, the Baltic, the Mediterranean and the Black Sea.

But at the very first attempts to pass from theoretical calculations to practical measures, it became plainly apparent that the events of the past years had considerably reduced the possibilities for the rapid organization of a fleet of privateers. On the one hand, the sad end that befell the attempt of freebooters to plunder certain provinces in Mexico, and on the other hand, the arrest, shortly before the events we have described, of the Mexican consul in San Francisco who was trying, by order of the Mexican President Santa-Anna, to organize a privateering squadron--both these happenings rendered extremely difficult the attempts of the Russian vice-consul to start a privateering fleet.

No happier results, it soon became apparent, were to be
expected of the fictitious agreement with the San Francisco
merchants. The signed contract, which was to assure the
protection and the defense of the Russian colonies on the
part of the United States, proved to be, at the crucial moment
only a scrap of paper with nothing binding about it.

This is what Stoeckl, the Russian ambassador to the United
States, reported, in part, to the Minister of Foreign Affairs
on the results of his conversations with a number of American
statesmen:

> "In spite of their willingness to protect our colonies
> and their genuine interest in them, they regard it as im-
> possible to prove to the English that the contract is not
> fictitious and that, in particular, it was drawn up before
> the war and cannot, therefore, be of any real use."[15]

Such a declaration by the leaders of American foreign
policy was construed as an unequivocal intimation that the
best course for Russia to adopt would be to sell its colonies
to the United States. And to be sure, immediately thereafter
a concrete proposal was made to the tsarist government.

But it was not at all to England's interests to have America
employ the threat of the English fleet in order to come into
possession of new territory. Consequently, just when the
Americans thought, according to the agent of the Russian-
American Company, that "the fall of our colonies had become
inevitable,"[16] help came, as we have noted, not from friendly
America but from hostile Britain. More than that, England's
apprehension of forcing Russia into a position where she
would have to sell the colonies to the United States was so
great, that she not only gave strict adherence to the agreement between the Russian-American Company and the Hudson
Bay Company, but also decided not to utilize the privileges
she had retained even after the conclusion of the neutrality
pact.

The British State Secretary for Foreign Affairs, Adding-
ton, informed the Hudson Bay Company that the neutrality
"will be only territorial in scope and will be limited only to
the land, and that the operation of the neutrality pact will not
be extended to the seas, and that, therefore, all Russian
ships encountered at sea and the property both of the Company
and the government and of private persons, that are on the

way to or from the colonies, will be subject to seizure by English cruisers, and that the coast and the ports of those possessions may be subjected to blockade."[17]

However, during the entire war not one of the ports in the Russian colonies was blockaded, nor was any vessel seized. Only the island of Urup was visited in September 1855, by the English frigate "Peake" and the French "Sibylle," but those visits were not a violation of the neutrality pact which covered only the northwest coast of America and did not apply to the Kuriles.

Russian diplomacy gave due consideration, of course, at the proper time, to the situation that had newly arisen. Stoeckl, the Russian ambassador to the United States, in a letter to Prince A.D. Gorchakov, recalling the neutrality pact that had been concluded between the Russian-American and the Hudson Bay Companies, observed that neutrality had been "entirely to our benefit, since we were not in a position to attack the English possessions, whereas the English would have been able to seize ours." Stoeckl succeeded exceedingly well in bringing out into the open the real reasons for what seemed at first glance to be an incomprehensible British policy. He wrote to Gorchakov that "this act of affability, which is so little in harmony with English egotism, had a secret reason behind it. A rumor was gaining currency at the time that we were preparing to sell our colonies to the United States; and it was in order to block such a sale that the British government gave its approval to the agreement between the two Companies."[18]

According to the information given to Stoeckl by the former Secretary of State of the United States, Marcy, the British ambassador in Washington made repeated attempts, during the Crimean War, to find out in the State Department whether the sale of the Russian colonies had actually been discussed. It should be added at this point that, in spite of the military preponderance of the allies over Russia in the Pacific, the allied fleet was pinned down to a considerable extent, by the Taiping rebellion. While an attack on the Russian colonies was an easy matter, the subsequent retention of the seized territory, in view of the danger of a clash with America, required the presence of considerable forces in that area. The Taiping rebellion, though, diverted almost the whole allied fleet to Chinese waters and it was there that decisions were being hammered out on problems that were of

the most pressing importance to the European colonial powers.

It was the Crimean War, then, which was instrumental in
bringing to the fore the question of the sale of the colonies in
the guise of a fictitious agreement. This opened up the perspective of the formulation of the same problem as a genuine
agreement.

Although the agreement concluded by Kostromitinov with
the American-Russian Company was of no juridical consequence to the Russian-American Company whatsoever, nevertheless he was repeatedly reproached--and not without rea-
son-- by the management for having allowed the expression
"cession of lands" to figure in the pact at all. As early as
August of that same year of 1854, Stoeckl reported to the
Director of the Ministry of Foreign Affairs, Sinyavin:

"This draft of the contract and the rumors spread by the
English press as to the intention of the Imperial government
to sell its possessions, gave the Americans the idea that we
might want to yield those possessions to them."[19]

In the fictitious agreement with the American merchants
the sum was approximately specified--seven million dollars--
around which the subsequent negotiations for the sale of the
colonies were to be conducted.

In reply to an inquiry made in 1845 by Senator Givin of
California and Secretary of State Marcy regarding the possibility that Russia might sell the colonies, Stoeckl declared
that Russia "never had such intentions." But it was no longer
possible to underestimate the political significance of such
a proposition. It became apparent that a new claimant to the
Russian colonies, besides England, had made his appearance
on the political scene.

Immediately upon the end of the war and the conclusion of
the Peace of Paris the problem of the future destiny of the
Russian colonies in America came up again. The necessity
for a solution was dictated by the weighty lessons of the
Crimean war. "In the event of war with a naval power, we
are not in a position to defend our colonies,"[20] wrote Grand
Duke Constantine in a letter to the Minister of Finance
Knyazhevich.

The term "naval power" was intended to apply, first of all,
to England. "The United States of North America," wrote
Constantine at the same time to Foreign Minister Gorchakov,
"should, in the natural course of events, be eager to conquer

all of North America, and will, therefore, meet us there
sooner or later, and there is not the slightest doubt that it
will seize our colonies without great effort, and we shall
never be in a position to recover them." Constantine then
proposed that the colonies be sold to the United States, thereby "solving in a friendly fashion and in a way that would be
profitable to us a problem which will otherwise be solved in
a way disadvantageous to us and in addition by conquest."[21]

The Ministry of Foreign Affairs, while it agreed in principle on the necessity of liquidating the colonies in North
America, was afraid that such a step might undesirably aggravate the relations with England. It insisted, therefore,
upon a postponement of the proposed sale until the franchise
of the Russian-American Company had expired, that is, until January 1, 1862.

The ambassador to the United States was charged"to sound
out the opinion of the cabinet in Washington on that subject."
The memorandum we have on the proposed conditions of the
sale carries a notation that nothing expounded in the memorandum "was to be carried into execution until the question
of the cancellation of the contract between our Company and
the San Francisco Company has been settled, since by the
provisions of that contract the value of our possessions in
North America might be considerably reduced."[22]

The above notation was made on April 29, 1857. But in
December of that year, when Stoeckl's observations on the
subject had been received, the question of the sale of the
colonies again came up for consideration. Grand Duke
Constantine in his second letter to Gorchakov on the sale of
the colonies noted that a monopolistic company, like the
Russian-American, could no longer serve to cloak official
government policy, and that in the given period, the Company was merely pushing Russia into aggravating her relations with America and that essentially the Company's
policy would be detrimental to Russo-American trade as a
whole. These disconsolate conclusions were based on
Stoeckl's declaration that "the time for monopolies has passed, and that they are no more possible in the Pacific than
anywhere else."[23]

The appearance of the new claimant to the Russian colonies seemed the more threatening to the tsarist government
as the wresting of the colonies might well come as a result
not only of an official exacerbation of the relations between

America and Russia--a course which Russia would certainly
not want to follow so soon after the Crimean War--but also
of what, in diplomatic language, is called "peaceful penetration."

This is what actually happened in the case of the Mormon
rebellion. The Russian government was put on guard by reports of Mormon attempts to migrate northward, into the
territory of the Hudson Bay Company or the Russian-America
Company. "The President," wrote Stoeckl, "smilingly al-
luded to such a possibility. . . . I asked him whether the Mormon
were coming as conquerors or as peaceful citizens. 'You,'
he said, 'will have to answer that question; as for us, we
shall be mighty glad to be rid of them.'"[24]

While noting that the rumors of the Mormon migration to
Russian territory were premature, Stoeckl added that in the
event such migration should become a fact, Russia would be
faced with the alternative of armed resistance or of ceding a
part of its territory. It had become necessary to force a
decision on the question of the sale of the colonies. On Stoeckl
telegram reporting on his audience with the President with
regard to the above rumors, Alexander II jotted down the
following remark: "This confirms the idea of settling right
now the question of our American possessions."[25]

Towards the end of 1857 it fell to Gorchakov to bring up
again the question of the sale of the Russian colonies, though
in a slightly different manner.

The Russian envoy was directed "without compromising
himself or the Imperial government, cautiously to suggest
the idea to the cabinet in Washington that it might be possible
to induce Russia to relinquish her colonies on favorable
terms."[26]

The defenselessness of the Russian colonies was the consequence not only of Russia's military weakness which was
disclosed during the Crimean War, but also of tsarist Russia's renunciation of its expansionist aims in that direction.
We have noted before that the tsarist government had been
compelled in the middle 1820's to give up any hope it ever
entertained for further active expansion on the American continent. Beginning with about the middle 1840's, Russia's interest in the Orient was completely focused on the continent
of Asia. This change is cognizable in the correspondence
devoted to the sale of the colonies of Grand Duke Constantine
and of almost all of the ministers. Stoeckl, who took an ac-

tive part in the sale of the colonies, also takes this reorientation into consideration. He write, for instance, to Gorchakov in 1859:

"Our interests lie on the Asiatic coast, and we should direct our energy thither. In that area we are in our own territory and in a position to exploit the production of a vast and wealthy region. We shall take part in the extraordinary activity that is being developed in the Pacific, our establishments will vie with similar establishments of other nations, and, in view of the solicitude which our august monarch has given to the coastal region of Amur, we must not miss the opportunity to attain in this vast ocean the high position of which Russia is deserving."[27]

In the meantime, there was a new development in the 1850's which tended to render the situation even more complicated. Unmistakable signs were discovered in Alaska of the presence of gold ore. The Russian-American Company had long before received information to that effect from individual gold seekers. It was also attested by the finding on many occasions of gold nuggets. But in gathering the information about the presence of gold in the various regions, the Company did not intend to utilize it for the purpose of starting a survey of the territory. More than that, fearing that the reports of the presence of gold might arouse the government to take away its monopoly, the Company opposed in every way it could the making of any surveys, studies, and so forth, on its territory. For this reason, even the richest deposits of coal and copper remained unexplored. In reply to the repeated offers to exploit the copper along the Mednaya River, the Company declared that it had already begun the work on its own, although this did not square with the facts.

It became impossible, however, to conceal the presence of gold in the colonies, once the attention of the whole world had been attracted to the western part of North America by the gold fields of California, and once, too, it appeared from the discovery of deposits in the boundary area between the territory of the Hudson Bay Company and the Russian-American Company that some of the main deposits must be within Russian territory.

In the report of the survey of the Russian colonies made by Captain Golovin, who, together with Councillor of

State Kostlivtsov, was sent on an inspection tour of the colonies in 1860, we have a very precise notation: "Along the
Mednaya River they found large nuggets of native copper, and
on the shores of Kenai Gulf the presence of gold was conclu-
sively proved."[28]

The reports, however, as to the presence of gold in the
colonies impelled the government to allow the Company to
retain its rights to that territory, though not, as the management of the Company supposed, in order to enable it to start
the mining of the precious metals. On the contrary, the
government had arrived at the conclusion that it must take
decisive steps to dispose of its American possessions as
rapidly as possible. There were solid grounds for such an
apparently paradoxical decision.

The example of California, which, within a short time,
was overrun by fortune-hunters from all over the world,
was ever before the government's eyes. Were a similar
situation to develop in Alaska, Russia, the government believed, would under no circumstances have been able to retain its control over that territory.

The possibility of such an outcome became especially real
in 1862 when gold was discovered along the frontier between
the Hudson Bay and the Russian-American companies.

It so happened that the mouth of the Stakhine River, the
most convenient means of communication with the gold fields
discovered within the English sector, was within Russian
territory. This land was under lease to the Hudson Bay Company, and the terms of the lease was just then expiring. Consequently, all the transit goods and all the gold-prospectors
passed through the Russian area, which, as a result, came
into the actual possession of the English. The English newspapers appearing in the port of Victoria on the Vancouver
River hinted very broadly at the chances for wresting that
territory from Russia. At any rate, they dwelt on the necessity for extending the agreement between the Russian-American and the Hudson Bay companies covering the right of un-
hampered exploitation of the territory. "Even admitting that
negotiations would not succeed in inducing the Russian-American Company to cede that territory to us completely," said
the English papers with reference to the estuary of the Stakhine River, "we still must have that shoreline in our hands,
in one way or another." The newspapers called for open
seizure of the area in question: "Should the Sitka administra-

tion, however, set its mind upon attempting to stop our passing, we shall resort to our naval power to protect the inviolability of the pact. A small number of English troops would
be sufficient to render the Russian gryphon quite tractable.
Should we meet with some difficulty, we could very easily
push back the boundaries of the Russian possessions. Since
we have in our hands the area which is rich in gold, we should
also be in possession of its adjacent coastline."[29]

The problem reached an even more acute stage as a result
of the discovery of gold within the territory under Russian
control. After Cameron, United States Ambassador to Russia, had informed the Russian government "that the gold-
fields discovered in Oregon and British Columbia extended
as far as the Russian possessions in America," the administration of the Company, upon being questioned on this point,
showed its utter confusion by giving absolutely contrary information in the text of the same document. On the one hand
it hastened to assure the Minister of Finance that, according
to the Indians--as though the Company did not have other
sources of information at its disposal--"the nearest locality
where gold may be found in large quantities is no nearer than
200 versts from the river's mouth, or approximately a seven
days' journey away, a place which is already outside the
limits of Russian territory."[30] On the other hand, the Company reported that it had issued an order saying "that since
we cannot offer open and determined resistance--something
we have been enjoined to avoid at all costs--we should allow
gold-prospectors to dig for gold in our territory, upon the
payment of a certain amount to the Company." At the same
time the Company forwarded to the Ministry of Finance
copies of the reports submitted by engineer Andreyev, who
had been commissioned to explore the discovered gold-fields,
emphasizing categorically that "the gold-fields are rather
poor and the gold as fine as flour, and that the richest sections yield only five dollars a day."[31]

Andreyev said in his report that "coarser gold-dust is to
be found beyond the second lock-gates or rapids." The mining
of those fields must have been profitable, for, according to
Andreyev, the number of gold-prospectors in that area had
reached four hundred.

Not being strong enough itself to combat the influx of the
gold-prospectors, the Company hastened to petition the government to send over an armed cruiser from the Pacific

Squadron to the Stakhine River in order to protect the Russian possessions "against the arbitrary activities of the foreigners It soon became necessary, however, to give up the idea of sending a cruiser to the Stakhine, since events in China permitted of no weakening of the Pacific fleet. In addition, it was found that the Stakhine estuary was inaccessible to men-of-war. The problem of protecting the colonies demanded an immediate solution. At the instance of Baron Brunnow, the ambassador in London, the lease-agreement with the Hudson Bay Company, which had expired on January 1, 1862, was allowed to run until June 1, 1863. On that date the agreement, in view of the delay in the sale of the colonies brought about by the American Civil War, was extended for another two years, until June 1, 1865.

It was necessary to renew the agreement in order to defend the Russian colonies against the claims of the English until such time as these colonies could be liquidated without hindrance. The legend which grew up later that the tsarist government did not realize, when it sold the colonies, the resources of which it was depriving itself, finds no substantiation in any official sources. Such a version of the sale is the more naive as the presence of gold-fields in Alaska was not only known to the government in the 1860's but was also discussed over and over again in the press.

In an editorial on the rumors concerning the prospective sale of the Russian colonies to the United States, "Golos" (The Voice), one of the most authoritative newspapers in St. Peter burg, wrote that the sale of the colonies would deprive Russia of them precisely at the time "when, as has recently been reported, numerous promising indications of the presence of gold have been discovered on their soil, the mining of which, assuming the reports are true, would bring in more in two or three years than the amount that the United States is prepared to pay for them."[32]

The New York Herald in an article devoted to the purchase of the Russian colonies by the United States did not preclude the possibility that "resources ten times more valuable than the amount [paid to Russia.-Au.] are hidden away in the entrails of the eternal snows which cover all of the 17,000 feet of towering Mt. St. Elias. That mountain is the beginning and the head of the gold-bearing chain running through California, Nevada, Mexico, Central and South America; why, then, may we not suppose that it hides gold-fields richer than all the others, provided we can find one way to know them?"[33]

The government not only knew of the presence of gold-fields in Alaska but was actually afraid of the consequences of such a find; for in the wake of an army of prospectors armed with spades there might follow an army of soldiers armed with guns. Tsarist Russia knew very well what she was selling, and the United States knew equally well what it was buying.

The real reasons which impelled the tsarist government to sell Alaska were the following: first, Russia's inability to defend her colonies in the event of war, secondly, her inability to pretect them even in a period of formal peace, in consequence of the wide-spread rumors about the presence of gold there and the inevitable conflicts resulting therefrom, and, finally, the shift of Russian interests to the continent of Asia.

Yet these factors are far from exhausting all the circumstances that favored the sale of the colonies. There were other reasons which tended to force the sale, some of which were inherent in the Russian-American Company itself.

Since the Company was not in absolute possession of all the territory that belonged to it, it was not in a position to oppose the exploitation of separate sectors in the guise of leases by other powers. This process began with the Hudson Bay Company, which was allowed to lease a certain sector in order to render the colony secure against any claims on the part of England. A considerable battle developed over the question of leasing, which affected the relations between Russia and England, and the United States.

On the one hand, the Russian ambassador in England, Baron Brunnow, out of diplomatic considerations and out of fear that the territory that had been leased might be subject to direct seizure, insisted categorically upon the renewal of the lease with the Hudson Bay Company; and on the other hand, the Russian ambassador to the United States, Stoeckl, out of the same consideration, insisted just as categorically upon the leasing of the same territory to the company of American citizens that was laying claims to it. In 1859, in view of the expiration of the contract with the Hudson Bay Company, Stoeckl proposed to the Company, in the name of a group of Californian citizens, that it lease the territory to them. The negotiations with the Governing Board were conducted by Clay, United States Ambassador to Russia, who "made an oral offer to pay more per year for the territory

leased by the Hudson Bay Company than that Company had
been paying."[34] In the event that his offer was rejected, Clay
expressed his readiness to initiate negotiations at least for
the islands which were not under lease to the Hudson Bay
Company.

The Company, threatened with the forced loss of a portion
of its territory, could not oppose such insistent "suggestions."
It was compelled to bring before the government the question
as to the extent to which the simultaneous conclusion of a
lease-agreement with Hudson Bay Company for territory on
the mainland was in harmony with the pact to be concluded
with the Company of Californian merchants for the lease of
the islands to them.

It was quite evident that in these conditions, when the territory of the Company had become an object of importunities
on the part of its neighbors, the Company was no longer of
any use to the tsarist government. The political importance
of the Company was reduced to nothing. As for its commercial importance, the Company had, as we have seen, lost
any it ever had and was now a semi-parasitic organization
that could exist only by government support.

In 1866, the total income of the Russian-American Company amounted to 706,188 rubles, of which 200,000 constitute
a treasury subsidy. The office of the Governing Board in St.
Petersburg consumed more than 10 per cent of the gross income, or 71,660 rubles.[35] A sum totaling only 10,828 rubles
or 1.45 rubles per 150-ruble share, was left for the payment
of dividends.[36] During the last years of the Company's existence these 150-ruble shares of the Company were selling on
the stock-exchange at 70 rubles, and only when the reports
on the sale of the colonies became widespread did the price
of the shares show a sharp rise.

It appeared from the most accurate calculations that the
Russian-American Company would be able to continue in
operation only in the event that it receive a further annual
subsidy of no less than 200,000 rubles, and on condition that
its whole indebtedness to the Treasury, amounting to 725,000
rubles, be cancelled. "Should this come about," reported
the management, "there would be no possibility at first of
figuring on the payment of dividends to the stockholders.
Only when the selling price of the main product of the Company, namely, peltry, has been raised after the terms of the
contracts have expired, will it be necessary to figure on paying between 4 and 6 per cent per share annually."[37]

However, even a subsidy could not restore the financial strength of the Company completely. In addition to the subsidy , the Company needed a single loan, since any ill-timed payment it might make on the loans it had contracted in Russia and abroad would threaten it with bankruptcy. In spite of the Company's difficult financial situation, the London banks were more than willing to grant it such a loan.

The decline in the political importance of the American colonies for the Russian empire and Russia's growing inclination to sell them to the United States compelled the English government to come to the aid of the Russian-American Company in every way possible. Preferring as neighbors the Russian-American Company, which was incapable of large-scale colonization, rather than the Americans, the English government, acting through Britain's financial circles, made an effort to assist the Company by putting at its disposal the loan it so desperately needed. The prospective sale of the colonies was kept a dark secret even from the members of the management. The latter attributed the delay in the promulgation of the new charter to purely financial difficulties of the government which, for that reason, did not want to give any further subsidies.

During the period between 1862 and 1867, when the Company's franchise was due to expire and the question of a new charter was left unsolved, London appeared to some of the members of the management as the surest hope. The Company had long maintained contacts with London's commercial circles, inasmuch as that metropolis was the center of the fur-trade. During the time, then, that the decision on the question of the franchise was being delayed, the Company started negotiations with a number of influential spokesmen for British finance, who promised to float a loan of between £150,000 and £200,000 on the London stock-exchange.

"We have had many conversations," wrote the owners of the banking firm of Albert Pelley and Co. to the Governing Board of the Russian-American Company in March, 1864, "with influential people in these parts. They were not all of the same opinion, and the expectations on the part of many of them of profits for themselves were so great that we were unable to arrive at any decision. But some of my friends agreed to underwrite this loan at 92 per cent and 6 per cent for a period of twelve years, with the payment of 1/20 every half year, after the first two years, together with the interest." 38

But in arranging the loan, the City wanted to have a definite guarantee that franchises would continue to be granted
to the Company in the future, and that, consequently, the
Russian colonies would not be sold to the United States. The
London stock-exchange demanded that the loan should be
guaranteed by the Tsar himself and by the Minister of Financ
Such a demand, the stock-exchange believed, would lead to
the retention of the Company and, hence, to the preservation
of the Russian colonies in America.

This is the text of the guarantee as worked out in London:

"[We] The Emperor or the Russian Government in con-
siderate of the trust we have placed in the company established in our empire and known by the name of 'Russian-American Company,' and in the desire to facilitate
the operations of the said Company by offering it an opportunity to collect funds in the United Kingdom with whicl
to conduct the business of the Company, herewith give our
consent to this guarantee of the dutiful fulfillment by the
Company of the obligations it has taken upon itself."

Then came the terms of the loan. As Pelley said in his
letter of May 27, 1864, "that document should be signed by
the Emperor and countersigned by the Minister of Finance
or the Prime Minister."[39]

The London banks would indeed have opened their coffers
wide to the Russian-American Company, if they had the
slightest assurance that they would thereby prolong its existence. "Give them the guarantee, and the £200,000 in cash
will be ours,"[40] wrote Rutkovsky, an official of the Company
who had been sent to London to look into the question of the
loan. The government, however, intent on liquidating its
colonies in America, would not, of course, give the required
guarantee, but limited itself to granting permission, in gener
terms, to the floating of the loan.

Just as unsuccessful was the attempt to obtain a loan in
government notes on the Petersburg stock-exchange from
insurance companies and the like. Negotiations for a loan
of 1,200,000 rubles, silver, in treasury notes, out of the
amounts coming in as poll tax and customs duties, were also
doomed to failure.

In summing up its financial status, the Company was
forced to declare "in all frankness that without money to pay

its debts, nothing can save the enterprise from having to
suspend its operations altogether."[41]

On January 1, 1862, the term of the charter of the Russian-American Company expired. In view of this, the Company had in the meantime--in 1860--submitted the draft for
a new charter to the Ministry of Finance. This draft did not
provide for any changes from the old charter and only gave
additional juridical sanction to the status existing in fact.
For instance, Article 1 of the charter which, in the old text,
read that the Company "is being established for the purpose
of engaging in hunting on the mainland of northwestern America and on the islands," was formulated much more candidly
in the new charter. "The Company," it said, "is being established for the purpose of administering the Russian colonies in America." All authority over the colonies was, as
before, concentrated in the hands of the governor, who was
elected by the management of the Company from among the
staff-officers of the fleet.

In order to cloak the lagging negotiations for the sale of
the colonies, the government did not refuse immediately to
grant its approval to the new charter, but pretended to be
studying it from 1860 to 1867, or to the very moment of the
sale. During that whole period the Company existed by virtue of an Imperial decree of May 29, 1861, according to
which "until such time as the question of the future destiny
of the Russian-American Company has been examined and
decided," the Company was permitted to continue its activities "according to the principles obtaining heretofore."

As the new charter was being considered by the government hierarchy, especially sharp attacks were leveled at the
monopolistic rights of the Company--the basic condition which
distinguished the Company from the other Russian joint-stock
companies of the time and turned it into a camouflaged weapon for the administration of the colonies by the government.

The sharp criticism aimed at this article in the charter
of the Company by the Ministry of Finance, the State Council,
and other departments was symptomatic of the nascent coun-
try-wide conflict between the middle class elements and the
monopolies which were characteristic of the seventeenth and
eighteenth centuries.

The spokesman for these views with regard to the Russian-
American Company was Grand Duke Constantine who, in order
to gain a measure of popularity, was demagogically parading

his "liberalism." He began by declaring that, under the conditions prevailing in Russia, "in the absence of any publicity
and in view of the fact that one cannot write anything against
the Company, the harm the Company does is even more pal-
pable."[42] He then demanded, without reference to the course
of the negotiations for the sale of the colonies, that the Company be reduced in all respects to the same status as the
other stock-companies, and that the administration of the
colonies be put under the governor-general of Eastern Siberia

In its intention to liquidate the Company, the government
began to prepare public opinion for such a development. It
was the fight against the serfdom existing in the colonies that
was invoked to justify the liquidation of one of the earliest
stock-companies, during the very period of "griunderstvo"[43]
when stock-companies were springing up in Russia with in-
credible rapidity.

The Directors of the Company, who, apart from reasons
of state, had a personal stake in the matter, inasmuch as
the liquidation of the Company would deprive them of a size-
able income, tried in every way to save it. The stockholders
and the directors, having for so many years been obedient
tools in the hands of the government, could not understand,
when the last moment came, that there was no sense in the
further existence of the Company, since the Russian colonies
in America had lost their importance. The Governing Board
made the fur fly in attempting to justify its course of action
with respect to the accusations brought against the Company,
without realizing that the question at issue was not that the
Company had been bad, but that it had lost its raison d'être.

Rear Admiral Etolin, a member of the Governing Board,
made a valiant effort in a memorandum to refute the accusations hurled against the Company of exploiting the native population, by pointing to the "philanthropic" works in which it
was ostensibly active. "It is unjust...," he wrote, "to accuse the Company of keeping the Aleuts in a state of slavery.
No one has deprived them of their property, and whatever
they manage to procure, whether on land or on water, belongs
to them. But since they would not be able, without the assistance of the Company which is supplying them with everything
to engage in their pursuits of hunting and fishing, they are
naturally under obligation to surrender their catch to the
Company, for which it remunerates them at a fixed price and
often even at a higher one. Rather, the Aleuts may be called

members of a family of which the American Company is the
head. As head of the family, or as the solicitous guardian,
the Company has a certain obligation, and it has indeed always abided by the principle that it is responsible for the welfare of the native and for the betterment of their existence,
as well as for their moral and intellectual development, according to the means it has at its disposal."[44]

The most serious charge brought against the Company
were the statistical figures themselves, which showed that
the Aleuts were dying out under the Company's "solicitous"
protection. To be sure, the Governing Board advanced a
strong argument against this weighty, and on the fact of it,
irrefutable accusation. The Company did not try to exculpate
itself or to disprove the fact that the Aleuts were dying out.
It merely resorted to an analogy. It was a fact, admitted
the Company, that fewer Aleuts were born than died, but was
it not also a fact that in Kamchatka, which had from the very
first been administered by the Crown and where the natives
were not sent out on any labor projects, they were also dying
out at the same rate as those in the Russian colonies in America? The management then cited the figures on the death-
rate of the Kamchatkans: in 1854 there were 274 births and
480 deaths of both sexes.

As to the other points of the indictment against the Company, the Governing Board was unable to take exception to
any of them.

The explanation offered by the Company in refutation of
the report that was drafted after an inspection-tour, came
in for especially harsh criticism at the hands of the Director
of the Navy Ministry, N. Krabbe.

The Company, the Governing Board tried to show, could
not but be full of solicitude for the Aleuts, in view of the fact
that its own welfare depended on them: "The interests of
the Company are intimately bound up with the well-being of
the natives, the Aleuts, and the Company is, therefore, obliged, for its own sake, to look after their welfare and contentment, in accordance with their local usages and conditions,
and not in accordance with the European mode of life." In
the margin Krabbe wrote: "Obliged it is indeed, but it has
not fulfilled its obligation, and has been concerned only with
stuffing the pockets of the monopolists."[45]

The Governing Board insisted on the necessity for a guard-
ianship over the Aleuts. "If he [i.e., the Aleut.-Au.] were

to be left to himself," wrote the Governing Board, "without
Company supervision, he would frequently starve to death."
Again Krabbe noted in the margin: "It does not necessarily
follow that he must be a slave, and that he is a slave is
attested by the report itself."[46]

In concluding its explanation, the Company, in an attempt
to justify its policy with regard to the Aleuts, wrote that "it
would be highly improvident to train them to eat bread" and
that their situation "should, in all justice, be called well-
managed and secure." Krabbe indignantly exclaimed: "Only
the devil knows what this means." Yet, only a short time
since, the same Krabbe regarded all this in the order of
things and was not at all indignant. Now, however, it was
being bruited in government circles for every one to hear
that the relations between the Company and the Aleuts were
based on force and should be altered.

In its memorandum on the Russian-American Company
the Department of State Economy said openly that the Company "being guided, properly speaking, by the principles of
serfdom, has regarded, and still regards, the hunting of
fur-bearing animals as its own peculiar possession and the
natives as its slaves."[47]

On the eve, then, of the liquidation of the tsarist colonies
in America there was finally talk of abolishing the institutuion
of serfdom in those remote Russian possession since the
necessity for such serfdom had now passed.

The fight against the Company was being waged not only
by government commissions but in the press as well. At
the initiative of Grand Duke Constantine "Materialy dlya istori
russkikh zaselenii po beregam Vostochnovo okeana" (Material
on the history of the Russian colonies on the coast of the
Eastern Sea), [48] consisting of extracts from official documents and memoirs, were published as a supplement to the
"Morskoy Sbornik" (Navy Journal). These papers cited facts
illustrating the predatory policy of the Company.

At the same time there appeared the capital work of P.
Tikhmenev,[49] a stockholder of the Company, who attempted
on the basis of official documents to set forth the Company's
humane attitude towards the natives and the benefits that
Russia had received from that organization. But the fate of
the Russian-American Company as well as that of the
Russian colonies in America was sealed; to all the considerations that we have enumerated which impelled Russia to sell

Alaska there was now added a new consideration that was
truly decisive in its effect. That was the attempt of the tsarist
government in the latter 1860's to orient itself toward America as an ally in the battle for the abrogation of the Treaty of
Paris and for the partition of Turkey.

In later times a certain amount of surprise was expressed
in the opposition press at the disinterested attitude evinced
by the tsarist government towards the sale of its colonies.
"We must remember...," wrote "Golos" "that our North American possessions lie adjacent to those of the English Hudson
Bay Company, to whom the passing of the Russian colonies
in the hands of the Americans can be least beneficial and
desirable, and, if only to rid itself of having the Americans
as its neighbors, the English company would undoubtedly have
been glad to pay three or four times the amount offered by
the United States."[50]

The truth is that if the Russian government had been guided
only by the desire to sell its colonies to the highest bidder, it
would have been able to get considerably more from England
than from the United States, since the American purchase of
the Russian colonies was heavy with complications for England.
But it was much more important for the tsarist government
to win an ally, especially one whose interests went counter
to those of England.

From the very moment that the question of selling the colonies to the United States arose, the Russian diplomats never
had the slightest doubt that the projected sale was a direct
challenge to England. In the account that Stoeckl gives in
his dispatch, dated December 23, 1859, of the course of the
negotiations for the possible sale of the Russian colonies to
the United States, he lays special emphasis on this circumstance.

"Before closing this report, I find it necessary to inform
Your Excellency that the plan for the cession of our colonies,
if it should be realized, has been worrying the British government to the highest degree."[51]

There were solid grounds for Stoeckl's observation: the
union of California with the United States was a serious blow
to British domination of the Pacific. England's efforts, in
turn, to intensify the colonization of Vancouver Island and a
section of Oregon met with a serious obstacle in the severity
of the climate. In such conditions, "if the United States,"
wrote Stoeckl, "should win mastery over our possessions,

then British Oregon would be squeezed together by the Americans from the north and the south and would hardly be able
to escape aggressive attempts on their part."[52]

In her aim to undermine English power in North America,
and, at the same time, bring about a clash between the United
States and the British empire, Russia decided to sell Alaska,
and the aspiration of the United States to dominate the American continent induced this empire that was vigorously in the
making to buy Alaska. In a conversation with Senator Gwin
of California Stoeckl pointed out that the amount of five millio
dollars which the United States had offered for Alaska would
hardly satisfy the Russian government. "I agree to raise my
offer," said Gwin, "and in this connection I shall have the
support of my colleagues from California and Oregon, but I
am not certain of the consent of the other states of the Union
that have no direct interest in the matter. The only reason
that might induce them to want to buy your colonies are the
prospects of increasing the power and influence of the United
States in the vast expanses of the Pacific, to the detriment
of Great Britain." "It is this political consideration," added
Gwin, "which the delegates from California and Oregon will
not fail to employ, and which will, without the slightest doubt,
have a favorable influence on Congress."[53]

The economic ties between England and the United States
did not at all prevent the protagonists of the South, when they
came into power, from being just as eager as those of the
North to oppose British expansion on the American continent.
Also, both the North and the South, in their desire for new
territory which would be admitted in the Federal Union as
an independent states, each nurtured the secret hope of winning the new state over to its side and thus increase its
strength in Congress.

The negotiations for the purchase of Alaska, directed, as
we have seen, primarily against England, were initiated
during the presidency of Franklin Pierce, who was under the
thumb of the Southerners. They were continued during the
incumbency of another protagonist of the South, James
Buçhanan, and finally assumed a definite form during the
presidency of Andrew Johnson who , although he opposed the
secession of the Southern States, did represent their interests

In 1859 the negotiations for the sale of the colonies passed
from the stage of generalities into the realm of concrete proposals. In one of his conversations with Stoeckl, Senator

Gwin again raised the question of the sale of the colonies,
emphasizing that President Buchanan was very much in favor
of it and that he had authorized him and the Assistant-Secre-
tary of State Appleton to conduct the necessary negotiations.
Stoeckl reported that Appleton had told him, in the President's name, that he, the President, "believed that the acquisition of our colonies would be beneficial to the powers
that are situated on the Pacific, that he was prepared to
start the plan moving, but before he went any further he
thought it necessary to find out whether we were inclined to
cede our possessions."[54] Should Russia's reply be favorable, Buchanan intended to discuss the question with members of his cabinet and with a few influential members of
Congress.

However, the sharpening of contradictions between the
North and the South, and the approaching presidential elections which held out the possibility of a number of changes
in the domestic policy of the United States, forced Russia
to desist for a time from giving a definitive reply to Buchanan's proposal. "Everything depends on the coming presidential elections, which will take place in November," wrote
Stoeckl at the beginning of 1860. "Until that time, we shall
continue to live in the state of chaos which now reigns everywhere, both in the administration and in the federal legisla-
tive assembly."[55]

Under these conditions, the sale of the colonies to the
United States had lost its meaning, as far as the tsarist government was concerned. Appleton and Gwin were informed
that "the Imperial government, without definitively declining
the proposition for the sale of its American colonies, regards
it necessary, though, to postpone the matter for a more opportune moment."

Officially such an "opportune moment" was stated to be the
expiration of the Charter of the Russian-American Company
in January of 1862. That date coincided with the conclusion
of the election campaign, which now made it possible to obtain a clearer picture of future United States policy.

The sale was postponed, then, for, what seemed at first
a year and a half, but for, what proved to be, seven years.

While sympathizing with the North as an enemy of England,
Russia could not, nevertheless, desire a break between the
North and the South, inasmuch as such a development would
certainly weaken the United State as a military power. "The

disintegration of the United States as a nation," wrote Stoeckl
to Gorchakov, "would, from our point of view, be something
to be deplored. The American confederation has acted as a
counterpoise to British power, and, in this sense, its continued
existence constitutes an important element in the balance of
power."[56]

Russia was interested in a compromise solution and in the
election to the presidency of a representative of the South,
to the extent that it might prevent a final break between the
North and the South. "Every one who is at the head of affairs
is scarcely above mediocrity," wrote Stoeckl with reference
to the domestic situation in the United States. "There are
only two exceptions. One is Senator Douglas of the Democra-
tic Party; he is talented and energetic, but is at odds with
the administration, which is using all the means at its disposal to keep him from the presidency. The other exception
is Senator Seward, a real statesman, but he is one of the
anti-slavery champions, and, were he to become president,
the South would leave the Union altogether."[57]

After the election of Lincoln, whom Stoeckl was evidently
unable to evaluate correctly, Russia made certain efforts to
bring about a reconciliation between the North and the South,
while preserving the Union. We are referring to the attempt
made by the Russian minister plenipotentiary to be allowed
to take part in the negotiations which Secretary of State
Seward was conducting with the representatives of the South.
Although in October, 1862, Russia declined France's proposal
to intervene in the conflict on the American continent, she
did, nevertheless, together with Great Britain, preserve her
full freedom of action, while striving to effectuate a reconciliation between the warring parties. In a conversation that
same October, (1862), with a representative of the United
States, Gorchakov laid particular stress on the fact that
Russia wanted above everything else "the preservation of the
American Union as an indivisible nation."[58]

In 1863, for a number of reasons, a Russian naval squadron was dispatched to America, under the command of Admiral Lisovsky. The squadron, together with the one under
Admiral Popov which was already stationed in the Pacific,
was intended, by its mere presence, to act as a deterrent
to the smuggling that the English were carrying on with the
South and which enabled the Confederate States to continue
their resistance.

After the end of the Civil War and the victory of the North,
Russia had reason to believe that she would be able to utilize
an alliance with the United States in her conflict with England
over the solution of the Near Eastern question in general and
the abrogation of the Treaty of Paris in particular. There
was no longer any need, then, of postponing the sale of the
colonies.

In July, 1866, an American delegation, headed by Assis-
tan Secretary of the Navy Fox, arrived in Russia. It extended
its felicitations to Alexander II, in the name of Congress, on
his "miraculous escape" from assasination on April 4. That
was an open demonstration of the United States as an ally of
Russia against Great Britain.

From the point of view of the nobility, the address sent
over by Congress was, to a considerable degree, rather
tactless. Congress, in sending its representative to St.
Petersburg "in a state of flaming indignation" over the April
4 incident, did not, evidently, find time to learn the official
version of the motives behind the attempt on the Tsar's life.
Karakazov, therefore, is pictured in the address as a representative of the nobility, taking his revenge on the Tsar for
having emancipated the peasants. But the necessity for winning an ally forced everybody concerned to make a happy face
while playing the miserable game. "There is no harm," shouted
the "Moskovskiye Vedomosti," "in that the Congress of a transatlantic republic, which as yet has no communications with
Europe by transatlantic cable, should err in the interpretation
of the causes of an event the substance of which it could not
possibly understand."[59]

There was "no harm" in it because, as the same "Moskovskiye
Vedomosti" declared, "the two nations have common foes."

The whole Russian press of the time was full of discussions
of the "community of foes" that Russia had with one power or
another. "Golos," and the other papers after it, were putting
out all varieties of propaganda to the effect that America
should become a "European power." "A great new power had
made its appearance on the European horizon," wrote "Golos,"
"which, without owning a patch of land in our hemisphere, may,
in alliance with Russia, really become a European power,
exerting a profound influence on the course of European events."

Yet, how did the Russian press picture this "conversion" of
America into a European power?

The "conversion" was to be accomplished by means of the

joint partition of Turkey. This was precisely the meaning of
the "Europeanization" of America, as far as Russia was concerned. "No doubt," wrote "Golos," "our harbors will henceforth be open to American warships; but the harbor of a
friendly power is still not the same as one's own; that is why,
while the rumors about the desire of the Washington government to obtain from the Sublime Porte one of the islands of
the Archipelago may be premature, they are not at all incon-
ceivable; and if the partition of Turkey's legacy should really
be in the offing, then our own interests impel us to want to
see the United States secure a share of that legacy. With a
naval station at its disposal in the Mediterranean, the American flag will prevent any incursions into the Black Sea by
fleets from the West, while our Baltic fleet will always be
on the alert to defend America's interests in northern
Europe."[60]

The fate of the Russian colonies was definitely decided
during Fox's stay in St. Petersburg. Stoeckl, who returned
to the Russian capital immediately after Fox had departed,
set to work on the official drafting of the sales agreement.
"The transfer of our colonies to the United States seems to
me especially desirable politically," wrote the Minister of
Finance, M.Kh. Reitern, to A.D. Gorchakov in December,
1856, after a conversation with Stoeckl.

Apart from the utter impossibility of defending the colonies in the event of war "with one of the naval powers,"
Reitern frankly pointed out that the most important reason
for selling the colonies to the United States was that the
United States would thereby "become a neighbour of the
English colonies not only to the south but to the northwest
as well." In his opi ion "such a development cannot but result in the strengthening of our friendly relations with the
United States and in increasing the chances for a disagree-
ment between the States and England."[61]

A similar view was expressed by Grand Duke Constantine,
who stressed "the exclusive advantages accruing to us from
a close association with the United States of North America
and from the elimination of any problem that might cause
discord between the two great powers."[62]

This aspect of the sale of the Russian colonies as a move
against England was also noted by Marx in a letter to Engels,
written on the eve of the drafting of the sales agreement. On
March 27, 1867, Marx wrote to Engels:

"The Russians are more active than they have ever
been before. They have cooked up a pretty mess between
France and Germany; Austria is rather impotent by herself. And they are also going to stir up a good deal of
trouble for the honorable English in the United States."[63]

It is worth noting that both the increased opportunity for
aggravating Anglo-American relations and the strengthening
of the association between Russia and America through the
sale of Alaska were thoroughly scrutinized in the foreign
press. To be sure, the English press passed over the subject in silence, but the French press, which was interested
in drawing England's attention to affairs in Russia and away
from what France was doing in Italy and Spain, devoted a
great deal of attention to the sale. Said the "Temps": "The
cession of the territory by Russia merely sets the seal to
the paradoxical alliance between Emperor Alexander and
President Johnson. What will come of it? Perhaps the naval squadron that America has for some time been keeping
in Greek waters will one day provide the answer to this question."[64]

Marx decisively rejected the possibility of United States
intervention in Turkish affairs and regarded all these rumors
as "Russian invention." In a letter to the editor of the
"Courrier Français," Vermorel, Marx wrote in August,
1867:

"You are reproducing canards (of Russian origin) to
the effect that North America will take the initiative in a
conflict with the Turks. You ought to know that the President of the United States does not have the right to declare
war. That right belongs only to the Senate.[65] If President
Johnson--that dirty tool of the slave-holders (although
you are so naive as to picture him as a second Washington)
--is trying to win some popularity by making a muddle of
international relations and by issuing a boastful declaration abroad, then remember that, after all, the Yankees
are not children or Frenchmen. The mere fact that the
initiative in all these attempts comes from him is sufficient
to deprive them of all real significance."[66]

But even while it disseminated such canards, the Russian
government did not put much credence in the possibility that

the United States would intervene directly in the conflict over
the partition of Turkey, in the event it became necessary to
use armed force. At the same time, though, the Russian
government realized full well that the complications arising
for England on the Pacific coast, as a result of the sale of
the Russian colonies in America to the United States, would
be of tremendous importance in reducing England's activities
on the continent of Europe.

In his analysis of Lilienfeld's pamphlet Marx wrote to
Kugelmann: "Another example of the gross ignorance of the
author of the pamphlet. In his eyes, the cession of the Russian part of North America was nothing more than a diplomatic trick of the Russian government, which, let me note
in passing, was in grave financial straits. But that is not
the point at all, and the American Congress has recently
published the documents that have a bearing on this deal.
Included is a report by an American agent, addressed directly to Washington, which says that the acquisition of the Russian colonies is as yet of no economic value whatever, but
that, as a result, the Yankees will be able to cut off England
from the sea on one side and so hasten the acquisition of all
of British North America by the United States. That is precisely the point."[67]

As early as the beginning of 1857, when the discussion of
the sale of the colonies was resumed, the Ministry of Foreign
Affairs tried to estimate the figure with which to start the
bargaining. Taking into consideration the fact that the Company
had, during that period, paid out the sum of 134,712 rubles
in dividends on 7,484 shares, had added 13,471 rubles to the
basic capital, and spent 673 rubles on various subsidies, the
Ministry calculated the annual profit of the Company at
148,856 rubles. Proceeding from the consideration that the
average annual rate of profit for the country was equal to 4
per cent, the Ministry arrived at the conclusion that the Company proper should be compensated to the amount of 3,721,400
rubles, silver. A like sum was specified for the benefit of
the government. The full price, then, of the colonies was
figured at 7,442,800 rubles, silver. This was the "minimum
program."

Another version, that was worked out at the same time as
the first, was based on a different set of figures. The basis
for the calculations in this case was not the profit, but the
total expenses of the Company on dividends, maintenance of

the staff, administration, and so forth. This sum, figured at 800,000 rubles, silver, according to data supplied by the Ministry, the Company "spent annually for the benefit of Russian subjects." Since it regarded this amount as equivalent to a 4 per cent profit on the total value of the colonies, the Company arrived at an evaluation of those colonies at 20 million rubles, silver.

However, the Utopian quality of the last version was apparent even to its authors, so that during the whole course of the negotiations the amount asked for the colonies fluctuated between 5 million dollars, or the amount of the first version which was equivalent to approximately 7,500,000 rubles, silver, and 7 million dollars, or the sum mentioned in the fictitious agreement between the Russian-American and the American-Russian companies.

According to Stoeckl, Senator Gwin of California, who conducted the negotiations, observed more than once that, in determining the price of the colonies, "it may be possible to go as high as 5 million dollars."[68] It was especially difficult to get a larger bid at that time, so soon after the end of the Civil War, when the Treasury was really empty.

Russia did not expect to get more than 5 million dollars. Reitern, the Minister of Finance, figured that the monetary remuneration should not go below 5 million dollars,"[69] or $2,200,000 less than Russia was able to get when the agreement was actually concluded. "I exerted myself to the utmost to get $7,200,000," Stoeckl informed the Minister of Finance. "I gradually brought Mr. Seward up to 6-1/2 million, but he would not go any higher. The negotiations were broken off temporarily, but I stood my ground, and the Secretary yielded."[70]

The last offer of an additional $200,000 was made on condition that the territory in question "be freed and released from all claims, special privileges, exemptions, grants or possessions of the united companies, corporate or non-corporate, Russian or foreign."

The $7,200,000 which Russia received for the colonies was equivalent to a little less than 11 million rubles, since the average value of the dollar in 1867 was 1.50 rubles and a fraction. According to the claims submitted by the Director of the Ministry of Finance on August 31, 1868,[71] that is, after the Company had been liquidated, Russia was still to be compensated to the amount of 728,600 rubles for moving

the Company's employees to Russia and for breach of contract, and 959,716 rubles for the loss of colonial property.
Moreover, the Company was to be made to pay its debts to
the Treasury, amounting to 677,883.70 rubles, including
interest.[72] In this way, of the total amount received from
the United States, the Company, after all its debts had been
deducted, was to receive 1,010,432.30 rubles. As for all
the other private debts, they, too, were to be paid off by
the Company out of the remaining amount.

The Treasury had left, then, a net amount of over 9-1/2
rubles--an insignificant sum, of course, but still equalling
more than one-half of the annual budget of a government
department such as the Navy, which had a budget of 16 million
rubles in 1867.

In discussing the material interests that prompted Russia
to sell the colonies, one cannot pass over in silence the indirect hints in the foreign press of the negotiations that were
going on between the United States and Russia about a loan.
Indeed, the tsarist government during that period considered
a foreign loan the only solution for the financial crisis in
which it was mired. "The deficit in current expenses, both
estimated and unestimated," wrote Minister of Finance
Reitern, in a secret report to Alexander in 1866, "will amount
to some 45,000,000 rubles in the next three years [i.e.,
1867-1869.--Au.], or an average of 15,000,000 annually.
This amount we must try to obtain through a foreign loan."[73]

The two loans obtained during 1862-1865, one a so-called
foreign loan at 7 per cent and the other a joint Anglo-Dutch
one at 5 per cent, did not solve the problem to any extent.
The story, therefore, that some sort of negotiations for a
loan were being carried on between Russia and the United
States might have some foundation in fact.

"The Russian government," wrote the "Temps," "has
tried not so long ago to sell the Petersburg-Moscow Railroad.
In this it did not succeed, but through the sale of its American possessions it will enrich its treasury by 7 million dollars, and there are also rumors that Russia has entered into negotiations with the United States on the subject of a
loan."[74]

The treaty for the sale of the Russian colonies to the
United States in 1867 was drafted in the greatest of haste.
"The circumstances in which the deal was consummated
seem to indicate a realization of the future importance of

that inhospitable portion of the North American continent, "
notes A. Babin. [75]

The son of Secretary of State Seward describes in his
memoirs the following incident that took place during the
drafting of the treaty:

"On Friday evening, March 29, Seward was playing whist
in his parlor with some of his family, when the Russian Minister was announced. I have a dispatch, Mr. Seward, from
my Government by cable. The Emperor gives his consent
to the cession. Tomorrow, if you like, I will come to the
department, and we can enter upon the treaty.'" In reply to
the news, according to Seward's son, "Seward...pushed
away the whist table, saying: 'Why wait till tomorrow, Mr.
Stoeckl? Let us make the treaty tonight."[76]

The secretaries were summoned, and in the presence of
Charles Sumner, chairman of the Senate Foreign Relations
Committee, the instrument was signed at 4 A.M. and sent
to the Senate for approval.

Rumors of the sale of the colonies to the United States per-
colated into the press even before the treaty was published.
Some Russian papers, especially Krayevsky's "Golos," came
out with sharp criticism of the transaction. An editorial in
"Golos" of March 25, 1867, had this to say:

"Today there are rumors that they are selling the Nikolayevskaya Railroad, tomorrow they will tell us that they
are selling the Russian-American colonies. Who is to assure
us that day after tomorrow those same rumors will not be
selling the Crimea, Transcaucasia, the Baltic provinces?
The thing least likely to happen would be a shortage of eager
buyers."[77] At the same time "Golos" made the point that
the Russian-American Company did not merit such treatment,
and that the sum realized from the cession of the colonies
was quite insignificant compared to their intrinsic value.

This editorial caught the eye of the censor. The chairman of the St. Petersburg Censorship Committee in a memorandum to the Main Office on Affairs of the Press quoted a
number of passages from the "Golos" editorial and observed
that "although the press is not prohibited by censorship regulations from discussing any steps taken by the government,
still, there is no excuse whatsoever for the expression of
offensive opinions on measures by the established authorities,
which, while not yet instituted, are known to be contemplated." [78]
In the editorial the censor discerned "something in the nature

of a studied inclination on the part of the editorial office of
the paper to disapprove of the actions of the government."
On this point the censor won the agreement of the chairman
of the Censorship Committee.

This marked the end of the "seditious" opposition on the
part of the Russian press to the sale of the colonies.

A section of the American press was even more strenuously opposed to the purchase of the Russian colonies by the
United States. Only individual papers, especially the New
York Herald, gave more or less a positive appraisal of the
event.

"Looking at the proposed cession of Russian America to
the United States from a certain point of view," wrote the
New York Herald, "it seems trifling and unimportant, but
looking at it from a different point of view, it is, without a
doubt, one of the most important international transactions
in modern times."[79]

Another article in the same New York Herald dwelt anew
on the great political significance of the sale. "The cession
of that region," wrote the New York Herald, "points to the
probability of a political, commercial, and military alliance,
defensive and offensive, between Russia and the United States
against England and France, to be followed in the future by the
setting up of a balance of power in the two hemispheres."[80]

The majority of American newspapers, though, took a
different position, on principle. One of the most authoritative newspapers, the New York Tribune, came out sharply
against the purchase of the Russian colonies and subjected
Seward's policy in the matter to withering criticism. In an
article captioned "Russian Charlatanism," the New York
Tribune gave a caustic picture of the Russian colonies according to Seward. "To judge by Seward's description," said
the New York Tribune, "there is no place in the world like
Russian America. A pleasant climate, quite warm in the
winter, where the Eskimos are trying to find protection in
the shade from the burning heat of the Arctic summer. The
countryside is covered with pine-trees and blooming green
gardens along the coast. There you can also find vast fields
of wheat and barley, herds of seals, white bears, icebergs,
whales, and gold veins--all the way up to the 60th parallel
of north latitude. All the comforts and all the necessities
of life are gathered in one place and, as Mr. Seward assures
us, we shall find the white bear lolling on a bed of roses,

barley ripening on the icebergs, grass growing in abundance in the fields, with Eskimos going sleigh-riding all over the place."[81]

In another article on the same topic the New York Tribune declared that in the whole history of diplomacy "there has not been another mad folly like that agreement, and yet there is actual danger that the plan will pass the Senate without publicity and without examination and will immediately win the necessary recognition."[82]

The articles in the New York Tribune, which appeared on the eve of the Senate discussion of the treaty, demanded the rejection of the agreement in sharp terms. Said the New York Tribune: "The Secretary of State has shyly and timidly made public the treaty in his address, and has asked the Senate to confirm it and the people to approve it. We are convinced that the Senate will say 'No.'; we know that the people will say 'No.'"[83]

Actually the Senate debate on the treaty aroused some apprehension on the part of the Russian envoy in the United States. At the end of March an official telegram was sent announcing the government's consent to the sale of the colonies. It was sent just at that time, because a new Congress was now in session, the makeup of which held out the hope of a solution of the question that would be favorable to Russia.

In a letter dated February 24 (March 8), 1867, that is three weeks before the treaty was drawn up, Stoeckl wrote to Reitern:

> "It would have been impossible for me in the midst of the stormy debates in the last session of Congress to begin negotiations that call for the height of discretion. The new Congress, which met four days ago, will not be so turbulent, and I shall then be able to devote myself to that question."[84]

But even in the case of the new Congress there was some doubt that it would approve the treaty. "I am not even certain," wrote Stoeckl in the same letter, "that our proposition will be accepted, and I am anticipating great difficulties."

It seemed, then, at times, especially when the opposition campaign was launched in the newspapers, that the Senate might not approve the treaty and that the affair might end up as an international scandal, since "Senate rejection of the treaty," as Stoeckl said, "would appear in the eyes of the world as an act of incivility towards the Imperial government."[85] However, everything ended happily.

On April 18, 1867, New Style Calendar, the Treaty was approved by the Senate, by a vote of 37 to 2, in spite of the fact that it bore the signature of Seward, "the implacable foe of three-fourths of the Senators." The approval was given first because, as Stoeckl correctly observed, " the opposition in the Senate was not against the treaty, but against the Secretary of State," and, secondly, because, as an American historian remarked, "the whole transaction was tainted with...[the] aroma of corruption...."[86] So that, notwithstanding the frenzied campaign by the newspapers, there were no untoward incidents.

In Russian literature on the subject, which in general sheds very little light on the complications that developed around the sale of the Russian colonies in America, the question of the bribery taking place during the consummation of the deal is naturally passed over in silence. In spite of the rumors circulating about it, even American students of the subject have, until a certain time, kept silent about this touchy question.

"The circumstances which led to the transfer [of the Russian colonies.-Au.]," writes Bancroft, the author of an important American work on the history of Alaska, "are still supposed by many to be enshrouded in mystery, but I can assure the reader that there is no mystery about it. In diplomatic circles, even so simple a transaction as buying a piece of ground must not be allowed consummation without the usual wise winks, whisperings, and circumlocution."[87]

The question has finally become clarified with the publication of contributions by Golder,[88] Dunning,[89] Farrar,[90] and other American students of the problem.

Mr. Dulles, whom we have quoted above, and whose work, published in 1932, summarizes all the information found in the work of his predecessors, states unequivocally that if some members of Congress had not been bribed, the treaty would most likely have run into undesirable congressional opposition. He says: "Just what happened we do not know, but no doubt exists as to the fact that bribery was used to smooth the path of congressional action. The whole transaction was tainted with that aroma of corruption which was to become so familar to post-war Washington."[91]

Dulles, calling in questions Seward's allegation that there
were no agreements as to the transfer of any funds, utilizes
the same source material discrediting Seward that other historians have used. He mentions Stoeckl's dispatch to his
government that he had spent the greater part of "the funds
allowed for secret disbursements," and finally, cites a revealing document found among the papers of President Johnson. In that document the President, referring to what
Seward had told him, relates that the Russian ambassador,
in connection with the Alaska treaty, had paid $30,000 to
John W. Forney, $20,000 to R.J. Walker and F.P. Stanton,
$10,000 to Thaddeus Stevens, and $8,000 to N.P. Banks.

What was it, however, that impelled the press, the New
York Tribune in particular, to come out so vociferously
against Senate approval of the treaty that closed the deal for
the purchase of the Russian colonies?

The most likely explanantion is that the treaty was brought
up for consideration by the Senate on the eve of elections in
certain of the states. The campaign launched by a number of
newspapers, especially by the New York Tribune, against
the purchase of the Russian colonies, was evidently intended
to help the election of those candidates who, among their
other campaign slogans, voiced the demand that not one cent
be appropriated for the acquisition of new territory. Such an
appropriation, they maintained, would add to the tax-burden
of their constituents. Naturally, under conditions of a post-
war depression, a slogan like that might have been partially
successful.

Then there was a connection between the election campaign
and the attack of the press on the purchase of Alaska may be
surmised on the basis of a very revealing paragraph in the
New York Herald.

"There are rumors," says the "Herald," "to the effect
that the treaty will not be approved. We suspect that the
rumor has been spread for the purpose of affecting the elections in Connecticut. But since the elections there have already been held, we hope that the Senate will be in a position
to discuss more carefully the question of whether our great
republic should stop on its course of destiny or should go on
forward to the north pole itself." [92]

But at the same time it must be taken into account that
the idea of expanding the territory of the United States at
the expense of Alaska was not without a certain fascination

to some influential circles. And the New York Tribune re-
sorts to a rather clumsy insinuation. It writes that the Tsar
of Russia purportedly intended to make a present of Alaska
to the United States, since he had no use for it anyway and
since it brought him nothing but trouble. "That is obvious,"
asserts the New York Tribune. "And it is just as obvious,"
continues the paper, "that Secretary of State Seward knew
about it. Unfortunately for our treasury and for our taxpayers, it is impossible to secure any fame in diplomacy by
receiving a simple gift. Instead of announcing the acquisition
of a territory apt to fall into our hands in the form of assistance to the Russian treasury, Mr. Seward is conducting
negotiations about it, squandering a sum of ten million dollars, mysteriously clothing the whole deal in a secret treaty,
then suddenly making his appearance in the Senate with it,
after the conclusion of the regular session of Congress and
urging the immediate approval of the treaty."[93]

The appeal to the taxpayers in the above paragraph does
not seem to us to have been accidental. It was those taxpayers who were afraid that their pocketbooks would be ad-
versely affected by new territorial acquisitions.

The further promulgation of the treaty proceeded without
undue delay. On May 3 (15) the convention was ratified by
the Tsar. On June 8 (20), 1867, the exchange of ratifications
took place in Washington, and on October 7 (19) the government commissioners arrived at Sitka. That same day the
Russian flag was hauled down. Together with the territory,
the United States, in accordance with Article II of the treaty,
received title to all buildings not privately owned. But since
there were no government buildings in the Russian colonies,
the United States was given all the buildings belonging to the
Russian-American Company.

CONCLUSION

"THE TSARIST GOVERNMENT has tried for centuries to gain possession both of Constantinople and of an ever-increasing portion of Asia, pursuing the appropriate policy in every case and utilizing every kind of contradiction and conflict arising among the great powers."[1]

By seizing a base on the west coast of North America, tsarist Russia was trying to further her aspirations for expansion in the western hemisphere. But when Russia encountered en route a powerful opponent in the person of England, and then clashed with a rising great power, the United States, she finally abandoned her fight for consolidating her influence on the North American continent.

A glance at the map will suffice to show that the defense and maintenance of those remote outposts require large forces and ample resources. But Russia's attention, beginning with the 1840's, was riveted on those problems on the European and Asiatic mainlands that were of prime importance to her. She was forced to renounce all further expansion in the western hemisphere and, consequently, to abandon her colonies in America which she had established as bases for such expansion; Russia's expansion stopped at the west coast of the Pacific. It was on this natural frontier which offered an outlet to the open sea that Russia was determined to defend her vital interests.

The Russian-American Company, an organization that was characteristic of a certain period of history, played its part in that expansion. The tsarist government was able to make an attempt to such far-reaching expansion without precipitating international complications, only under the cover of an organization that was private in form but governmental in substance.

The tsarist government acted cautiously. When it became clear that any further expansion was impossible, there was nothing easier to do than to liquidate the Company; and it was even possible to accomplish the sale of the colonies, as we have seen, with certain compensatory benefits in the international field.

273

The existence of the Company was of comparative short duration. Its destiny was predetermined. In the conditions of developing capitalism there was no room for state monopolies of that kind. In the course of a few decades the Pacific Ocean became the battlefield of states that had become imperialistic. A new complex of problems began to assume shape in that area, and tsarist Russia takes her place among the plunderers, entering on a new stage of the same conflict right on her own eastern borders.

It was not, however, only in the unsuccessful attempt made by the tsarist government to expand on the American continent that the Russian-American Company played its part.

In describing the activities of the East India Company Marx had this to say: "The pages of history that relate to British rule in India tell of almost nothing except wrack and ruin; their constructive work is scarcely visible through the pile of rubble. Nevertheless, that constructive work has begun."[2] Elements of such constructive work were also present in the Russian colonies in America.

By scattering the Aleuts along the whole coast and by making them virtually its slaves, the Russian-American Company civilized them to a certain extent. Under the Company's direction, a certain proportion of the native population acquired special skills. The area, thanks to the Company's intensive commercial activities, was linked with all the forward nations, with the whole world of trade.

In analyzing the part played by tsarist Russia in the Orient and in comparing Russia colonization with Polish colonization, Engels wrote to Marx:

"...Russia is actually playing a progressive role with respect to the Orient. In spite of all its loathsomeness and Slavic filth, Russian domination is playing a civilizing role in the areas of the Black Sea, the Caspian Sea, Central Asia, as in the case of the Bashkirs and Tatars. And Russia has absorbed many more elements of enlightenment and of industry in particular than all of Poland, by nature haughty and lazy. Russia has it all over Poland by the very fact that the Russian nobility, beginning with the Tsar and Prince Demidov and ending with the least important boyar of the fourteenth rank who is distinguished only by his noble birth, manufactures, speculates, swindles, takes bribes, and is mixed up in all sorts of Christian and Jewish transactions."[3]

This was a step forward, this was progress, but the sort
of progress that is peculiar to a capitalistic world.

The Company organized a whole series of voyages around
the world. It fitted out thirteen round-the-world expeditions
in the period between 1804 (Krusenstern's expedition) and
1840 (Zarembo's expedition). These expeditions are of very
great importance in the history of geographical discoveries.
They enriched the sciences of cartography, oceanography,
and a number of other related fields of knowledge. The results of all these investigations became, within a short time,
the common property of universal science. On the basis of
research done by the preceding expeditions, Kashevarov was
able in 1847 to compose new maps of the shores of the Pacific, and in 1852 Tebenkov was able to issue his "Atlas severo-
zapadnykh beregov Ameriki, ostrovov Aleutskikh i nekotorykh
mest Severnovo Tikhovo okeana" (Atlas of the northwestern
shores of America, the Aleutian Islands, and some places
in the North Pacific), with a supplement of hydrographic
observations. As cartographers who are specialists in their
field have said, the Russian maps and atlases of the Pacific,
including the coast of America, were executed in such a way
"as to arouse even today the envy of many places on the
globe."[4]

But the positive aspects of the activity of the Company
are not limited to the civilizing role (pointed out by Engels)
that Russian expansion played in the Orient as a whole, nor
to the round-the-world voyages and expeditions which, in
the literal sense of the term, opened up the northern part
of the Pacific. The importance of the activity of the Russian-
American Company is more comprehensive. The Company
helped not only to discover that vast region but also to
strengthen Russian influence there; it helped with the acquisition of the west coast of the Pacific, of those natural
frontiers where even today the U.S.S.R., a great Pacific
power, is keeping a watchful eye over the vital interests of
her peoples.

NOTES

Preface
   1. "Russian Expansion to America: Its Bibliographical Foundations,"
in The Papers of the Bibliographical Society of America, (University of
Chicago Press, 1931), Vol. XXV, pp. 111-129. Useful bibliographical
items, especially on more recent contributions, will be found in Stuart
Ramsay Tompkins,"Alaska: Promyshlennik and Sourdough" (Norman,
University of Oklahoma Press, 1945), pp. 305-308.
   2. "Russkie otkrytiia v Tikhom Okeane i Severnoi Amerike v XVIII-
XIX vekakh" (Russian Discoveries in the Pacific and in North America in
the Eighteenth and Nineteenth Centuries), Moscow, 1944, p. 6.

Introduction
   1. P. Tikhmenev, "Istoricheskoe obozrenie obrazovaniia Rossiisko-
amerkianskoi kompanii" (Historical Review of the Formation of the Russian-American Company), St. Petersburg, 1861-62.

Author's Preface
   1. According to certain sources, no provision was made in the budget of the Ministry of Finance for transporting the company archives,
and the material was left without any supervision.
   2. F.A. Golder, Guide to Materials for American History in Russian
Archives, Washington, D.C., 1917-(37).
   3. P. Tikhmenev, "Istoricheskoe obozrenie obrazovaniia Rossiisko-
Amerikanskoi kompanii i deistvii do nastoiashchevo vremeni" (Historical
Survey of the Formation of the Russian-American Company and Its Activities to the Present Time), Pt. I-II, St. Petersburg, 1861-63.
   4. S.S. Shashkov, "Rossiisko-amerikanskaia kompaniia," Sobr. soch.,
t. II (The Russian-American Company, in His Collected Works, Vol. II),
St. Petersburg, 1898, pp. 632-652.

Chapter I
   1. Ia. Shternberg, Etnografiia, sb. "Tikhii okean," izd. Akademii
nauk SSSR, (Ethnography, in collection Pacific Ocean, pub. by Academy
of Sciences U.S.S.R.), 1926, p. 147.
   2. Arkhiv vnutrennei politiki, kul'tury i byta (AVPK i B), Leningrad,
fond Nepremennovo soveta (Archives of Internal Politics, Culture and
Way of Life, Leningrad, Archives of Permanent Council), file no. 103.
   (Footnote references to archive materials in the Russian language will,
after the first mention, be given in English. --Ed.).
   3. Wm. Petty, "Traktat o nalogakh i podatiakh" (Treatise on Taxes
and Contributions), in collection "Mercantilism,"Leningrad, 1935, p. 213.
   4. "Torguiushchee dvorianstvo, protivu polozhennoe dvorianstvu voen-
nomu, ili dva rassuzhdeniia o tom, sluzhit li to k blagopoluchiiu gosudarstva, chtoby dvorianstvo vstupalo v kupechestvo (Trading Nobility, Contrasted with Fighting Nobility; or, Two Discourses on Whether It Serves
the Welfare of the State for the Nobility to Enter the Merchant Class.
St. Petersburg, 1766), p. 10.

5. "Torguiushchee dvorianstvo, " p. 58.

6. "Morskoi istoricheskii arkhiv" (MIA) (Historical Naval Archives, Leningrad, Collection of Count I.G. Chernyshev) in file no. 44.

7. Op. cit. in note 2.

8. P. Tikhmenev, "Istoricheskoe obozrenie obrazovaniia Rossiisko-amerikanskoi kompanii i deistvii ee do nastoiashchevo vromoni (Historical Survey of the Formation of the Russian-American Company and of its Activities to the Present Time, Pt. II, St. Petersburg, 1863), Suppl. p. 22. In quoting from documents published by Tikhmenev I have disregarded, for the convenience of the reader, certain orthographic peculiarities of the text; I have separated the conjunctions and prepositions from the verbs and, where necessary, have put in my own punctuation.

9. I quote from extracts of a manuscript translation cited by a correspondent of the Russian-American Company (AVPK and B), Archives of the Chancery of the Procurator-General of the Senate, 1800, No. 2402, ll. 13-24.

10. Ibid.

11. AVPK and B, Archives of the Chancery of the Procurator-General of the Senate, 1800, file no. 2402, letter of N.P. Rezanov, correspondent of the Russian-American Company, to P. Kh. Obol'ianinov, Procurator-General of the Senate, dated October 1, 1800, ll. 13-24.

12. Op. cit. in note 2.

13. Ibid.

14. Complete edition of laws, Vol. VII, No. 4348.

15. Ibid, Vol. XV, No. 11489.

16. "Politicheskii opyt o kommertsii" (Essai politique sur le Commerce, translated by S. Bashilov, St. Petersburg, 1768), p. 45.

17. Ibid, pp. 45-46.

18. V. Berkh, "Khronologicheskaiia istoriia otkrytiia Aleutskikh ostrovov, ili podvigi rossiiskovo kupechestva"(Chronological History of the Discovery of the Aleutian Islands; or, The Exploits of the Russian Merchant Class, St. Petersburg, 1823), p. 114.

19. Ibid.

20. Ibid, p. 113.

Chapter II

1. "31 prisuzhdeniie uchrezhdennykh N.N. Demidovym nagrad" (Thirty-one awards of prizes established by N.N. Demidov, St. Petersburg, 1882), p. 67. Analysis of P. Tikhmenev's "Istoricheskoe obozrenie obrazovaniia Rossiisko-amerikanskoi kompanii." Cf. note 1, chapter I.

2. In 1791 was published the book "Rossiiskovo kuptsa imenitovo rylskovo grazhdanina Grigor'ia Shelikhova pervoe stranstvovanie s 1783 po 1787 god iz Okhotska po Vostochnomu okeanu k amerikanskim beregam" (The First Voyage of the Russian Merchant, Honorary Citizen of Rylsk, Grigorii Shelikhov, 1783-1787 from Okhotsk on the Eastern Ocean to the American shores); and in the following year, the book entitled "Rosiiskovo kuptsa Grigor'ia Shelikhova prodolzhenie stranstvovania po Vostochnomu Okeanu k Amerikanskim beregam v 1788 godu" (Continuation of the Voyage of the Russian Merchant Grigorii Shelikhov on the Eastern Ocean to the American Shores in 1788). Shelikhov himself did not take part in the second voyage, the so-called "continuation." The memoirs that were published comprise Izmailov's and Bocharov's journal of the

expedition. Still, both the text and the provenance of the first book which
deals directly with Shelikhov's "voyage," long gave rise to a certain scep-
ticism. Obscure, too, was the role Shelikhov played in the preparation
of the work for publication. Thus, Tikhmenev noted as early as 1861,
that "his (i.e., Shelikhov's) journal of the voyage was, as is well known,
published without his knowledge" (pt. I, p. 8). A number of American
scholars, Bancroft in particular, have pointed out that the description
of Shelikhov's voyage contains whole pages which were lifted bodily from
books about the Aleuts (for details cf. Shelikhov's Voyage to Alaska, a
Bibliographical "Note" by Avrahm Yarmolinsky). Bancroft asserts that
Shelikhov's journal which lay at the base of the text of the book, had been
presented by Shelikhov to Yakobii, the Governor of Irkutsk. After the
governor had retired, the journal was purloined from the chancery by
his successor Pil and published "against the wish of the late" Shelikhov.

We were able to find confirmation of the view that Shelikhov's journal
was published against his will, in sources relating to the year 1798, which
belonged to Shelikhov's widow who was conversant with all his undertakings. The document, which, at first glance, fully confirms Bancroft's
opinion, is a "Memorandum on the Solid Establishment of the American
Company," presented by the widow Shelikhov to the Board of Commerce
on October 7, 1798.

I quote in full § 7 of the memorandum:

"Although all the activities and operations of the American Company
are such that it would not harm the glory of our nation for them to become
known to the whole people, still, taking into consideration the circumstance that the northeastern section of America is not yet effectively
consolidated, explored, or made completely submissive to the Russian
scepter, and that the English, out of envy and greed, may sometimes
create difficulties, this matter must, of course, be regarded as so important, that all the operations of the company are to be concealed for a
time from the public, in order that foreigners may not learn too soon of
the activities being carried on in that region. With this purpose constantly in mind, my late husband did not venture to come out boasting before
the public with an edition of his journal about his American discoveries.
He merely felt it necessary to present that journal to the governor of
Irkutsk, inasmuch as he had been ordered secretly to bury in some
marked spots a number of plates with the inscription that the land was
a Russian possession. However, there were discovered among the public some little printed books, issued without the benefit of censorship,
under the title of 'Shelikhov's Travels. Later on printed accounts appeared dealing with other private naval explorations and discoveries as
well as the political intentions of the Court of all the Russias became
known to foreigners, while we, in return, have had only scanty information about them and their discoveries, information that is lacking in
much that is necessary and important. This happened, I believe, because
the doings of the Company were passed along from government to government, and became known to many persons. At the present time, though,
the Company has been put under the patronage of the State Board of Commerce. Still, with all the information passing through the hands of many
persons, a secret could hardly remain so for long. Taking the liberty
of expressing myself most humbly on this matter, I am presenting all
the material, as well as everything written above for the sagacious ex-

amination and benevolence of your Excellency." (MIA, G.G. Kushelev Collection, file no. 79, l. 241-258).

Notwithstanding such convincing corroboration of Bancroft's opinion, certain parts of his hypothesis give rise to substantial doubts. The first reason for such doubts lies in the circumstance that two editions of the journal came out during Shelikhov's lifetime, and that the official statement about the publication of "Shelikhov's Travels" supposedly against his will was not made till seven years after the event and three years after the author's death. In any case, to judge by the source material at our disposal, there were no protests on the part of Shelikhov or of his heirs until 1798. Also, Shelikhov learned immediately of the publication of his journal. In one of the letters of A. Radishchev of Irkutsk to Count Vorontsov, dated November 14, 1791, that is the year that the first edition of the "Travels" appeared,we find the following bit of information: "I have made the acquaintance" writes Radishchev, "of Mr. Shelikhov, who has just returned from Okhotsk where he goes every spring to meet his vessels on their return from America. Your Excellency knows him and has read the journal of his travels which has just been printed in Moscow and with which he is displeased." (Archives of Count Vorontsov, v. V, p. 330; translated from the French.) So, to judge by Radishchev's letter, it is a question only of Shelikhov's "being displeased," which, perhaps, was related not to the mere fact of the publication of the supposedly purloined journal, but to the editing which had, apparently, been entrusted to someone. As to Natalya Shelikhov's statement, that may hav been made during the bitter battle of Shelikhov's heirs for the privilege of exclusive exploitation of the American colonies. The statement may have been made to turn aside the objections against the granting of such privileges to a private company, on the ground that it might lead, as it had led once before, to the divulging of state secrets.

Furthermore, Pil, Governor-General of Irkutsk, whom Bancroft suspects of purloining Shelikhov's journal, was one of the most active proponents of granting Shelikhov exclusive privileges; it is doubtful whether he would have published, against the author's will, a document which might have harmed Shelikhov in any way.

3. Cf. "Vedomost' mekham, vyvezennym chastnymi kompaniami" (Information about furs exported by private companies) and "Vedomost' mekham, vyvezennym kompanieiu Shelekhova i Golkova" (Information about furs exported by the Shelikhov-Golikov Company), supplement to V. Berkh's op. cit.

4. Arkhiv Gosudarstvennovo Geograficheskovo obshchestva, fond G. IV. I, plan ustroistva kompanii, predlozhennyi Shelikhovym v 1787 g. (Archives of the State Geographical Society, Collection G. IV. I, plan for establishing the company, proposed by Shelikhov in 1787), ll. 4-7.

5. Ibid, petition of Shelikhov and Golikhov to Empress Catherine, February, 1788, on ll. 47-50.

6. Ibid, ll. 4-7.

7. Ibid.

8. Ibid, petition of Shelikhov and Golikov to Catherine, February, 1788, on ll. 47-50.

9. Complete edition of laws, Vol. XXII, no. 16709.

10. Ibid, Vol. XVII, no. 12589.

11. Op. cit. in note 35, Vol. XXIII, no. 17135.

12. Morskoi istoricheskoi arkhiv (Historical Naval Archives, MIA) G.G. Kushelev Collection, file no. 79, letter of Shelikhov to Baranov, dated August 9, 1794, on ll. 34-42.

13. Op. cit. in note 4, Shelikhov's representation to Gov. -Gen. Pil of Irkutsk of February 11, 1790, on ll. 52-57.

14. Ibid, report of Gov.-Gen. Pil of Irkutsk to Catherine, 1790, on ll. 89-99.

15. Ibid.

16. Op. cit. in note 8, file no. 140, letter of Shelikhov to Baranov, dated August 9, on ll. 24-35.

17. Op. cit. in note 12.

18. Ibid.

19. Op. cit. in note 3, file no. 140, letter of Shelikhov to Baranov, dated August 9, 1794, on ll. 24-35.

20. AVPK and B, Archives of Chancery of the Procurator-General of the Senate, 1799, file no. 1672.

21. AVPK and B, Archives of Permanent Council, doc. no. 140, 1. 2.

22. Ibid.

23. Ibid, file no. 176, 1. 58.

24. Quoted from P. Tikhmenev, op. cit., Pt. II, suppl. p. 86.

25. A Shelikhov employee.

26. Op. cit. in note 24, pp. 41-42.

27. Op. cit. in note 3, file no. 176, memorandum of G.I. Shelikhov's heirs to the Board of Commerce entitled "Opritchinakh soedineniia Ameri-kanskoi kompanii s Irkutskoi, o sostoianii poslednei do soedineniia i o posledstviiakh so vremeni soedineniia" (The Reason of the Union of the American Company with the Irkutsk Company, the Situation of the Latter Prior to the Union and the Consequences Since the Time of the Union), 1799, on ll. 58-75.

28. Marx and Engels, "Sochineniia" (Works), Vol. IX, p. 332.

29. MIA, G.G. Kushelev Collection, file no. 79, 1. 95.

30. Ibid.

31. MIA, Fond G.G. Kusheleva (G.G. Kushelev Collection) file no. 79, Memorandum of the Board of Commerce, entitled "O vrednosti mnogikh v Amerike kompanii i pol'ze ot soedineniia ikh voedino" (On the Harmful-ness of Many Companies in America and on the Advantages of Combining Them into One), August 5, 1797, on ll. 95-97.

32. Ibid.

33. AVPK: B, Archives of the Permanent Council, file no. 176, 1. 24.

34. Op. cit. in note 20, 1797, file no. 203, ll. 16-17.

35. Arkhiv Instituta istorii Akademii Nauk, Materialy o Rossiisko-amerikanskoi kompanii (Archives of the Historical Institute of the Aca-demy of Sciences, Source Material on the Russian-American Company), doc. no. 126.

36. AVPK and B, G.G. Kushelev Collection, file no. 79, "Memorial o sposobakh k prochnomu vosstanovleniiu Amerikanskoi kompanii" (Memo-randum Concerning the Methods for the Solid Establishment of the Ameri-can Company), October 7, 1798, on ll. 241-258.

37. Ibid.

38. Op. cit. in note 36, doc. no. 7.

39. Ibid, doc. no. 8.

40. Ibid, doc. no. 7.

41. A. Kotzebue, Das merkwürdigste Jahr meines Lebens, Berlin, 1802, t. II, p. 149.

42. Op. cit. in note 36.

43. Complete edition of laws, Vol. XXV, no. 19030.

44. MIA, G.G. Kushelev Collection, doc. no. 79, "Obiasnenie N. Shelikhovoi o pol'zakh uchrezhdaemoi Amerikanskoi kompanii" (Madam N. Shelikhov's explanation of the advantages of the American company to be founded), on ll. 239-240.

45. AVPK: B, Archives of the Permanent Council, file no. 176, memorandum of G. I. Shelikhov's heirs to the Board of Commerce, entitled "O pritchinakh soedineniia Amerikanskoi kompanii s Irkutskoii, o sostoianii poslednei do soedineniia i o posledstoiakh so vremeni soedineniia," 1799, on ll. 58-75.

46. Op. cit. in note 61.

47. Op. cit. in notes 8 and 53.

48. See P. Tikhmenev, op. cit., Pt. I, p. 70.

49. AVPK and B, Archives of the Chancery of the Procurator-General of the Senate, 1800, file no. 2404, entitled "Opisaniie pervonachal'novo osnovaniia nakhodiashcheisia pod vysochaishim e.i. v. pokrovitel 'stvom Rossiisko-amerikanskoi kompanii, nastoiashchevo onoi polozheniia i sredstv k usovershenstvovaniiu onoi" (Description of the First Beginnings of the Russian-American Company under the Patronage of His Majesty, about its Present Condition and the Ways to Improve It"), written by N.P. Rezanov, October 10, 1800, on ll. 13-24.

50. Ibid, 1. 40.

51. Op. cit. in note 75.

Chapter III

1. Arkhiv vneshnei politiki (AVP) (Archives of Foreign Relations) Moscow, Collection of Ministry of Foreign Affairs, Asiatic Dept., 1803, file no. 11, 1. 1.

2. Ibid.

3. Ibid, file no. 8, ll. 2-5.

4. Marx and Engels, "Sochineniia" (Works), Vol. IX, p. 357.

5. AVPK and B, Archives of His Majesty's own Chancery, 1802, file no. 152.

6. Op. cit. in note 1, 1805, file no. 12. ll. 4-5.

7. Ibid, file no. 8, Memorandum of the Governing Board of the Russian-American Company to the Consul-General in the U.S., on ll. 18-28.

8. The data about the size of the Russian and the native population in the settlements of the Russian-American Company and other information about them are borrowed from "Obozrenie sostoianiia i deistvii Rossiisko-amerikanskoi kompanii s 1797 do 1819" (Survey of the Condition and Operation of the Russian-American Company of the General Chancery of the Minister of Finance, sec. 2, 1819, file no. 10, on ll. 7-83.

9. ANKH, Archives of the General Chancery of the Ministry of Finance, 2nd div., 1819, file no. 10, 1. 49.

10. Known after 1817 as the Nizhny-Novgorod Fair--(Tr.).

11. Op. cit. in note 86. 1. 51.

12. ANKH, Archives of the Russian-American Company, 1802, file no. 1, Letter from the Governing Board to A.A. Baranov, Governor of the Colonies, 1803, on ll. 72-83.

13. Arkhiv Gosudarvstvennovo geograficheskovo obshchestva (Archives of the State Geographic Society), K. Khlebnikov's Memoirs of America, pt. III, p. 208.

14. ANKH, Archives of the Department of Manufacture and Domestic Commerce, sect. 2, 2nd bundle, 1815, file no. 237, report of the Governing Board to the Ministry of the Interior, 1815, on ll. 38-43.

15. Ibid.

16. Ibid, 1826, file no. 706, Report of the Company Director I. Prokofyev to the general meeting of the stockholders, on ll. 93-110.

17. Archives of the Chancery of the Procurator-General of the Senate, ll. 40-41.

18. Ibid, 1. 24.

19. General Archives of the Chancery of the Ministry of Finance, 1. 24 v.

20. Op. cit. in note 13, Veselago Collection, file no. 8, report of the Governing Board for 1807, on ll. 1-7.

21. By Company calculations, its capital at that time was 3,028,334.615 rubles.

22. Op. cit. in note 90, Veselago Collection, file no. 29, report of the Company Director I. Prokofyev, 1824, on ll. 1-12.

23. Ibid.

24. Ibid.

25. Suppl. to "Moskovskiia Vedomosti," (Moscow News), 1783, no. 79, p. 311.

26. K.F. Ryleev, "Polnoe sobranie sochinenii" (Complete Collected Works), 1934, p. 490-491.

27. AVPK and B, Archives of the St. Petersburg Censorship Committee, 1825, file no. 206778, 1. 1.

28. "Severnaia pchela," (Northern Bee) 1861, no. 109, S. Yanovsky's notes to Tridechny's article.

29. Ibid, no. 72, review of "Materialy po istorii russkikh zaselenii po beregam Vostochnovo okeana" (Materials on the History of the Russian Colonies Along the Shores of the Eastern Sea, signed by Tridechny).

30. Op. cit. in note 14, 1826, file no. 706, Lobanov's petitions addressed to the Tsar, on ll. 93-110.

Chapter IV

1. P. Tikhmenev, op. cit., pt. I, supp., p. 41.

2. K. Khlebnikov's memoirs of America in "Materialy dlia istorii russkikh zaselenii po beregam Vostochnovo okeana" (Source Material for the History of the Russian Settlements on the Shores of the Eastern Sea), Vol. III, St. Petersburg, 1861, p. 88.

3. AVP, Archives of the Chancery of the Ministry of Foreign Affairs, 1817, file no. 12180-12184, 1. 31.

4. Archives of the Department of Manufacture and Domestic Commerce, 1811, file no. 47, Memorandum of the Governing Board to the Tsar, December 18, 1811, on 1. 1-4.

5. Ibid.

6. Ibid, letter of the Minister of the Interior, O.P. Kozodavlev to State Chancellor N.P. Rumiantsev, first half of 1812, on ll. 12-14.

7. Op. cit. in note 3, 1819, file no. 12160, 1. 9. Translated from the French.

8. Ibid, 1815, file no. 12174, 1. 33.

9. Op. cit. in note 14, chapter III, 1819, file no. 440, V. Golovnin's letter of September 10, 1819, to the Directors of the Russian-American Company, on ll. 10-17.

10. Ibid.

11. Ibid.

12. MIA, Documents from various sources, file no. 123.

13. Ibid.

14. Ibid.

15. Ibid.

16. Complete edition of Laws, Vol. XXXVII, no. 28747.

17. Op. cit. in note 3, 1822, file no. 3645, letter of State Chancellor K.V. Nesselrode to Minister of the Interior D.A. Guryev, of June 3, 1822, on ll. 29-34. [In the text Guryev is referred to as Minister of Finance.--Translator's note.]

18. Ibid.

19. Ibid.

20. British Minister of Foreign Affairs.

21. Barral-Monferrat, De Monroë à Roosevelt 1823-1905. Paris, 1905, p. 15 [Translated from the French by C.G.]

22. Arkhiv grafov Mordninovykh (Archives of the Counts Mordvinov), Vol. VI, St. Petersburg, 1902, pp. 642-643.

23. Archives of the Chancery of the Ministry of Foreign Affairs, 1823, file no. 3646, 1. 19.

24. Ibid, 1. 21.

25. Vospominaniia kn. E.P, Obolenskovo, "Obshchestvenne dvizheniia v Rossii v pervuiu polovinu XIX veka" (Memoirs of Count E. P. Obolensky, in Social Movements in Russia in the First Half of the Nineteenth Century), Vol. I, St. Petersburg, 1905, p. 237.

26. Archives of the Chancery of the Ministry of Foreign Affairs, 1827, file no. 7316, letter of N. S. Mordvinov to K.V. Nesselrode, February, 1824, on ll. 7-9.

27. Ibid, 1824, file no. 3717, letter of K. V. Nesselrode to N.S. Mordvinov, 1824, on ll. 21-26.

28. Op. cit. in note 22, pp. 656-657.

29. Op. cit. in note 23, 1824, file no. 3650, 1. 6.

30. Ibid.

31. Gosudarstvennyi arkhiv feodal'no-krepostnoi epokhi (GAFKE, State Archives of the Period of Feudalism and Serfdom), Moscow, Archives of the Investigating Commission, file no. 48, 1. 228.

32. Ibid, 1. 240.

33. Ibid, 1. 242.

34. Op. cit. in note 23, 1824, file no. 3717, 1. 21.

Chapter V

1. Extract from Langsdorf's journal, "Materialy dlia istorii russkikh zaselenii na beregu Vostochnovo okeana" (Source Material for the History of the Russian Colonies of the Eastern Ocean), 1861, pt. IV, p. 187.

2. Archives of the Department of Manufacture and Domestic Commerce, 1826, file no. 747, 1. 4.

3. Ibid, 1813, file no. 143, 1. 3.

4. Ibid.

5. Ibid, 1811, file no. 38, 1. 6.

6. Ibid, 1. 12.

7. Op. cit. in note 9, Chapt. III, 1. 55.

8. Quoted from the supplement to Pt. II of P. Tikhmenev, op. cit.,
p. 210.

9. Ibid, p. 221.

10. K.F. Ryleev, "Polnoe sobranie sochinenii" (Complete Collected
Works), Academia, 1934, p. 491.

11. GAFKE, Gosudarstvennyi arkhiv, I.V. (Government Archives)
file no. 12, 1. 66.

12. M. Dovnar-Zapol'skii, "Memuary dekabristov" (Memoirs of the
Decembrists) 1906, pp. 130-131.

13. AVPK and B, Archives of the State Council, Department of Economy, 1827, file no. 23, special opinion of Count N.S. Mordvinov, on ll.
6-16. It is difficult to say to what extent the figures cited by N.S. Mordvinov are true to fact, since this whole question has not been treated at
all in historical literature. At any rate, the correctness of the basic
conclusions of Mordvinov with respect to the difficult situation of Russia's
foreign trade, is not open to question.

14. Ibid.

15. Op. cit. in note 2, 1815, file no. 222, memorandum of the Directors of the Russian-American Company to the Minister of the Interior,
O.P. Kozodavlev, of June 12, 1817, on ll. 123-126.

16. Archives of the Institute of History of the Academy of Sciences,
Materials on the History of the Russian-American Company, doc. no. 49.

17. Ibid, doc. no. 44.

18. Ibid.

19. "Sochineniia i perepiska," (Works and Correspondence) 2nd edition,
K.F. Ryleeva, edited by P. Efremov. St. Petersburg, 1874, pp. 309-310.

20. "Russkiye propilei" (Russian Propylaea) Vol. II, p. 104.

21. N.I. Grech, "Vospominaniia o moei zhizni" (Memoirs of My Life),
Academia, 1930, p. 452.

22. GAFKE, Archives of the Commission of Inquiry, 1826, file no. 78,
testimony of Romanov, on ll. 6-10.

23. "Vosstanie dekabristov" (The Decembrists' Insurrection), vol. I,
Tsentrarkhiv. 1925, p. 21.

24. Ibid, p. 179.

25. Op. cit. in note 163, file no. 359, 1. 121.

26. AVPK and B, Archives of the Senate, Heralds' College, unnumbered
file, entitled "Ob opeke nad imuschchestvom Ryleeva" (Trusteeship Over
Ryleyev's Property), 1. 15.

27. Op. cit. in note 23, p. 155.

28. Op. cit. in note 21, p. 442.

29. N. Kotlyarevsky, "Ryleev," St. Petersburg, 1908, pp. 49-50. In
his desire to prove Ryleyev's utter lack of interest in the activities of the
Company and the limited opportunities which his position offered him,
Kotlyarevsky sometimes falls into gross errors. In his comment on the
paragraph quoted above he has this to say about Ryleyev's work for the
Company: "The sphere of his activities was rather narrow and precisely
circumscribed. Schnitzler is hardly correct when he speaks of some
sort of protest by Ryleyev against the irremovability of the Directors of
the Company and of a proposal that they be elected annually." But, in

calling to witness Schnitzler's work (J.H. Schnitzler, Histoire intime
de la Russie, II, Paris, 1847), Kotlyarevsky failed to take notice of the
fact that, in speaking of Ryleyev's protest apropos of the irremovability
of the Directors, Schnitzler had in mind not the Company, but the Northern Society. A translation of the paragraph on which Kotlyarevsky bases
his conclusions leaves no doubt on that score. "But his [i.e., Trubetskoy's.--Au.] departure for Kiev...brought about Ryleyev's becoming a
member of the Board of Directors (at the end of 1824), and from that
time on Republican tendencies gained the upper hand there. A pupil of
the American school, Ryleyev had signalized his becoming a member of
the Council by protesting against the irremovability of the Directors--in
his opinion they should have been elected annually" (Schnitzler, p. 80;
translated from the French.--Tr.) It is absolutely indisputable that in
the given case it is not a question of the Company but of the Northern
Society, of which Ryleyev was also elected Director, and that the reference to the American school is to his constitutional ideals and not at all
to the Russian-American Company.

30. Op. cit. in note 10.
31. Ibid, p. 481.
32. Ibid, p. 484.
33. Vospominaniia Kn. E.P. Obolenskogo (Memoirs of Count E.P.
Obolensky), "Obshchestvennye dvizheniia v Rossii" (Social Movements
in Russia), Vol. I, St. Petersburg, 1905, p. 236.
34. Op. cit. in note 19, pp. 309-310.
35. Ibid, p. 284.
36. GAFKE, Archives of the Commission of Inquiry, file no. 358,
1. 32.
37. MIA, Archives of the Navy Department, 1822, file no. 2595, 1. 4.
38. Op. cit. in note 36, file no. 78, ll. 6-10.
39. Cf. Baron Steingel's memoirs in "Obshchestvennye dvizheniia v
Rossii" (Social Movements in Russia), Vol. I, p. 379.
40. Op. cit. in note 12, p. 165.
41. Ryleyev and Somov lived in the Company building. A. Bestuzhev
lived in a room in Somov's apartment. Steingel also stopped off there on
his return from St. Petersburg.
42. Op. cit. in note 12, p. 187. [Emphasis mine.--Au.]
43. M. Azadovskii, 14-e dekabria v pis'makh A.E. Izmailova, "Pa-
miati dekabristov" (December 14 in the correspondence of A.E. Izmailov,
in "In Memory of the Decembrists"), Leningrad, 1926, Akademiia Nauk
SSSR, Vol. I, p. 242.
44. D. Zavalishin, "Zapiski dekabrista" (The Memoirs of a Decembrist), St. Petersburg, 1906, p. 88.
45. ANKH, Archives of E.F. Kankrin, file no. 35, 1. 12.
46. Ibid.
47. Op. cit. in note 44, p. 91.
48. AVPK and B Archives of the Council of State, Department of Economy, 1841, doc.·no. 3914, draft for the new charter of the Russian-
American Company, on ll. 123-124.
49. Marx and Engels, "Sochineniia" (Works), Vol. IX, p. 353.
50. Ibid, p. 332.
51. Ibid.

Chapter VI

1. Archives of the State Geographical Society, IV, 1, Shelikhov's representation to Gov.-Gen. Pil of Irkutsk, on ll. 52-57.

2. Ibid, l. 89.

3. Archives of the Institute of History of the Academy of Sciences, Materials on the Russian-American Company, doc. no. 183.

4. P. Tikhmenev, Pt. II, suppl. p. 260.

5. Ibid, p. 267.

6. Ibid, pp. 233-234.

7. AVP, Archives of the Chancery of the Ministry of Foreign Affairs, 1823, file no. 3645, l. 116.

8. Ibid.

9. P. Tikhmenev, Pt. I, p. 208.

10. That was the name of the colony in California.

11. H. Bancroft, The Works, Vol. XIX, California, Vol. II, San Francisco, 1885, p. 630.

12. ANKH, Archives of the Department of Manufacture and Domestic Commerce, 1819, file no. 442, Report of the Governing Board of the Russian-American Company to the Minister of Foreign Affairs, August 13, 1817, on ll. 87-93.

13. Op. cit. in note 7, file no. 3646, Communication of the State Chancellor to the Governing Board of the Russian-American Company, December 1, 1809, on ll. 25-26.

14. Ibid, 1809, file no. 12160, draft of the instructions to Count Pahlen, 1809, on ll. 9-29. Translated from the French.

15. Ibid.

16. Complete edition of Laws, Vol. XXXII, no. 25178.

17. Archives of the State Geographical Society, Veselago collection, file no. 101, "Istoricheskaya zapiska o selenii Ross na beregakh Novovo Albiona" (Historical Note Concerning the Colony of Ross on the Shores of New Albion), on ll. 1-4.

18. The first "proclamation," sent over to California with Baranov in 1810, is quoted in full in V. Potekhin's article, "Koloniia Ross," in "Zhurnal manufaktur i torgovli," 1859, Vol. VIII.

19. GAFKE, Archives of the Ministry of Foreign Affairs, P-3, 1816, file no. 24, "Proclamation of the Russian-American Company," 1813, on ll. 18-21.

20. Op. cit. in note 12, 1819, file no. 442, Report of the Governing Board of the Russian-American Company to the Minister of Foreign Affairs, August 13, 1817, on ll. 87-93.

21. Ibid.

22. Op. cit. in note 7, 1823, file no. 3646, l. 24.

23. Ibid, file no. 8735, l. 5. Translated from the French.

24. Ibid.

25. Quoted from Tikhmenev, Pt. I, p. 222.

26. Op. cit. in note 7, 1820, file no. 7562, ll. 54-55. Translated from the French.

27. Ibid, 1823, file no. 8735, l. 6. Translated from the French.

28. Op. cit. in note 19, sect. XXIV, 1825, file no. 68, ll. 11-12.

29. Ibid, l. 10.

30. Op. Cit. in note 12, 1823, file no. 582.

31. Op. cit. in note 7, 1823, file no. 3646, l. 19.

32. D. Zavalishin, "Delo o kolonii Ross" (The Matter of the Colony of Ross), in "Russkii vestnik," 1866, t. 62, p. 55.

33. Op. cit. in note 19, file no. 358, 1. 2.

34. Ibid, file no. 47, 1. 17-18.

35. Ibid.

36. Ibid.

37. Ibid, 1. 171. [Emphasis mine.--Au.]

38. Ibid, file no. 48, 1. 22.

39. Ibid, file no. 47, 1. 84-85.

40. Ibid, 11. 17-18.

41. Ibid, file no. 48, 1. 88.

42. One dessiatine is equivalent to 2.7 acres. One sagene is equivalent to seven English feet.--Tr.

43. K. Khlebnikov's memoirs about America, entitled "Materialy dlia istorii russkikh zaselenii po beregam Vostochnovo okeana" (Material for the History of the Russian Settlements on the Shores of the East Sea), Vol. III, St. Petersburg, 1861, p. 152.

44. The areas away from the sea yielded a crop that was between ten and twenty times as large as that of the areas belonging to Russia.

45. Archives of the State Geographical Society, Veselago Collection, file no. 58, Report of the Governor of the Colonies to the Governing Board, April, 1834, on 11. 1-20.

46. Ibid.

47. Op. cit. in note 12, 1819, file no. 409, 1. 35.

48. Op. cit. in note 45, Veselago Collection, file no. 58, Report of the Governor of the Colonies to the Governing Board, April 1834, on 11. 1-20.

49. One verst is equivalent to about two-thirds of a mile.--Tr.

50. Op. cit. in note 45, Veselago Collection, file no. 58, Report of the Governor of the Colonies to the Governing Board, April, 1834, on 11. 1-20.

51. Governor of the colonies of the Russian-American Company.

52. Op. cit. in note 91, 1825, file no. 692, 1. 3.

53. Op. cit. in note 45, Veselago Collection, file no. 58, Report of the Governor of the Colonies to the Governing Board, April 1834, on 11. 1-20.

54. Ibid.

55. Ibid.

56. Op. cit. in note 12, 1834, file no. 61, 11. 161-162.

57. Op. cit. in note 45, 1834, file no. 1116, 1. 13.

58. Ibid, 1. 15.

59. Ibid, 1. 17.

60. Ibid, 1. 18.

61. Op. cit. in note 12, 1836, file no. 71, 1. 98.

62. Ibid.

63. Op. cit. in note 45, Veselago Collection, file no. 62, 1. 1.

64. Ibid, 1. 7.

65. Op. cit. in note 12, 1839, file no. 1305, 1. 11.

66. Ibid, file no. 1305, Report of the Governing Board of the Russian-American Company to the Minister of Finance, March 31, 1839, on 11. 1-6.

67. Ibid.

68. Op. cit. in note 7, 1839, file no. 217, Exchange with Washington, on 11.238-239. Translated from the French.

69. Ibid, 1848, file no. 184, Exchange with Washington, on l. 54. Translated from the French.

70. Op. cit. in note 12, 1849, file no. 1727, l. 23.

71. Ibid, l. 51.

Chapter VII

1. ANKH, Archives of the Department of Manufacture and Domestic Commerce, 1819, file no. 406, Memorandum presented by Scheffer to Alexander I, February 1819, on ll. 1-6.

2. Op. cit. in note 1, 1819, file no. 406, extract from Scheffer's journal on his visit to the Hawaiian Islands, on l. 35-37.

3. Ibid, 1817, file no. 350, l. 42.

4. Ibid, ll. 19-20.

5. Op. cit. in note 1, 1819, file no. 406, extract from Scheffer's journal on his visit to the Hawaiian Islands, on ll. 35-37.

6. "The Hawaiian Spectator," Vol. I, p. 50, Honolulu, 1838.

7. Op. cit. in note 1, 1817, file no. 350, l. 20.

8. O. Kotzebue, "Puteshestvie v Iuzhnyi okean i v Beringov proliv dlia otyskania severo-vostochnovo morskovo prokhada, predpriniatoe v 1815, 1816, 1817, i 1818 godakh izhdiveniem gr. N.P. Rumiantsova na korable Riurike" (Voyage to the South Sea and the Bering Strait for the Purpose of Finding the North-East Passage, Undertaken in the Years 1815, 1816, 1817, and 1818 at the Expense of Count N.P. Rumyantsov on the Ship "Riurik"), Vol. II, St. Petersburg, 1821, p. 18.

9. Op. cit. in note 1, 1817, file no. 350, l. 12.

10. Ibid, l. 13.

11. Ibid, l. 21.

12. Ibid, l. 38.

13. Ibid, ll. 32-33.

14. A species of edible root.

15. Op. cit. in note 1, 1817, file 350, l. 43.

16. Ibid, 1819, file no. 406, extract from Scheffer's journal on his visit to the Hawaiian Islands, on ll. 35-37.

17. Ibid, 1817, file no. 350, l. 45.

18. Op. cit. in note 1, 1819, file no. 406, letter of the Head of the Ministry of Foreign Affairs, L.V. Nesselrode, to the Minister of the Interior, O.P. Kozodavlev, dated June 24, 1819, on ll. 52-55.

19. [K. Khlebnikov] Zhisneopisanie A.A. Baranova, glavnovo pravitelia rossiiskikh kolonii v Amerike (Biography of A.A. Baranov, Governor of the Russian Colonies in America), St. Petersburg, 1835, p. 168.

20. From the letters and testimony of the Decembrists, edited by A.K. Borozdin, St. Petersburg, 1906, p. 71. [Emphasis mine.--Au.]

21. GAFKE, Archives of the Investigation Committee, file no. 47, l. 156.

22. Zavalishin, "Zapiski dekabrista" (The Memoirs of a Decembrist), p. 229.

23. Ibid.

24. GAFKE, Archives of the Commission of Investigation, file no. 48, Zavalishin's testimony of October 4, 1826, l. 156.

25. AVPK and B, Archives of the State Council, Department of Economy, 1827 file no. 23, l. 2.

26. Ibid, Separate opinion of Count N.S. Mordvinov, on ll. 6-16.

27. Ibid, In the text: "Panaminskii peresheek" [--Au.] (Panaminian Isthmus).

28. Ibid.

29. Ibid.

Chapter VIII

1. ANKH, Archives of the Department of Manufacture and Domestic Commerce, 1818, file no. 361, 1. 30.

2. Ibid, 1. 31.

3. Ibid, 1815, file no. 222, 1. 108.

4. Ibid, 1835, file no. 1139, 1. 3.

5. Supplements to the Report of the Committee on the Establishment of the Russian-American Colonies, St. Petersburg, 1863, supplement III.

6. Ibid, p. 291.

7. ANKH, Archives of the Commercial Department, 1804, file no. 146, 11. 2-3.

8. Ibid.

9. AVPK and B, Archives of the Chancery of the Prosecutor-General of the Senate, 1799, file no. 1672.

10. Ibid.

11. Archives of the Institute of History of the Academy of Sciences, Materials on the History of the Russian-American Company, file no. 14.

12. AVPK and B, Archives of the Senate, 5th Department, 1821, file no. 989, extract composed in the Criminal Court of Justice at St. Petersburg, 1816, on 11. 26-113.

13. Op. cit. in note 1, 1825, file no. 222, Report of the commandant of Okhotsk to the Ministry of the Interior, 1815, on 11. 34-63.

14. Ibid.

15. Quoted from Tikhmenev, op. cit. Pt. II, suppl., p. 49.

16. Op. cit. in note 1, 1812, file no. 78, 1. 2.

17. Quoted from K. Khlebnikov, "Materials for the History of the Russian Colonies on the Shores of the Eastern Ocean," p. 27.

18. Ibid.

19. Archives of the State Geographical Society, Veselago Collection, file no. 58, Report of the Governor of the Colonies to the Governing Board, April 1834, on 11. 1-20.

20. Op. cit. in note 297, pp. 106-107.

21. Op. cit. in note 1, 1826, file no. 709, 1. 9.

22. Extract from the account of Captain Krusenstern's voyage around the world on the "Nadezhda" (Hope), 1803-1806, in "Materialy dlia istorii russkikh zaselenii po beregam Vostochnovo okeana" (Materials for the History of the Russian Colonies on the Shores of the Eastern Sea), St. Petersburg, 1861, Vol. IV, p. 72.

23. Extract from Langsdorf's memoirs, in op. cit. above, p. 190.

24. Ivan Grigor'evich Polomoshnov, a clerk of the Company.

25. Quoted from Tikhmenev, op. cit., Pt. II, suppl., p. 95.

26. Ibid, p. 109.

27. Memoirs of Capt. Golovnin on the present condition of the Russian-American Company (1818), in op. cit. in note 17, Vol. I, p. 53.

28. Khorunzhii, a cornet in the Cossack cavalry. --Tr.

29. Op. cit. in note 12.

30. Ibid.

31. Ibid.
32. Ibid.
33. V.M. Golovnin's remarks on Kamchatka and Russian America in 1809, 1810, and 1811, in op. cit. in note 12, Vol. II, p. 79.
34. Ibid.
35. Op. cit. in note 12, 1. 172.
36. Ibid, 11. 270-271.

Chapter IX
1. Extract from the travel notes of Simpson, Director of the Hudson Bay Company, 1841 and 1842, in op. cit. in note 314, Vol. IV, p. 231.
2. MIA, Archives of the Chancery of the Ministry of the Navy, Managing Division, 1860, file no. 162, Pt. 1, 1. 4.
3. S.S. Shashkov, "Rossiisko-amerikanskaia kompaniia" (The Russian-American Company,) in Sochineniia (Works), Vol. II, St. Petersburg, 1898, pp. 633-634.
4. GAFKE, State Archives, 1789, file no. 2742, 1. 4.
5. A. Markov, "Russkie na Vostochnom okeane" (The Russians in the Eastern Sea), Moscow, 1849, p. 53.
6. AVPK and B, Archives of the Chancery of the Procurator-General of the Senate, 1797, file no. 203.
7. Archives of the Historical Institute of the Academy of Sciences, Materials on the history of the Russian-American Company, doc. no. 181.
8. Op. cit. in note 6, 1797, file no. 203.
9. Ibid.
10. Op. cit. in note 7, doc. no. 181.
11. Supplement to the Committee Report Concerning the Establishment of the Russian-American Colonies, p. 78.
12. "Pravila dlia toenov, izbiraemykh v starshiny nad obshchimi seleniiami aleut v Kadiakskom otdele" (Rules for the Toyons who have been Selected as Elders over the General Settlements of Aleuts in the Kodiak Division), §2, in op. cit. in note 11.
13. Ibid, §3.
14. "Dvukratnoe puteshestvie v Ameriku morskikh ofitserov Khvostova i Davydova, pisannoe sim slednim" (Dual Voyage to America of the Naval Officers Khvostov and Davydov, written by the latter), St. Petersburg, Pt. II, 1812, p. 116.
15. Op. cit. in note 11, p. 61.
16. Ibid, pp. 49-50.
17. Parka, a garment made out of the skins of birds or mammals.
18. Op. cit. in note 14, p. 127.
19. Sarana--Martagon, or Turk's-cap lily, the bulb of the wild lily used in food.
20. Ishkat, about a chetverik (roughly a bushel).
21. Op. cit. in note 14, p. 129.
22. "Doklad komiteta ob ustroistve russkikh amerikanskikh kolonii" (Report of the Committee on the Establishment of Russian-American Colonies), St. Petersburg, 1836, p. 108.
23. The references are to banknotes.
24. Cf. op. cit. in note 11, Suppl. XI.
25. ANKH, Archives of the Department of Manufacture and Domestic Commerce, 1824, file no. 603, 1. 19.

26. Op. cit. in note 14, p. 74.

27. Op. cit. in note 25, file no. 222, 1. 69.

28. Ibid, line 70.

29. Ibid.

30. Ibid.

31. Ibid, 1824, file no. 635, 1. 11.

32. Archives of the State Geographical Society, K. Khlebnikov's Memoirs Concerning America, pp. 118-119.

33. Op. cit. in note 25, 1824, file no. 635, 1. 11.

34. Op. cit. in note 32, Veselago Collection, file no. 49.

35. Op. cit. in note 14, p. 115.

36. Ibid, p. 121.

37. ANKH, Archives of the Ministry of Finance, Sect. 2, 1819, file no. 10, 1. 47.

38. Op. cit. in note 11, p. 66.

39. Ibid, pp. 66-67.

40. AVP, Archives of the Ministry of Foreign Affairs, P-3, 1805, file no. 7, 1. 28.

41. Baranov is referring here to the Aleuts who were with him.

42. AVPK and B, Archives of the Permanent Council, file no. 140, letter of A.A. Baranov to G.I. Shelikhov, 1792, on ll. 36-45.

43. Op. cit. in note 11, p. 310-311.

44. A. Markov, "Russkiye na Vostochnom okeane" (The Russians in the Eastern Sea), p. 35.

45. Op. cit. in note 25, 1842, file no. 1430, 1. 1.

46. Ibid, 1. 2.

47. Ibid, 1. 13.

48. Quoted from Tikhmenev, op. cit., Pt. II, suppl., p. 103.

49. AVPK and B, Archives of the Synod Chancery, 1809, file no. 273.

50. Op. cit. in note 25, 1826, file no. 738, 1. 7.

51. ANKH, Archives of the Department of Commerce, 1809, file no. 435, ll. 3-4.

52. AVPK and B, Archives of the Synod on the Kamchatka Eparchy, 1847, file no. 2743, 1. 18.

53. Tikhmenev, op. cit. Pt. II, supple, p. 214.

54. Ibid.

55. Op. cit. in note 25, 1818, file no. 222, 1. 108.

56. Ibid, file no. 361, 1. 1.

57. Op. cit. in note 11, p. 35.

Chapter X

1. AVP, Archives of the Chancery of the Ministry of Foreign Affairs, 1839, file no. 217, ll. 238-239. Translated from the French.

2. ANKH, Archives of the General Chancery of the Ministry of Finance, 5th Secretariat, 1866, file no. 58/25, Letter of the Minister of Foreign Affairs, K.V. Nesselrode, to the Minister of Finance E.F. Kankrin, dated January 4, 1839, on ll. 32-38.

3. AVPK and B, Archives of the State Council, Department of Economics, 1841, file no. 3914, 1. 144.

4. ANKH, Archives of the Department of Manufacture and Domestic Commerce, 1849, file no. 1727, 1. 51.

5. Ibid, ll. 51-52.

6. Supplement to the Committee Report Concerning the Establishment of the Russian-American Colonies, p. 545.

7. Quoted from Tikhmenev, op. cit., Pt. II, p. 62.

8. Report of the Committee on the Establishment of the Russian colonies in America, p. 63.

9. AVPK and B, Archives of the Department of Public Instruction, 1847, file no. 3179, l. 11.

10. Op. cit. in note 6, p. 226.

11. Beginning with the year 1844 the number of shares was firmly stabilized at 7,484. From 1845 on the shares were figured in silver. The value of a share of 500 rubles in banknotes, in round numbers, was figured at 150 rubles, silver.

12. AVPK and B, Archives of the State Council, Butkov Collection, file no. 15.

13. Op. cit. in note 9, l. 12.

14. MIA, Archives of the Chancery of the Navy Department, Management Section, 1860, file no. 162, Pt. II, ll. 71-72.

15. Op. cit. in note 4, 1834, file no. 1103, l. 21-22.

16. Op. cit. in note 9, 1848, file no. 3179, l. 34.

17. Op. cit. in note 4, 1849, file no. 1727, l. 37.

18. Op. cit. in note 14, Pt. II, l. 72.

19. Ibid, Pt. I, ll. 317-318.

20. Ibid, Pt. II, ll. 41-42.

Chapter XI

1. Lenin, "Sochineniia" (Works), Vol. XV, p. 143.

2. ANKH, Archives of the Governing Board of the Russian-American Company, 1854, file no. 28, l. 55.

3. H. Bancroft, op. cit., Vol. XXVIII. History of Alaska, 1730-1885, p. 570.

4. Op. cit. in note 2, l. 2.

5. Ibid, l. 9.

6. Ibid, l. 13.

7. Ibid, l. 18.

8. Ibid, l. 50.

9. Ibid, l. 51.

10. Ibid, l. 48.

11. Licenses to engage in privateering.

12. Privateer, a vessel owned by private persons, that, under license of one of the warring powers, preys on the merchant-men of the enemy, and is given the booty as a prize.

13. Op. cit. in note 2, l. 51.

14. Ibid, ll. 53-54.

15. Ibid, ll. 61-62. Translated from the French.

16. Ibid, l. 52.

17. Ibid, l. 20.

18. AVP, Archives of the Ministry of Foreign Affairs, Asiatic Department, 1857, file no. 4, letter of December 23, 1859 (January 4, 1860, New Style), on ll. 36-41. Translated from the French.

19. Op. cit. in note 2, ll. 61-62. Translated from the French.

20. ANKH, Archives of the Chancery of the Ministry of Finance, letter "Sh.," 1857, file no. 1., l. 11.

21. Ibid, 1. 6.

22. Ibid, 1. 1. The reference in this case is to the agreement between the Russian-American and the American-Russian companies.

23. Op. cit. in note 18, 1856, file no. 4, letter of November 1/13, 1857, on ll. 21-23. Translated from the French.

24. Ibid, 1857, file no. 4, 1. 27, letter of November 20 (December 2), 1857. Translated from the French.

25. Ibid.

26. Op. cit. in note 20, ll. 9-10. [Emphasis mine.--Au.]

27. Op. cit. in note 18, on ll. 16-41. Translated from the French.

28. Supplement to the Committee Report Concerning the Establishment of Russian-American Colonies, p. 283.

29. "The British Colonist" of January 14, 1862. Quoted from the translation preserved in the Archives of the State Geographical Society, F. Veselago Collection.

30. MIA, Archives of the Chancery of the Navy Department, Management Division, 1862, file no. 113, 1. 11.

31. Ibid, ll. 24-25.

32. "Golos," 1867, no. 84.

33. New York Herald, 1867. Quoted from "Golos," no. 103.

34. ANKH, Archives of the General Chancery of the Ministry of Finance, 5 business correspondence, 1866, Report no. 58/25, 1. 32.

35. Even after the proposed expenditures had been drastically reduced at the demand of the Minister of Finance, the maintenance cost of the Governing Board amounted to 51,660 rubles.

36. Op. cit. in note 30, 1860, Pt. II, secret study of the income and expenses of the Russian-American Company, on ll. 18-28.

37. Ibid, 1. 22.

38. AVPK and B, Butkov collection, 1864, file no. 15, letter of March 12, 1864. [Emphasis mine.--Au.]

39. Ibid.

40. Ibid, letter of March 15, 1864.

41. Op. cit. in note 34, 1. 3.

42. Op. cit. in note 20, 1. 6.

43. Cf. the German "Gründer-Jahre," a period marked by the mushroom growth of corporations in industry, banking, transportation, etc.

44. Committee Report Concerning the Establishment of the Russian-American Colonies, pp. 377-378.

45. Op. cit. in note 30, 1860, Pt. II, 1. 84.

46. Ibid.

47. Ibid, 1. 85.

48. Supplement to "Morskoi Sbornik," nos. 1-4, 1861.

49. P. Tikhmenev, "Istoricheskoe obozrenie obrazovaniia Rossiisko-amerikanskoi kompanii," (Historical Survey of the Formation of the Russian-American Company), St. Petersburg, 1861.

50. "Golos," 1867, no. 84.

51. Op. cit. in note 18. Translated from the French.

52. Ibid.

53. Ibid, letter of July 4/16, 1860, on ll. 48-49. Translated from the French.

54. Op. cit. in note 18. Translated from the French.

55. Ibid, on ll. 44-46. Translated from the French.

56. Soedinennye Shtaty v epokhu grazhdanskoi voiny i Rossiia (The United States in the Period of the Civil War and Russia), in "Krasnyi arkhiv," 1930, no. 1 (38), p. 154.

57. Op. cit. in note 18 on ll. 42-43. Translated from the French.

58. Op. cit. in note 56, p. 155.

59. "Moskovskie Vedomosti," (Moscow Record) 1886, no. 171.

60. "Golos," 1866, no. 232.

61. Op. cit. in note 34, l. 2.

62. Ibid, ll. 1-2.

63. Marx and Engels, "Sochineniia" (Works), Vol. XXIII, p. 399.

64. "Temps," 1867. Quoted from "Golos," 1867, no. 86.

65. According to the United States Constitution, Congress, not the Senate alone, has the power to declare war.--Tr.

66. Op. cit. in note 63, Vol. XXV, p. 494.

67. Ibid, Vol. XXVI, p. 43.

68. Op. cit. in note 423, letter of November 23, 1859 (January 4, 1860, New Style), on ll. 36-41. Translated from the French

69. MIA, Archives of the Chancery of the Navy Department, 1858, file no. 1, l. 19.

70. Op. cit. in note 34, l. 61. Translated from the French.

71. Op. cit. in note 20, 1860, Pt. II, l. 178.

72. Op. cit. in note 20, 1866, file no. 3, l. 24.

73. Ibid.

74. "Temps," 1867. Quoted from "Golos," 1867, no. 86.

75. A. Babin, "Istoriia S.-A. Soedinennykh Shtatov" (History of the United States of North America), St. Petersburg, 1912, Vol. II, p. 221.

76. F.W. Seward, "Seward at Washington, as Senator and Secretary of States," N.Y., 1891, p. 348.

77. "Golos," 1867, no. 84.

78. AVP, Archives of the Chancery of the Main Office on Affairs of the Press, 1865, file no. 15, Pt. I, ll. 189-190.

79. New York Herald, 1867. Quoted from "Golos," 1867, no. 104.

80. Ibid, no. 103.

81. New York Tribune, 1867. Quoted from undated clippings on file at the ANKH, Archives of the General Chancery of the Ministry of Finances, 5th Secretariat, 1866, file no. 58/25. The New York Tribune for that year was not available at any of our libraries.

82. New York Tribune, 1867.

83. Cf. note 81.

84. Op. cit. in note 34, ll. 47-48. Translated from the French.

85. Ibid, l. 66. Translated from the French.

86. F.R. Dulles, "American in the Pacific," Boston, 1932, p. 92.

87. H. Bancroft, Works, Vol. XXVIII, "History of Alaska," p. 595.

88. F. Golder, "The Purchase of Alaska," in American Historical Review, Vol. 25, 1920.

89. W. Dunning, "Paying for Alaska," in Political Science Quarterly, Vol. 27, 1912.

90. V. Farrar, "The Background of the Purchase of Alaska," in Washington Historical Quarterly, Vol. 13, 1922.

91. F.R. Dulles, op. cit., p. 92.

92. New York Herald, 1867. Quoted from "Golos," 1867, no. 103.

93. New York Tribune, 1867.

Conclusion

1. Lenin, "Sochineniia" (Works), Vol. XIX, p. 281.
2. Marx and Engels, "Sochineniia" (Works), Vol. IX, p. 363.
3. Ibid, Vol. XXI, p. 211.
4. "Tikhii okean," (The Pacific, Collection of Articles), Akademiia Nauk SSSR, 1926, p. 35.

INDEX

New York Tribune, The, 268-69, 271-72

Nicholas I., 104, 136, 146-48, 151, 167, 209-10, 237

Nihau, see Onihau

Nikolayevsk, 57, 224

Nikolayevskaya Railroad, 267

Nilov, Capt., 190

Nobility, and trade, 12-13, 45-46, 63-64, 100, 116, 172-73, 261, 274

Noriega, Don, 139

North, U.S., 258-59, 261

North American colonies: consolidation, 73-93; effect of Conventions (1824-25) on, 73-93; exploitation of, 15, 20, 63, 119, 198, 202, 280n; first history of northwest shores of, v, vii, 4; first Russian promyshlenniky on, 7-21; labor in, 171-92; natives in, 193-216; politics on, see Politics; population, 10; Ross, California, 118-52; Russian expansion of, 50, 53-54, 167, 170, 244, 273; Russian trade, 12, 27, 169, 198; sale of, 3, 234-72; U.S. to dominate, 258

North American Union, 88

North Pole, 31

Northeastern Sea, see Pacific Ocean

Northern Company, 34

Northern Duma, 108

Northern Sea, see Pacific Ocean

Northern Society of Decembrists, see Decembrists

"Notes on America," K. Khlebnikov, 5

Novoarkhangelsk: defense of, 208-209, 234-35, 237-38; settlement, 3, 54, 57, 70, 81, 122, 129, 175, 184, 238; trade, 74, 86-87

Nutka (Cape King George), 14, 42

Nutka Sound, 51, 73

Oahu Is., 155-57, 159-60, 162-63, 165-66

Obolensky, Ye.P., 88, 110

Obolyaninov, Procurator Gen., 48

Offices, Company, 56-57, 59, 67, 105, 250

Okhotsk: and colonies, 10, 25, 27, 31, 32-33, 59, 98-99, 224, 280n; trade, 61, 75, 178; Sea of, 221; workers, 175-76, 180, 191, 204

"On the Creoles," 214

"On the Harmfulness of Many Companies in America and the Advantages of Combining Them into One," Board of Commerce, 39

Onihau, 155, 157

"Opinions of the Management," 165

Opium, 226

Opium War, 222

Oppenheim and Co., 227

Order of Restoration, 137-39

Oregon: British colonization of, 257-58; Russia in, 73, 247, 257-58

Orient, 18, 52, 221, 244, 274

Orlov, 224

Otters, see Sea otters; River otters

Pacific Coast: privateering, 239; Russia on, 55-56, 73, 81-82, 136, 153; U.S. interest, 73, 80, 155, 257, 259, 273

Pacific Ocean: Britain on, 51-52, 155, 238, 264; maps, 275; Russian domination of, v-vi, 6-7, 16-17, 44, 50, 72, 140, 167, 220; Russian expansion, 1, 6, 14, 17, 24-25, 31, 38, 102-103, 153, 232, 274; trade, 16-17, 22, 36, 243, 245

Pahlen, Count P.A., 43-44, 75-76, 124-25

Palmerston, 218

Panama, Isthmus of, 169

Panov, merchant, 21, 23

Paraguay, Jesuits, 213

Paris: 15, 242, 257, 261; Peace of, 257, 261

Passports, colonist, 26-27, 172-73

Pasture, Ross, 141

Paul I: natives and, 41, 195-97; Russian expansion, 15, 37-39, 42-45, 73